"Since starting the meditation I crave bein~ ¨  ”
like I used to crave alcohol. When I feel o
it is me who is paddling around in the selfis
this new inner knowledge I am starting to t   ⊥ellhole
quicker. Amazing, after nearly 17 years of sc

Cheryl R. - Australia

"I have been practicing the meditation as you suggest, Danny. I wasn't sure how helpful it was but now I can see clearly the contrast between wakeful and being asleep. Thank you for what you do. I have never met you but you have helped me immensely."

Brad M. - Michigan, USA

"Thanks. I can feel the results from this."

Stephen H. - Alexandria, Virginia

"Gosh.... Big, big changes since I started the meditation. Yesterday I was out walking. . . . I stopped and saw the sparkles...with my eyes open. I have felt much closer to God and feel His presence on a regular basis since starting the meditation. I have become so much more aware and just in the last few days my faith in God and trust has grown tremendously...just when I was looking for an effective meditation. God gives me what I need always. I'm keeping this up. Thank you."

Charmian O. - Elgin, Scotland

"Awesome! Where have you been all along? I've tried other forms of meditations to no avail. I just finished my first 20 minutes of the Meditation Sampler. I have noticed the changes! I cannot thank you enough for your help! Peace and All Good!"

Don W. - Louisville, KY

"I have been meditating using the links you sent me for the last week and I have been feeling real good. All in all I feel great and positive now thanks."

Shaun - Los Angeles, CA

"Thanks to this meditation I have achieved a quality of sobriety I have been needing and yearning for almost 30 years. I have had a lower back problem dating back to 29 years ago from which I have not had a single undisturbed night of sleep until making the meditation a part of my life. I now sleep well with no disturbance and I have even stopped my pain medication. This is a spiritual and psychic awakening facilitating more tolerance and patience, better, easy relationships with others and more confidence than I ever had before. To say I am grateful is an understatement. What I owe you is beyond evaluation. Thanks."

Mark F. - NSW, AU

"It has given back hope, which I had lost. I had feeling of empathy instead of all the festering hate. There is hope and thank you again for sending that."

Deborah M. - Shaws Bend, TX

"Awesome. I love your site. It has helped me so much through the years. Between you and my meetings and sponsorship I will be sober ten years in November even though I have been a member of AA for thirty years."

Deborah N. - Harbor Hts., WA

"Since I met you I started using your 11th Step meditation practice and I have made some milestones. I'm in my 17th year and it shouldn't have taken so long."

John L. - Salt Lake, UT

"I am absolutely amazed at how quick the meditation has worked on my ability to watch and not identify with ego. I have only been at it a couple of weeks and I feel only just scratched the surface. Thank you Danny."

Pat C. - London, UK

"Thank you for the meditation. I have searched for guidance in meditation and what I found has been completely useless and absolutely incompatible with the Big Book spirituality. Thank you so much. I am amazed."

Suzanne - USA

REAL MEDITATION
FOR
REAL ALCOHOLICS
and those who love them

A companion book to meditation
as practiced by the author

danny j schwarzhoff

ISBN-13: 978-1481118729

ISBN-10: 1481118722

CONTENTS

Contents

DEDICATION

To Nancy, my wife of thirty three years, our two children, Danny and Kristen and every single alcoholic and addict on earth.

INTRODUCTION

There are two possible parallel universes in which we can live. Whichever one we choose determines the course of our existence and is the difference between living a happy, healthy, useful life that is free from depression, anxiety, and fear or living a sick, emotionally handicapped life dowsed with physical and mental ailments.

Alcoholism, drug addiction, *all* obsessions, such as food and sexual addictions, do not cause themselves. They are not inherited or contracted like a classic *disease*. They are *symptoms* of the spiritual disease that emanates out of an original, wrong choice. All alcoholics have chosen wrongly and in that one indiscretion, gave up their power of choice in favor of obsession. The meditation practice spoken of in this book ends this insanity. Forever. It returns all those who practice it back to the place where the bad choice can be reversed; *corrected* if you will; and you can do it even before you finish reading this book.

The technique proposed is a nonreligious but spiritual procedure for separating from the lower self—that dark, *inhuman* part of our existence called *ego* that keeps us cruelly hooked to our instincts. In separating from this false "Self," we automatically reestablish our lost connection to God and commence an instant, spiritually intuitive download into our psyche. Direction, discipline, knowledge, and power come to us, but *only* while in this "state."[1]

Christians call this a state of *grace*; *theosis,* for Buddhists; *wu wei* and *te,* in Taoism; *kripa,* for Hindus. Christ referred to this state as "the Kingdom." It is possible only when we access it through awareness; then all forms of anger; annoyance, irritation—even frustration and fear—fall away harmlessly. There is an inner Heaven that is always *at hand*; meaning we can access it any time we choose—*if* we choose. But do we? Do we know how?

---

[1]Please visit the "How To Get There," page in the back of this book for fast access to the meditation exercise. It is available for streaming or download. It is free and always will be.

For all alcoholics, the problem is always the same: too much of life has passed, while that inner *state* has been ignored. Despite inheriting the gift of free-choice, we have all been preconditioned by events and lifestyles to shy away from this state of awareness and God-consciousness, to instead become dependent upon instincts and self-centered longings. This has left us wide-open to anger, resentment, and fear. What alcoholic is not familiar with *all* of these?

This unawareness is a lack of protection that permits cruel, controlling people to command an odd power over us—as we compensate by manipulating others in kind, generating a cycle of misery for all involved.

We are *intended* to be at odds with our natural instincts, learning to set them aside in favor of receiving and living from spiritual intuition instead. However, this takes the exercise of choice, a disposition that our lower, instinctual nature (ego) hates for *us* to make. It literally *angers* at the very prospect and will utilize all of It's cunning and baffling powers to see that we willfully avoid this truth.

Intuition, on the other hand, is God's will, a vision that would have us live in perfect peace and ease—if only we would sit still long enough to let it. Instincts are those things that pull us away from this serenity, for which reason we selfishly struggle for happiness that we have no power to deliver to ourselves.

This is a book for people who are in recovery, doing what they believe is the best they can to remain recovering, maybe even following the Twelve Steps to a T, and yet lingering doubt and bedevilments beg the question of growth—people who are feeling held back by depression, anxiety, or anger and plagued by physical health issues springing out of addictions to nicotine, caffeine, or even the abusive use of foods and sex. This book shows exactly what has been going wrong and proposes a free, simple, immediate solution that works.

The meditation made available through this book should not be confused with daily meditations, visualization prayers, reflections, affirmation-styled mantras or religious textual meditations that are targeted toward the recovery-addiction market by religious practitioners. I am not a religious person and do not embrace or promote any doctrines of any religion or spiritual movement. You will not find those here.

What you will find is access to an ancient technique that is the missing link to spiritual recovery. You will also find something you will not find anywhere else: *Proof* that the state of consciousness this technique induces actually does work.[2]

You could spend twenty years of your life in the Himalayas visiting Tibet and Nepal in a quest for enlightenment; you could study with teachers and gurus in India, immersing in ancient mysticism and principles; and you will not receive what you can discover through *this* meditation in less than ten minutes. Study and the accumulation of knowledge, spiritual or otherwise, increases stores of information but it gets in the way of the wordless intuitive spiritual "data" soon to become available to you. There is no place to go to obtain the solution to any obsessive addiction, except within. Access to your *within* is being presented to you right here, right now.

Awareness is a state of spirituality that God has endowed and is already "known" to us regardless of whether we have words to express it. Through the meditation I have used for many years and am now making available to you, I have simply reduced *knowing* into words in order to convey a message — one that has the potential to reawaken you and prompt you to remember what you have already been preprogrammed to understand, long before you ever read these words. Even before you were born.

This meditation allows us to separate from the false *Self* that says, " I am God," and this severance becomes effortless and automatic the very moment we become mindful of the *Self* that exists inside; as we default back to our original state of God-consciousness.

People who contact me often refer to the meditation exercise I use with alcoholics as "your meditation," and "Danny's meditation". I can understand them saying this. However, there is no owner or leaseholder to what you are about to be exposed. I am just one author of this one book, bringing your attention to something that already exists and has no human origin.

---

[2]You are invited to go online to download my medical files. Visit the "How To Get There," page in the back of this book which includes a complete history of my mental and physical conditions for nearly the last decade.

The ability to choose *conscious contact* with God in preference to unconscious contact with *Self* and the world is our true spiritual inheritance. There is no human guru who "invented" it. Neither did I manufacture it. I have simply rediscovered what has already existed, and if we must acknowledge from where this originates, then I would have to say, "with God". Now you are rediscovering it too.

The Spirit behind the exercise says, *"Know that you are not God, that only I am God."* I cannot make anyone accept this at the level necessary for true spiritual living. My job as the writer of this book is simply to point you in a particular direction by showing you *how* to remember this. I can do that only if I am able to persuade you to sit still long enough to let Him catch up with you. Then He will reveal this to you so deeply your world will be rocked forever. It will dash to pieces the ego-will living inside you that so desperately tries to become God. That lower *Self* that you *think* is a part of you, and isn't, will diminish. You will realize, at a level deeper than intellect, that you have played God, and it simply doesn't work.

I first came upon this meditation in 1964 as a little boy. I have since met others who are also familiar with the practice, as intuitively as I am. As the result of practicing it, their lives have become as ordered and their existences as meaningful and God-centered as mine. They enjoy similar mental, emotional, and physical well-being, living whole, unselfishly useful, and happy lives working with others, serving God and their fellows.

In saying that this has come about intuitively, I mean that it came naturally—just as natural as it has already come to you, when you were much younger, except you may not remember. If there is a physical DNA passed on from generation to generation, why not then a spiritual equivalent?

My twelve-year-old daughter already knew of this and practiced it on her own, before I was even able to show it to her. I first introduced my sixteen-year-old to this meditation when he was eight. Thus far, he has been navigating the treacherous waters of *teendom* in today's

America virtually free and safe from the typical teen angst many of us presume to be *normal* today. It isn't.

I have been asked on occasion, "Did Jesus meditate this way?" I would say He probably did not need to meditate the way you or I need to, because He was not born with the same ego-affliction with which *we* are cursed. When Jesus "meditated," He did so not to "get" centered, as He already was fully conscious. He already lived "under God"—and He tried to show us how to *get* there too—how to join Him in the *Kingdom of Heaven* within, so to speak. His mission was to demonstrate how to access the mind of God through joining with His mind, in consciousness.

Jesus would have "meditated" more to glorify His Father, your Father—*our* Father. This was something He did each waking moment of His life; a condition which we all must move toward. You will understand this in the weeks, months and years to come *if* you continue with this meditation and carry the state of awareness into your daily life.

All that is written in your Christian Scriptures about how Jesus guided his believers as well as the nonbelievers certainly does correspond with this practice, especially the one and only prayer he told his disciples to use. Even the life of Moses and observations of the prophets are in agreement.

Is it a Christian practice? Although entirely nonreligious, this technique is consistent with spiritual principles that are the basis for all Judeo-Christian faiths, regardless of denomination. It is fully amenable with the message of Moses and the life of Jesus Christ, and, although not associated with any religion, it is completely in accord with Christianity and Judaism.

If anything you experience and learn when you use this meditation seems vaguely familiar to you, that is because viscerally it is. You will receive a new understanding expressing truths already written in your heart. The exercise is simply opening up your heart and letting God's will inside, where it will reactivate that lost truth in you, so you will act and think in ways you never have before, without being told by any human being *how* to think or act. Your spiritual DNA, long lying dormant in your yearning psyche, will be reactivated.

You will be inspired, living each moment as if walking in new sunlight, the Sunlight of the Spirit, with no planning, no worries, and no stress.

Any similarity between what happens to you as the result of using this meditation and what you have seen and heard in your Scripture with regard to Jesus is not intentional—although they certainly may be well matched. Propitious changes in attitude, worldview and behavior affecting your mental, physical and emotional wellbeing can happen rather quickly. It can be startling.

Some of the insights presented in this book may seem quite extraordinary. You may wonder where they come from. Well, they come from experience and observation but even more importantly, they come from inner intuition as the result of clear awareness and conscious contact with God. I have no gurus. I do not get these extraordinary ideas or inspiration from any of the so-called spiritual guides, preachers and teachers. I have never been schooled in theology (aside from what I have learned in Catholic grade and high school) and aside from a few college courses in psychology and sociology and I hold no degrees or certifications in those fields. I do not follow any psycho-spiritual philosophies or religious doctrines and I have no interest or need for motivational speaker-tapes, self-help systems and no need to investigate spiritual courses of any kind. Frankly, neither should you. Virtually all of those are nothing more than revisited, revamped versions of ancient spiritual axioms that have been around for centuries, anyway. Many of them perversions of their original form.

Ten or twenty years from now, there will be some new best-selling guru, all the rage, having become a household name, as if he has stumbled upon something new. Yet it will be only a remarketing of some newer version of familiar self-help strategies derived out of a few hackneyed, pseudo-spiritual themes, all designed to attract throngs of new followers to accompany *the movement*. The is no need to fast-forward into any decade ahead to see this. Today's media is already overrun.

Today there are many spiritualists who have become popular on talk shows and in book clubs. Frankly, I would never have heard of any had their names not been brought to my attention by some of those protégés I have helped. I have only fleeting knowledge of the existence of these due to their being heavily marketed through talk-show hosts (and hostesses) or their attaining best-seller status.

I must admit, I am equally ignorant of the teachings from the list of this decade's pop culture evangelists and superficial self-help darlings of the Public Broadcasting System. I flip through their programs with my cable remote as if they were commercials for weight-loss pills. I do not need to know them. Once you use this meditation, then neither will you.

If you are one of those searching people who have taken such circuitous paths in the past, please do not see this as arrogance on my part. Some of these statements can be understandably disconcerting. That is because in effect, I am suggesting that you may have wasted your time, perhaps even a lifetime, following men and looking to gain wisdom from those who do not really have much to give—who are merely skilled at making it seem that they do.

When you have truth and understanding that comes from within, you will not be lured to others. You will instead be drawn to your Father Who comes through the kingdom inside you; and so you do not need ever worry whether anyone's teaching are valid. You will have *teachings* from God to absorb and from which to live confidently. You will come to trust these teachings.

The meditation I practice and now pass on to you with no charge is not available through any of the best-selling books available today. You also will not find it through late-night infomercials or religious-service broadcasts. Your priest, your rabbi, or your Sunday minister will not be able to show this to you. It would be the rare preacher who could come close to teaching anything like this powerful method. (I say this because I have come across several very enlightened preachers over the last twenty years.) But you can have it free of charge, no strings attached. Simply go to the download-listening instructions on the "How to Get There" page in the back of this book.

Not everyone who comes across this book will take kindly to the information in it, nor to the simple proposal it points them toward. For them it will appear too simple. It will mean reconsidering some old and comforting ideas and considering some painful ones. This is not a book for the fainthearted. It is likely to conjure up some deeply held, perhaps suppressed emotions. Unless you can remain calm and objective to this adventure, observing, not succumbing to fears—even those painful doubts the materials in this book may provoke, you may never get truly well. True open-mindedness, consideration without gullibility, is the order.

With this in mind I invite you to try something unique. I invite you to conduct a little due diligence—on me. You are invited to go online to download my medical files, which include a complete history of my mental and physical conditions for nearly the last decade. In it, you will see the results of every physical exam, blood test, and prescription for medication I have had for nearly ten years. Yes, this is very personal information to open up for public scrutiny but it authorizes me to say the things I do. It comprises my evidence-based curriculum vitae, which is a more powerful set of credentials than any formal accreditation issued through a learning institution.

As a rule, alcoholics do not trust academics. They can be wary of credentials. They do not trust authorities. And so, this book does not make an academic presentation. Those with a true spiritual inclination can be particularly apprehensive about secular solutions derived out of clinical halls and universities. The approach to real alcoholics must carry very special weight and depth. It cannot be cast from an intellectual platform that speaks down as if from some hilltop of superiority. No matter how hard a professional clinician tries to get into the trenches with the alcoholic there is always an *at-arm's-length* relationship, erecting a stubborn wall of resistance. That is why I have decided to open up my life for all to see in this manner, skeletons and all. It allows me to speak and write from a position of strength born of experience and verifiable results. I hope no one sees it as bragging or a reckless temptation of fate. I know it is not. I call it complete honesty. (Please visit the "How To Get There," page in the back of this book for download access to my complete medical history.)

Alcoholic radio curmudgeon Don Imus, the irascible ex-shock jock turned political pundit, recently complained during his morning drive broadcast that he could never entrust his health to a "fat doctor."

His complaining is not unsubstantiated. A recent study conducted by researchers at John Hopkins University[3] shows that primary-care physicians who were physically fit and of normal weight were very likely to provide recommended obesity care to fat patients. However, if a patient was *as fat* or fatter than his corpulent doctor—he received no diagnosis, nor was he prescribed treatment for his overweight condition. Who would take their advice, anyway? I mean if you went to the gym and your personal trainer had you doing lunges while sucking on a Newport Light, how much confidence would you place in his guidance?

In 2009 President Obama nominated a clearly obese and unhealthy Dr. Regina Benjamin as US Surgeon General. How does such an appointment translate down the line to the ranks of physicians, and how does that contribute positively toward helping establish credibility and public confidence in the health care system? It doesn't exactly instill faith in the acumen of public health advisers, does it? Conversely, another doctor in public view, Dr. Oz, appears to be fit as a fiddle, a credible role model for the good health routines he promotes. I don't know about you but I would definitely listen to Dr. Oz's advise on nutrition and exercise—in a heartbeat. Dr. Benjamin? I am not so sure.

This is not to impugn anyone personally. I am sure Dr. Benjamin is a lovely person, as I am sure there are many overweight persons in the healthcare field who are strong advocates for ethical, moral practice and champions of *"Primum non nocere."*[4] Yet "do as I say, not as I do" is a classic kind of pecksniffery that cannot possibly endow anyone, credentialed or not, with a credible personality authorized to play a leadership role or act as spokesperson on matters they claim to possess expertise. This is my only point.

Documented recovery, such as what you will find in my medical files, conveys actual experience and serves as a verifiable register of

---

[3] http://www.nature.com/oby/journal/vaop/ncurrent/full/oby2011402a.html "Obesity, A Research Journal" reporting of a national cross-sectional survey of 500 primary care physicians conducted between 9 February and 1 March 2011,

[4] "Do no harm" - akin to the promise within the Hippocratic Oath that includes the promise "to abstain from doing harm."

how spiritual growth translates into progressive mental and physical health—not because of what I have learned in school or through books but because I have practiced a particular type of conscious living through meditation; and I have experienced a particular kind of spiritual change. I have discovered the missing link to spiritual renewal and have something to pass on. Well, maybe it hasn't been missing, but certainly, it has been long ignored—even hidden. Someone neglected to pass on to you the *whole* truth.

I am sure you are well aware that there is value in philosophies like, "Love, don't hate," "Forgive and forget," and "Live now and not in the future or past." These are vital maxims of spiritual truth and hope. But the question has remained, "How?"

Surely, having pursued a searching, spiritual course, you have already been well advised to pray and to meditate. But even then, something has been missing. You haven't been shown *how* to do it properly. You have been told *what* to do but no one has been able to show you *how* to do it. That is because they don't know.

Alcoholism is the effect of a cause. The cause, spiritual disease, is itself an *effect* of a *cause* that went before it: anger.

Yes, I am saying that you must be free from anger. But more than that, through this special meditation of which I write in this book, I also show you *how*. I say, "You must give up judgment" but also, "This is how." This is the missing link in every Twelve-Steppers program of action and design for living. This meditation is the *how* that takes the original relief gotten through the Twelve-Step experience and makes it a permanent new nature that cannot be confounded. It makes all spiritual design for living as natural and consistent as breathing.

"A half truth is a whole lie." - *Yiddish proverb*

HOW THIS BOOK CAME ABOUT

This book did not start out trying to be a spiritual volume. Its purpose is not to inspire or guide. It is first to convince you of something very important. After that, to suggest that you need what is being offered. Then, finally to deliver it...pronto!

The first book I thought I'd publish was not this one at all. It began as a hideous memoir titled "Strangely Insane." The work was to be a rather self-serving, epic presentation that is the story of my life; a saga that is very important to me. The problem is that such a tome probably wouldn't be all that important to you.

The days of shocking exposes emanating out of the dark, alcoholic underworld have come and are long gone. I could almost hear alcoholics thinking, "Oh God. Not another memoir." Having already been shocked enough in body, mind and spirit by their own behaviors, the last thing the world needs is another alkie blowing tales of misery and recovery. Let's face it, after a while misery becomes a bore. There are more than enough folks already chronicling and publishing their tales of alkie druggie woe. I cannot imagine very much of it even getting read anymore unless the author is a celebrity.

I am no celebrity. I am not a very important person, except to my wife and kids, which is as it should be. Any attempt to compete with such authors in a market already saturated with heaping globs of recovery fat would make no practical sense.

Gratefully, I had the clarity and presence of mind to see how so many recovery genre books are not much more than post-rehab confessionals; passé, tear-jerking narratives chronicling woeful tales of personal downfall and redemption.

Alkies have heard it all before. There is only so much experience, strength and hope coming from another human being that is truly worthwhile. After that...(*yawn*). Reaching real alcoholics, especially already recovered ones, would require much weightier matter or else risk being considered just one more *also ran* in the recovery book-writing racket. When out in the field, approaching still suffering alkies, it is vitally important to present a personal story with which the prospect for recovery can identify – but for selling books . . . *eh, not so much anymore.*

"Strangely Insane" would have to be rewritten. If it could be molded into a fiction novel; the kind that could not only entertain and captivate the non-alcoholic or alcoholic reader's attention – it could also hold a viscerally spiritual, non-religious message deeply imbedded inside. The decision to break off the editing of the manuscript and to begin another project; something smaller, simpler and brief, was not easy. I had already invested at least four years into it. But it had to be set aside, even if only for a short while.

Now I am glad I did. You see, for years I had been meaning to whip up a pamphlet to accompany the meditation exercise I had been using in working with my own family and with alcoholics. *I have taken habit over the years of recording a small exercise for protégées that they use to put into their spiritual recovery practice. They love it because the language I use speaks specifically to alcoholics and especially Twelve Step oriented, recovered alcoholics. I have been distributing this practice worldwide over the last decade and receive astounding testimonials from all over the globe as to its efficacy.*

I felt such a thoughtful booklet could be a helpful accompaniment to the audio, helping streamline some of the directions I had been personally passing onto others, with good results. The idea was to make the exercise available over the internet and provide some written encouragement answering some questions regarding the experiences that meditators typically have as the result of using the exercise.

Writing began, sketching out an outline, based on personal experience and in helping others, of exactly how alcoholics are *created* and how they *recover*. Before long what developed was more than a pamphlet; it was a full-scaled book; the one you are reading right now. Not only that but I realized that I had completed a non-fiction outline that could serve as a framework for the remodeled "Strangely Insane." *That is coming next, as a novel, I hope.*

Alcoholics in recovery seem to have an insatiable appetite for books about spirituality, specifically prayer and meditation The list of titles is quite narrow and searching for a meditation technique suitable for alcoholics, especially one that is Twelve Step friendly, is not easy. There is a limited array of volumes which seem to be more along the lines of *visualization prayers*, *reflections* and positive *affirmation*-styles of "meditations." Very often these are laden with religious context that may suit some people, but certainly not all.

Real Meditation for Real Alcoholics is nothing like those. Here is an introduction to a meditation technique that has been practiced since ancient times by all people in a presentation tailored specially for alcoholics, because the author is one.

If you have come upon this book while looking for a non-religious, spiritual way to learn how to meditate, this is it. You have just come upon a real, tangible technique that you can use in your daily life, starting today.

There are millions of recovered alcoholics who have successfully adopted a spiritual design for living and for them the alcoholism problem has been solved. Perhaps you are one of those. If you are, then as the result of following a few simple rules, you have experienced a spontaneous abatement of the obsessive desire to drink and gotten your life back. But as is often the case, in time, there can be a return of unmanageability as a slow, excruciating unraveling of sobriety begins. Spiritual growth ceases and there is a re-emergence of anxiety, irritability and depression.

Perhaps you have also experienced this. Then this book is written for you. Maybe you have not experienced this but would like to avoid hitting the spiritual wall so many others seem to run into. Then this book is also for you.

Even if you are not alcoholic yourself but need an understanding of what you are dealing with—a way to rise above the inevitable morass that encroaches and surrounds the lives of those who love and live with alcoholics—then this book will seem a Godsend. While it may not be just what the doctor ordered (or the counselor for that matter) and may seem a little radical, it does offer what you need to set right the seemingly intolerable situation in which you find yourself.

Alcoholics seeking to get better often pass through the clinical maze of treatments and mistreatments, finally settling on a fundamental spiritual solution to their problems; hopefully a permanent solution.

Then, the self-centered human penchant to egotistically *kick into overdrive* intervenes.

Oftentimes ambitiously expanded spiritual pursuits fall flat—proposing principles or philosophical views that are divergent to the base principles an alcoholic has accessed with success, causing the unwitting searcher to experience grave, internal conflicts and spiritual crises they never expected. Personal difficulties emerge. As troubles mount, they wreak increasing havoc on life, health and living.

How do I know this? Well for one thing, it once happened to me.

Subsequently, I was blessed to have discovered the way out of that sticky predicament. Then, in working with others, I began to expand the scope of this tiny, personal calling across the U.S., even traveling abroad, speaking with many others. It seems that no matter where they live, all over the world, there are sober alcoholics who agree that spiritual stagnation is quite a daunting dilemma and going forward, they are as perplexed by this troublesome glitch in their recovery as I had been.

Having eliminated this problem for myself through an effective meditation, I began taking this solution to them and it has helped many. I have no idea *how* many. I have communicated with thousands and with the highest ranked recovered alcoholic blog on the internet I have reached millions over the years; I can only surmise the number to be up there somewhere. I am not about to erect a McDonald's style "Billions Served" sign on my front lawn. But rather than keep this proposition solely one-on-one and eyeball-to-eyeball (and since I am a writer by trade) I have decided to use my vocation and write this book.

Through it, I would like to introduce you to a free, non-religious technique that will not clash with the fundamental spiritual Principles laid into the foundation of *any* spiritual recovery. Whether you have solved your problems through a non-religious spiritual fellowship, religious organizations or any *other way*, it is my deepest hope to convince you that you can access a unique spiritual skill and apply it to your life successfully. No matter where you are in your recovery, whether you call yourself recovered or recovering; whether you are dry or an active drunk stepping on the toes of those around you like a drunken bull-clown in a Texas Rodeo, it is appropriate, non religious and fully compatible with every spiritual principle in the Twelve Step presentation.

It is an ultra-simple but powerful method of developing and maintaining ongoing God consciousness that is unlike any you have *ever* seen before. It will enliven your experience while still practicing the Principles you so cherish; thereby resolving any dilemma you may have had in the past regarding this aspect of spiritual recovery.

If you have been exposed to the world of recovery from alcoholism then no doubt you are already familiar with the fellowship named *Alcoholics Anonymous*. You probably know that back in the 1930s a group of a hundred alcoholic men and woman adopted some specific procedure and a spiritual lifestyle that endowed them with a spontaneous, enduring spiritual awakening. Through that experience they were relieved of their desire to drink. They decided to spread the word about the effective recovery method they used—through the *wholesale* distribution of a book delineating precisely *how* they recovered from alcoholism. "Alcoholics Anonymous: The Story of How Many Thousands of Men and Women Have Recovered from Alcoholism" endeavors to tell readers *where* to find God and *how* to find Him. It is one of the twentieth century's greatest "How To" spiritual works.

Since its publication in 1939, the "Big Book" as it is fondly called, has sold more than 30 million copies and has been translated into more than forty languages, with its Twelve Step principles now used as the model for more than sixty active recovery programs.

What many are surprised to learn is that the Twelve proposals don't actually remove the desire to drink. Not directly anyway. First, the twelve spiritual suggestions induce a spontaneous spiritual awakening, then that awakening finally expels the obsession. It was not designed as a long drawn out affair. Historically, the whole process took just a matter of days to accomplish and the co-founders of *Alcoholism Anonymous* chronicle this in their book.

Many of those following such a radical course as this also discovered something else. Not only did the experience remove the obsession to drink, but also along with it came a style of living which resulted in the removal of all the obsessive problems of the alcoholic.

Quite neat. Whether the practitioner is able to *keep* that awakened state and *continue* to live as a spiritually awake and aware person is something else entirely.

I can say from experience that it works. It happened to me. Like millions of others, I had the same spiritual experience as the result of following the simple prescription described by the co-authors of "Alcoholics Anonymous." It was ridiculously simple albeit extraordinarily difficult to endure. But once done, I experienced the spontaneous removal of the desire to drink—just as predicted. It took forty-four days to get through it. That was in 1999.

Now there is more to this.

There is a well-known factoid among the worldwide community of Twelve Steppers. Simply stated: As recovered alcoholics, we can access a spiritual program – as detailed in *Step Eleven* of the original text of "Alcoholics Anonymous." This program entreats the alcoholic to meditate. Then, as if some by some purposeful laxity on the part of the co-authors, the same book does not tell us how to do it.

These men and women have been as perplexed as I by this ironic hitch because it is an oversight that ultimately commits all effort to resolve all alcoholic problems to a lifetime of ultimate failure. Good health, relationships, emotional sobriety, stability and peace of mind escapes even those who do not drink. We have been left with no choice but to search outside of the Twelve Step fellowship in hopes of finding a suitable meditation technique – one that does not conflict with the Twelve Step Principles.

With no meditation directions in the Twelve Step instructions, the choice is to skip it or else go outside the Twelve Step program. I have spoken with many others, all over the world, who agree; trying to choose between two such equally undesirable alternatives, makes for quite a dilemma. Talk about being stuck between a rock and a hard place—a *catch-22* with neither choice being acceptable. This book, this meditation is the break in the dilemma.

Today people all over the world are using this technique to solve this dilemma. I regularly work with alcoholics who have also had their weight issues, chronic pain, depression, anxiety, smoking, sleep disorder and of course drinking problems; literally removed without effort. These folks range from alcoholics unable to stop drinking to recovered alcoholics who have hit a brick wall in their spirituality. Even spouses and loved ones of alcoholics have benefited.

For well over a decade now, I have reinstated the same practice I had discovered when I was but a tot and today endeavor to live in an aware state of consciousness every waking moment. I find I am able to do so reasonably well and I practice staying aware through exercising consciousness through practicing the very special meditation technique I now bring to the fore. I am convinced that the recovery world will be better for this introduction.

From this book you will be guided in learning this meditation, even though the specific directions are aurally presented and not textually. There is no reason for disappointment however, since we don't need scripted guidance in this text. I am not holding out, you can have it anyway, free of charge. (Those directions cannot be effectively reduced to paper and ink and with over thirty years experience using this technique it has been shown that it is unwise and possibly unsafe to do so. It is *that* powerful.)

This book is more of a pitch for, and companion to, a free download that will demonstrate to you exactly how to meditate properly and safely. *Yes, there is meditation that is most definitely unsafe. That idea will be expanded upon more fully later in this book.* The free meditation audio file address and download and listening instructions can be found on the "How To Get There" page in the back of this book.

I see that this book can be something else too. It can help a reader validate some of the understanding that comes once the decision is made to give this meditation thing a whirl. Some of the revelations; the understanding, sure to come, can be so astonishing there may be a strong temptation to doubt it is even possible. *Examples of this are presented later on as well.* By having this book, readers will get the real sense that they are not alone; that there really is a Fourth Dimension of existence and that it is possible to *know* without being *taught.* My testimony and many years of experience can help give fellowship through the written page to the trembling soul even though we may never meet.

Looking now at this project I can see that the presentation is something different from anything else in the genre. It has the look and feel of a self-help or "How To" work, but it is not. It is an attention-getter; a device to entreat you to sample what I have discovered for me and my family and those to whom I have helped. Any really good spiritual exemplar will, once getting your attention, deflect you off him and toward the source of all real answers to all your problems. That one is God. May he save you from all your human reliances.

"If you don't control your mind, someone else will." - *John Allston*

DISCOVERING MEDITATION

It was in the early 60s, when I was about six years old that I first became conscious of the meditation I today practice. I am sure that many of you who are reading this also knew of it. You were born with it too, but perhaps have since forgotten what it was like. Back then, using an *eye-head* method, I practiced rising above the stresses and cruelties surrounding my life. (More about these in the "Authors Biography.") Without the love and guidance of a father, I abandoned it in favor of chasing food, music, sex and…of course, alcohol.

Then when in my late teens, I rediscovered the experience and had a "spiritual awakening" that was of a very drastic nature. Immediately I was able to discard the immature drinking and drugging life, get off the Bronx streets, marry Nancy, my High School sweetheart and begin a promising career in Public Relations and Journalism.

Riding on that initial spiritual experience—without doing much of anything to maintain the moral lifestyle, life's unmanageability bore down. Discomfort mounted. The drinking solution reentered the picture. This was in the early 80s. With booze eventually failing to numb the pain of conscience well enough to remain comfortable in my own skin, I made a decision to reestablish the lost God connection. I came across a man who knew about the very same "meditation" experience with which I was already familiar but had based an entire career on it—helping others. He would help me. He had captured its essence and ingeniously snapped it into a box, ready for wholesale distribution, so to speak. I met with him at his home in Oregon where I spent two weeks with him and his family.

With his help, we were able to iron out some of the "kinks" in my life at the time. I also learned how to include the combined *hand-finger* method with the *eyes-head* technique[5] I had discovered as a child. I experienced a dramatic spontaneous awakening—the desire to

---

[5]These two techniques are references to the actual meditation you will learn if you decide to access to the meditation exercise. It is available for streaming or download on the "How To Get There," page in the back of this book. It is free and always will be.

drink left completely—*as did a real nasty spirit.* I left Oregon, came back to New York City and began meditating in earnest – once again. This resulted in a dramatic, "white light" variety of spiritual experience. I felt as I did when I was a child again.

I continued to meditate but within a year, I am ashamed to admit, began to exploit the meditation to fulfill some ambitious desires. I became enamored with the new understanding and insights I was given to receive. I had learned a little and something in me craved knowing more. As the normal clamor of the world drew nearer I doubted the simplicity of God consciousness and lost faith to *Self* consciousness. Latching onto *Self,* I was pulled into a state of prolonged unawareness, the same kind I had fallen into earlier during my High School years. Within a very short time, I was once again "of the world", enslaved to the bondage of *Self.*

This misuse of a great gift resulted in a settling back into the drinking I had given up only a few years before. It did not take long before I had damaged my body beyond the point of no return. The symptoms of spiritual disease began to manifest; mental obsession and post-drinking, physical craving, in what we know today to be classic alcoholism. Unable to stop drinking once I started, compounded by the utter inability to *not start,* I developed what I term as "Alcoholic Syndrome."[6] or as the cofounders of *Alcoholics Anonymous* would have said, I was a "Real Alcoholic". I was a goner.

As a "functional" alcoholic, there were inevitable twists and turns in the stream of life. Gains were always followed by heartbreaking setbacks. Despite each new low, I was able to keep up with practicing meditation for a number of years. By using the phrase "keep up" I am in no ways ingratiating myself, trust me. I was a fair weather "meditator" using it to patch up the wounds of my foolishness with a false hope that imagined spiritual acumen delivers so well. *Just look into some of the churches and you will know what I mean.* My "church" was not a spiritual structure—it was the temple of intellect; my own alcohol soaked skull, with me playing the role of a twisted, drunk and perverted

---

[6]Alcoholic-Syndrome - Mental Obsession and Physical Craving combined to form the singular description of "Alcoholism"

pastor; who like many others, manages to retain his corrupted position. Somehow I kept consciousness at some level, however low.

Amidst the highs and lows, life simply crumbled. There was never any real security or sanity for many years. For some time it appeared I was the pinnacle of success, riding around Wall Street in chauffer driven limousines, puffing on fat Cuban cigars, dining in the finest restaurants and "doing deals" all over Manhattan.

Associating with nefarious individuals, who were as spiritually lost and displaced as I was, it became easy to get embroiled in multi-billion dollar, international investment banking deals—schemes that ultimately would never get off the ground. But boy did the wheeler-dealer Wall Street lifestyle feel good; and I looked good doing it. I was *important.*

Other years I scrounged through couches collecting lost pennies so I could buy a forty-ounce bottle of Budweiser. It was a kind of life that wasn't a living. There is a difference between being humbled and degraded. This was not humbling. It felt as if my wife Nancy and I were riding on a roller coaster wearing blindfolds. All I could do was feel the rushing wind, gravity and fear straining around; while sucking in the whirling electrified air into my spiritually defeated psyche. The exhilaration felt like life. It was a nauseating but strangely addictive energy – a life force that powers some really creepy people. I had become one. It wasn't life at all but it's cruel imposter: Death.

Something vital was missing. It became clear that it would be necessary to get back to practicing conscious contact with God. God and Wall Street. What a merger this could be. Talk about He-Men of the universe!

Still clinging to the prideful vestiges of imagined spiritual prowess of the past, I was too ashamed and afraid to begin again; returning to Oregon was out of the question. The state of mind with which I was familiar and knew was possible to attain through the meditation practice was too painful to bear; at least in my self-centered, *pain-avoidance* mode. A few feeble attempts to relax and find peace resulted in going even further into the spiritual abyss. I had forgotten how to meditate properly. Big mistake.

Too 'proud' to restart – a decade had already passed since my first experience. I felt that by then *I should have been sporting a halo over my head*. I marked time waffling and wallowing in between depression and exhilarating drunkenness. Then in 1997, I came to the AA Fellowship. On the very first day of *meetings*, something really caught my eye and the attention of my soul and heart.

In my first AA meeting, I sat in the back of the crowded church basement, clutching my infant son under my arm like a football. I was intent upon hiding from the gavel wielding "elders" presiding."

Behind them, depended by frayed strings thumb-tacked to the cheesy dark wood paneling of the basement wall, were two shades – you probably know the ones. They were filled top to bottom with black and red lettering. From where I sat I could not make out the text very well, but I thought they resembled to two hideously large Chinese menus – the smaller version of which are periodically littered through the halls and under the doors of Manhattan apartment buildings; advertising the take-out and delivery fare of the local "Wall of China" or "Wang's Wok."

If I squinted hard and if I strained my neck far enough, I could just barely make out two words appearing on one of the grotesque documents hanging in front of the room—the shade on the left. They were "God" and "meditation", words which had previously conveyed the two most impactful ideas in my life. My heart was instantly lifted. I knew that I had stumbled upon a lifeboat that could get me back to God. I felt I had come home.

Not only was I in the midst of a spiritual fellowship but it was a meditation friendly fellowship too! I was overjoyed, to say the least. The rest is a classic AA recovery experience with which you may already be familiar. As part of adopting the Twelve Step lifestyle in order to "practice these principles" I began to engage in all of the daily prayers – straight out of the *Big Book* – finding the spirit behind the text of these prayers to be entirely in agreement with what I had come to see as *truth*. This brought a special fondness for the Twelve Step prayers and recognition of the impeccably genuine spirit of goodness behind them.[7]

---

[7]See the "Big Book" prayers in Appendices I and II

When directed to engage in daily "meditation" through Step Eleven I did not need to search for any special technique, religion or spiritual movement to teach what is commonly termed as "meditation" as I already had many years of practice and experience with the state of consciousness needed and a method for getting to it. This is why I am free from attachments to formal philosophies as I have never been corrupted by their doctrines in order to arrive at a practical meditation technique. I have the original; the untainted and effective method for human, conscious contact with God as espoused and chronicled in Scripture.

Spying that shade on the wall, I knew that this was my chance. I could simply pick up where I had left off years ago and as I had intuitively practiced as a child. I did so immediately and I was able to move easily into it without too much trouble.

If you look into my past you will see that I am a marketing person. I worked for many years in Public Relations and the food marketing business and for nearly twenty years, I was a broker on Wall Street where I marketed securities. So when investigating the business end of this book-publishing venture I saw it was necessary to evaluate at the product competition this book would be up against on bookshelves.

Among similar genres I found authors proposing many spiritual meditations and relaxation techniques. Several of them seemed on the surface to resemble the one I have discovered, at least in approach. But virtually every single one of them are inexact enough to set them far apart from the type of meditation exercises of which I write.

I have no aspiration to becoming a superficial, self-help, "abundance" guru or one of those life-coach, prosperity preaching types seen on late night infomercials, running around on stage with a microphone strapped to their heads, ranting about their newest redux of New Thought pseudo-spiritualism. I have no hopes of running a spiritual mountain retreat of meditating alkies and spirituality seeking "followers". There will be no spirituality cruises, sweat lodges, fire-walks, hotel ballrooms filled with padded banquet chairs or mega-church stadiums stuffed with hordes of fanatics *praising the Lord* through Marshal amps and backup singer accompaniment. I find that kind of stuff and those kinds of promoters very disturbing. You will never, see me trying to distribute this technique on any home shopping cable networks and you will never be able to matriculate a "course" in this spirituality.

What I offer you *free* is much too significant to require payment. This meditation is simply an exercise. The consciousness effect and the contact you make with God is between you and Him and there will never be any money, or quid pro quo of any kind to come in between you and that spiritual objective. You are never going to be asked to change your diet, send money, donate, take classes, adopt special jargon, attend any seminars, listen to me preach sermons, join in, sign up or in any way personally affiliate with any organization or with me. We will probably never personally meet. I do not seek "followers" or to become the head of any spiritual group, church or self-help movement.

I may continue to speak at some Twelve Step functions as I have been doing for years, here and abroad, but mostly I will write some books and as any good author would, do some readings—but that's it. What I present here is too simple and precious to complicate or contaminate by mundane commercialism. To turn conscious contact with God into a cottage industry or an empire will absolutely ruin it, rendering it worse than useless—but harmful. I will continue to give it away without cost and it will always be that way.

Raising my family and to continue giving away this meditation exercise for all the days of my life is my hope.

I have over thirty years of experience with this technique. I have done it right. I have done it wrong. I have let up on it. I have stepped it up to foolish levels. During decades I have made so many mistakes with it that it nearly ruined my life, bringing me close to death. I have had many "successes" as well and it is that success upon which I have settled and pine my life and the lives of my wife and two children. I have also taught it to others who have benefited and to those who have abused it and suffered as well. I teach it to my kids, my wife. I have overcome mental, emotional, and physical diseases through this technique.

So why should you believe me?

Well, I say, "Don't."

I also say, "Don't disbelieve."

If something resonates in your heart – if there is some inner recognition, the same kind I felt back in 1997 when I sat in that AA meeting room looking up at that those wall shades; then please consider that maybe there is something here that will change you forever.

I have discovered something priceless and I wish to share it with you. It is the missing link, the lost element of the Twelve Step practice for which you have been looking. There is ineffable human wellness resulting from a spiritual, physical, emotional and mental state that is attendant to improving conscious contact with God. If what I share through this book delivers the same access to perfect peace and ease in living that me and my family have, then your time, and mine, will have been well spent.

"How much more grievous are the consequences of anger than the causes of it" - *Marcus Aurelius*

HOW TO APPROACH THIS BOOK

This book directs you toward a form of meditation that liberates the mind from learning and from the limitations of that marvelous storage facility in your head called "brain". It is a tool to reconnect you to a lost, inner source of understanding totally free from intellectual knowledge.

Instead of attempting to go through this book from beginning to end as you would a "self-help" book or a novella, it is highly suggested that you read the Introduction and front sections first. Then before moving on to Chapter 1 enter the meditative state. Use the free audio download located on the "How To Get There," page in the back section. This suggestion is not mandatory, but many sincere readers will find this helpful prior to getting too deep into the book. There is much in this book that you simply will not grasp on the "first go around." This is to be expected and nothing to worry about.

Although you may not know it, your mind, your thoughts and attitudes have become ensnared by suggestions and seductive influences stemming from a lifetime of pressure. Some of these are stresses with which you are probably already familiar—others are not so apparent. Either way, these influences have wielded a certain sway, presiding over your behaviors. Under such a "spell" it can be difficult if not impossible to tell true from false. This is very similar to hypnotism such as you have seen on TV, or have noticed in product advertising, political propaganda, religious doctrines or anything designed to influence and motivate. The effects can be very subtle, often undetectable, and therefore quite powerful and dangerous.

The meditation exercise to which you are being introduced through this book is not merely one more of these seductive influences to compete for control over you and your attentions. Instead it will release you from the mental stranglehold of your prejudices and allow you to see for yourself. Perhaps for the first time.

With that new freedom you will gain clarity over the material presented in this book. It will reboot your thinking, shaking loose old cobwebs of thought, freeing you to perceive without prejudging. Should you have concerns over this idea, then please feel free to go ahead and read anyway. I believe the case will be made well enough in this book to encourage you to use this meditation on your own. Simply come back after earnest meditation and access this book again. You will find that your perception is entirely different and the topics discussed far more meaningful to you.

Please refrain from attempting to remember or memorize the concepts and presentation of spiritual ideas. Inciting the intellect through "learning" will only defeat the state of quiet consciousness being proposed. Trying too hard to grasp the contents of this book, especially if electing to skip the meditation exercise can only neutralize your spiritual progress.

This book is more meant to steer you in a direction than it is intended to enlighten. Those who read the material presented are known to have many 'aha' experiences of their own. If this is to happen genuinely, then such experiences must be yours alone. You do not need an author's "enlightenment" or the understanding of *any* other human being when you can access and improve wisdom, understanding and conscious contact with God on your own. Independence from people, gurus and things human is a main point of this book, as you are about to discover.

"Everybody has a plan . . . until they get punched in the face."
- *Mike Tyson*

1 OKAY. I'M RECOVERED

Now What?

*T*he door opened, the little bell on top of the door jingled, and the two children stepped out of the warm June sunlight and into the florescent dankness of the store. A frigid blast of air slapped their faces, and it felt good.

It smelled like candy, fresh tobacco and ink. Peering past the wooden newspaper stand and down the long row of empty chrome and red leatherette stools that dotted the length of the counter, Betty Wilson thought they looked like shiny, giant mushrooms.

Gary Greengrass walked along the row and eyed the red and white Coca-Cola fountain midway down the counter. It was flanked by a set of chrome-plated spigots and taps. "I wanna Coke!" he said. He imagined the sugary, cold burn scraping the back of his tongue, and it made him swallow spit. Reaching into one pocket of his blue Wranglers, Gary pulled out a quarter and smacked it down on the counter.

Betty stood considering the stools. "Hmm. Let's see now. Which one?" she thought.

She head-nodded a quick eye-count down the mushroom row. "It could be stool one," she reckoned.

"Uh-uh. It has electrical tape on it. Probably lost some of its stuffing and way too hard to sit on —not to mention ugly...How about stool two? Nope—too close to stool one. Stool three? No way! Too obvious." Her head stopped counting at four, and she walked toward it. "Four it is!" she thought.

"We can sit here," she announced, and with one finger gave Number Four a push. Instead of spinning, the stool wobbled around and in barely a quarter turn, came to a blood-curdling stop. It sounded exactly like the chalk on Sister Mary Margaret's blackboard.

Gary, still admiring the big Coca-Cola machine, gritted his teeth and cringed. "What was that?"

"Ree—ject!" she sang.

"Okay. Next stool." She gave it a spin. This one whirled like a top. It was suitable for the ultimate test—the butt spin. A complete three-hundred-and-sixty-degree dervish whirl.

One last glance toward Willie and—"Shoot," she said. "Here he comes."

"What did you say?" Gary asked. When he saw the old man approaching, he immediately knew. Willie always yelled when the kids spun on the stools. One time he chased Buddy Bloss, a repeat offender, all the way out of the store and around the corner. Buddy might have gotten away too, if he hadn't been so spin-dizzy and swerved right into Mrs. Melfi's bushes.

A quick back-and-forth, hippy swing of the butt cheeks would have to do. She swung. There was barely a squeak.

On the counter there was a cardboard box bearing a cartoon of the mustachioed sultan wearing a turban. "How much are these jelly rings?" she wanted to know.

"Two cents." Willie's cigar jiggled when he spoke, the gray ash at its end ever-threatening to fly off, but somehow it never did. Everyone in the Bronx neighborhood was convinced Willie never bothered to light it; that it was just the same old cold ash, on the same cigar, burned long ago.

"Sim Salabim," she said, and lifted the lid off the box. The smell of raspberry and chocolate rose to tease her nostrils. "Hey, there are marshmallows twists in this box too. I'm taking one."

"Same price. Two cents."

"Can I have a pretzel?" Gary asked.

Willie picked up the glass pretzel-rod cylinder and placed it on top of the cold, white marble counter. He lifted the lid, exposing a bundle of salty rods. They stood like crisp soldiers. Betty stuck her nose over them and took a whiff.

"These are fresh!" The proclamation made Gary smile. He watched her slide one rod out and crunch the end into her mouth. It was salty. Now they were both smiling.

2

"Yes, they are fresh. Of course, they are fresh. Now do you kids want soda, or what?"

"I wanna Coke," said Gary.

"Egg creams!" She smiled.

"Chocolate." Willie assumed.

Willie could make a vanilla egg cream too, even though hardly anyone ever ordered vanilla. It was always chocolate. He went through three gallons of Fox's U-Bet syrup a week.

"Yes, two." Her smile widened. She disregarded Gary. Not with her eyes.

Even if you have never been to New York City undoubtedly you have heard of the famous New York Egg Cream. Making one is very simple. Using the basic ingredients, mixing them properly, with the right utensils and in the right order, will always yield the same delicious beverage.

Substitute Hershey's chocolate syrup for Fox's U-bet? "Yup. It's an egg cream all right. Sort of." It doesn't taste quite like a New York Egg Cream, though.

Forget to bounce the seltzer off the spoon and instead allow it to splash directly into the bottom of the glass? You may think, *"Not bad. It looks okay."* But it is somehow…*different.* No frothy mustache for you.

How about using skim milk instead of fresh, whole milk? *Oh God. Puhleeze! Take it away. If I wanted a milky, chocolate soft drink, I would have bought a Yoo-hoo.*

Any way you tweak the formula, well intentioned or not, your efforts may result in some sort of decent-looking chocolate soda concoction. Heck, it may taste dammed good too. But, as any true blue New Yorker knows, making a real egg cream is a craft. If you toy with the conventional technique passed on through the generations you do so at your own risk. Betty Wilson would certainly not approve.

Are you getting my drift?

"Wait a minute. This is a book about meditation, right? What are we doing in the Bronx, and why are we talking about egg creams?"

I can explain.

Just as there are simple and fine elements to successfully making a genuine New York Egg Cream, genuine *conscious contact* with God also entails some elementary essentials vital to success. While the list of ingredients is short and the method employed simple, experience has proven time and time again that tampering with any of the fundamentals will make the difference between settling for a dull, unreasonable facsimile or having a genuine, effective egg cream. *Oops...I mean Step Eleven.*

It is the beginning of a new school year in the United States as the finishing touches go into this book and both my son and daughter look forward to a new year. I made a decision to take my fifteen-year-old son Danny out of the public school system and have him finish high school in a private school. He has always gotten straight A's and is on the Honor Roll and so I am sure that ultimately the switch will prove satisfactory.

Still there is concern that he may be at some academic disadvantage coming into a new discipline. It is only the beginning of his sophomore year; yet early in his secondary education. The hope is that if he is at any disadvantage, he will get caught up easily. Still a little chariness can't hurt, and so we have been preparing him, accelerating his reading and use of learning materials he would never be exposed to at the public level.

In the same way, since it is early on in this book, I wish to ensure that every reader is up to snuff in certain areas of recovery. I make frequent references throughout this book to the Twelve Steps. While I expect that many readers will already be familiar with those, it is also my hope that those who are not will also feel comfortable enough with my authority over alcoholic obsessions to be sufficiently encouraged to try the meditation technique I propose.

As you may have gathered, the subtitle of this book "and those who love them," infers that this will work for non-alcoholics too. My immediate family, all non-alcoholic, meditates just as I propose you allow me to show you. It works for all of us.

If you are a Twelve Step aficionado, I am of course writing directly to you. The good news for you is that now with this book, you have discovered the missing link to your Twelve Step practice that will change your life forever, making that design for living come alive like never before. You will not want to miss what this book delivers to you.

If you aren't, then as with my son, I am certain you can be brought up to speed very nicely. The good news for non-twelve-steppers is that this technique is so powerful and effective that even if you have not already established *conscious contact* with God by way of the Steps, you will now be able to do exactly that anyway.

Let's be clear. This is not to encourage would be Twelve Steppers to balk or scoff at the complete Twelve Step approach. Real alcoholics endeavoring to navigate the Twelve Step route are on a road to spiritual awakening and recovery and should continue. It is to welcome problematic, hard drinkers, whose lives suffer and yet may not qualify for the Twelve Step approach, to at least get on board with a spiritual lifestyle they will automatically have once prayer and meditation become of part of their existence. Those types can have a spiritual awakening too. They just do not have to go the drastic lengths of the Twelve Step procedure. For them, if they are non-alcoholic, there may be an easier softer way.

All you will need to be fully acclimated is a brief perspective so the language I use throughout this book makes sense. This book is not some deep introspective analysis of the Twelve Steps, or of *Alcoholics Anonymous*. By the time you finish reading this page you will be sufficiently caught up and not feel like you missed some 'classes'.

> *The Twelve Steps is a series of proposals that when acted upon, precisely as prescribed, in the order prescribed, are found to actuate a spontaneous spiritual awakening. It's an experience that sets off a sequencing of effortless answers to all of life's problems. For the alcoholic, the first of these being the dissolution of obsessive drinking.*
>
> *Once this spontaneous awakening occurs the practitioner never drinks again provided he live by certain spiritual principles codified in the Steps, each one vital to ongoing permanent sobriety and spiritual soundness. Practitioners who continue on with the precise spiritual*

principles conveyed through "Alcoholic Anonymous" become free from anger; life becomes perfectly ordered; emotional ties and personal dependencies upon people, places, things, even upon the Big Book itself, melt away in favor of reliance upon God. It is a useful, peaceful way to live that grows effortlessly.

The cessation of drinking under this spiritual order of human existence is incidental.

This recovery was experienced by a once agnostic and chronic alcoholic named Bill Wilson, who endeavored to replicate in other hopeless alcoholics, what he did to induce this apparent miraculous outcome. After getting a hundred others to successfully follow the same exact path, achieving the exact same result, he numbered and wrote them down. Then in 1938, they published it in a program of recovery under the auspices of a group of recovered, alcoholic co-authors. This launched the wholesale distribution of the procedure they had found.

Their book, titled "Alcoholics Anonymous", a how-to volume, presents a rapid, effective and permanent recovery plan that works where all other methods fail. It is one of the best-selling books of all time. In 2011, the A A "Big Book" as it is affectionately nicknamed, was pegged by Time magazine as being one of the "100 Best" and most influential books ever written in English. The solution to spiritual disease which causes alcoholism presented through that book is responsible for the release of thousands upon thousands of alcoholics from the clinical mazes of hospitals, rehabs and treatment centers that exist under the smothering patronage of the 21st Century U.S. Health Care system. No wonder it has sold over thirty million copies.

Today the Twelve Steps remains the granddaddy of all recovery plans. Despite many attempts to capture and market its essence; it has never been successfully commercialized without spoiling its effectiveness—a fact which makes it the competitive envy of the alcohol and addictions treatment industry to this day. Trying to do what only God can has proven to be quite impossible.

Step Eleven suggests prayer and meditation and reads as follows:

"Sought through prayer and meditation to improve our *conscious contact* with God *as we understood Him,* praying only for knowledge of His will for us and the power to carry that out."[8]

This is a Step often thought to be primarily about prayer and meditation. This is a common misconception, and very easy to make. The object of *Step Eleven* is not to pray and meditate. Prayer and meditation is merely the *means* to an *end.* That *end* is to "improve *conscious contact* with God," not to pray or to meditate. If that were true, then *any* prayer and *any* meditation would be appropriate and it is not.

Prayer and meditation are principally specific and to be congruous with the Twelve Steps there must be adherence to the spiritual principles discussed throughout the Twelve Step presentation. Prayer and meditation for the sake of prayer and meditation is *not* an element of this particular spiritual prescription. This is what this book proposes to introduce you to; a means to an end, a very special meditation technique that is fully reconcilable with the spiritual principles of the Twelve Step recovery presentation made through "Alcoholics Anonymous".

Praying to manipulate outcomes in the Stream of Life or meditating in order to attain what we believe to be enlightenment or wisdom; or say, to know the future or to achieve happiness—anything more than *conscious contact,* has nothing to do with *Step Eleven* meditation.

I am sure my editor will flag what follows for redundancy, but I must repeat this idea: *Any motive for meditation beyond improving conscious contact with God is inappropriate for our purposes.*

Step Eleven contains a powerful, one-two formula designed to improve *conscious contact with* God. "Improve" implies that an initial

---

[8]"Alcoholics Anonymous", 4th edition, Alcoholics Anonymous World Services, 59:2

contact has already been made. For the Twelve Stepper first contact has already been made through a spiritual awakening. Subsequently he becomes increasingly "God conscious" more of the time.

Typically this powerful experience occurs somewhere in between Step Four and Step Nine—frequently even sooner than that. *(I and many others have experienced such awakening even before beginning a Fourth-Step.)* The idea now is to *improve* upon that contact with Him. For the alcoholic who has not yet had that experience, that is about to change, if you are willing to try the method proposed here.

Improve means to *make better.* That does not mean willfully increasing with intensity or stepping up effort. In this case *making better* means *more often with lessening effort.* We are to live more and more of our days, taking life easy, each second of each minute in each day in *conscious contact* with God. We are either *conscious* or we are *unconscious*; either filled with Gods vision or else agnostically attached to *self*-vision. *I speak more about this idea in the meditation exercise recording I am hoping you will access and use.*

Sometimes a clever teacher will tell a student, "Forget what you *think* you know...I am going to set you straight with something better." Nonsense. Be wary of anyone who tries to erase from your mind what it already believes. Anyone who asks you to empty your mind, so they can replace it with something else, is demonstrating sure signs of brainwashing. First that *they* have been brainwashed and secondly that they seek to brainwash *you.*

I have not written this book in order to indoctrinate. I prefer showing how to become objective, to undo prior brainwashing. Through that, God will correct your attitude, not suggestions I plant in your head. Whatever you *think* meditation is or whatever you recon it *ought* to be, you are asked to please always remember those preconceptions. Do *not* forget what you already believe about meditation. Instead, please consciously contrast what I convey in this book with what you know. I want you to consciously observe the difference. Don't believe or disbelieve, just see.

With its powerful marriage of word to spirit, *Step Eleven* becomes the dominant prescription for success in the life of a spiritually awakened, recovered alcoholic; a simple recipe that promotes spiritual growth and progress. As with the beloved egg cream, removing or diminishing even one element of the *two-part formula*, prayer and meditation, alters the effect that those combined ingredients produce. Similarly, *conscious contact* with God will *not* increase with such tampering. Modification may *decrease* it.

Even the egg cream with its three scant ingredients is more complex than Step Eleven. In the Step the recipe has only two parts: It has prayer. It has meditation. The first part of the step... prayer? On that, we get plenty of help from the book "Alcoholics Anonymous". The second part, meditation...not so much. Hence, this book.

In the egg cream, milk is the nourishing new awakened life. Prayer is the sweet chocolate syrup. Meditation is the seltzer that makes it all fizz and come alive. Which would you rather have: a glass of seltzer, a glass of chocolate milk, or a New York Egg Cream? Yum... and *Sim Salabim*!

So this thing called meditation poses a bit of a problem for you.

Many alcoholics believe that in order to live a happy and whole life they will be required to do much more than stay sober. They are also sure that their very lives hang in the balance unless they can adopt a very specific design for living. This is no ordinary lifestyle. It proposes a very specific modality of daily existence that reflects a drastic departure from the way the typical alcoholic has lived for most of his life. For one thing, it prescribes daily prayer and meditation.

This design is expressed in the Twelve-Step plan, which is ingeniously delineated in a resourceful little how-to volume titled "Alcoholics Anonymous: The Story of How Many Thousands of Men and Women Have Recovered from Alcoholism".

Weighing in at a mere one hundred and sixty four pages and fondly referred to as the *Big Book*, this work contains proposals for a way of life that is currently being practiced worldwide by millions of people. These are legions of recovered alcoholics taking their lead from the coauthors of that book: "One hundred men and women" who had established a relationship with God. They shared a common problem and discovered a common solution. The problem, they discovered, was caused by spiritual dysfunction. The solution they found came quite simply, by means of a spiritual awakening.

One hundred somnambulant, obsessive miscreants discovered that upon awakening, the obsession to drink was lifted—removed permanently. The experience placed them onto a moral path leading to the discovery of God. Getting there took some simple acts of "human" will—just a smidge—but it was the *only* act of will that they would ever need to make for the rest of their lives. It was only fitting that they should stick together to form a spiritual bond and a fellowship of that spirit. They dubbed it *Alcoholics Anonymous*, eponymously named after their book explaining how it all came about.

It is the only book I have ever seen covering the Twelve Steps that is worth a darn. Everything anyone ever needs to understand and follow the directions for taking the Twelve Steps in order to invoke a spiritual awakening is right there in that book. Every time someone has ever tried to improve upon it, to re-systemize it in attempt to make it easier to understand, all they have ever managed to do is spin things just enough to screw it all up. I mention this in case you might get the idea that this is a book about the Twelve Steps or about "Alcoholics Anonymous." Again, *fuhgetaboudit!* This isn't *The Twelve Steps—Redux.*

What would be the point of rehashing what "Alcoholics Anonymous" has already covered well enough? What *this* book is about is the part of the Twelve Steps that is *not* covered by the coauthors of *Alcoholics Anonymous* in *their* book. We are going to talk about the *unaddressed* part of Step Eleven: *Meditation.*

Step Eleven implies that once an alcoholic recovers from alcoholism, in order to maintain his newly sane condition he will also need to meditate. Instructions on just how to go about it are glaringly absent. It is a mystical proposal with a specific aim; improving *conscious contact* with God through two activities, prayer and meditation. While not in the least bit vague about the prayer side of this dual proposal, the coauthors of "Alcoholics Anonymous" even go so far as to characterize the *kind* of prayer to use ("praying only for knowledge of His will for us and the power to carry that out"). Yet it seems they were outright negligent in presenting readers with a meditation technique to use. Not even a hint. It has been suggested that this obvious oversight was deliberate—and perhaps that is so. My conjecture on this matter is irrelevant. Whether the omission was intended or not, many practitioners are forced to seek outside sources for a technique.

Some are drawn toward traditional Eastern religions, well known for their meditation practices, while other recovered alcoholics seem to prefer a nonreligious solution. It is for them that this book is written.

There are other religions that are often associated with forms of meditative practices. Some of those may be wonderful religions, which could be considered, but the fact is that *most* of the religions that openly embrace and promote meditation are shot through with doctrine and spiritual ideologies that many alcoholics have no desire to test in their own lives.

This is not necessarily so because of prejudice. It isn't out of close-mindedness either. It is because the precepts and practices of such cultures belie the principles laid into the cornerstone of the Twelve-Step lifestyle. They contain concepts that countermand those they have already come to believe, out of experience with their personal miracle of recovery.

This goes beyond intellectual schisms between ideologies. It is the difference between living a happy and usefully whole life that is free from the stress of self-managing mental, physical, and spiritual health, and *not*. Eastern religions and Judeo-Christian principles such as those endorsed through the Twelve Steps just don't work together. Select one or the other—but picking both ... or worse, mixing and matching a smorgasbord of opposing spiritualities? Perhaps *this* is why you haven't found peace on earth and goodwill. *This* could be why you suffer from emotionally based maladies like bipolar disorder or depression and have physical ailments ranging from diabetes and cancer to food addiction and heart disease. Emotions have even determined what spiritual principles you *will* and *will not* accept. Conversely, non-emotional living ensures the automatic acceptance of truth *without* decision-making.

There are major, global religions—not mere cults, mind you, but large, spiritual organizations with major marketing outreaches—offering as part of their spiritual regimen, "meditation." In some of these practices, you may find some similar elements of what you will discover in the meditation offered in this book—and *more*. It is the *more* that can be disturbing. The *more* consists of pantheistic spiritual tenets and concepts inconsistent, not only with the principles of the Twelve Steps but also with the principles most Americans have come to accept and upon which their nation, the United States of America, was founded.

Of the 55 delegates to the Constitutional convention in 1787, save for a small handful of Deists, virtually all were of some denomination of a Christian faith. It is not a surprise to learn that our nation was founded on principles closely paralleling Judeo Christian spiritual values. Our founding fathers believed in universal, not relative morality, establishing our nation to run under a *God... Whom we trust.*

Today those values are recognizable as distinctly American. They are steeped in a belief in the biblical God of Israel, the Ten Commandments and biblical moral laws and they have prevailed for several centuries. The fabric of our society is shot through with this American experience; and most people reading this book will have been raised in environs and under laws that have been mightily influenced by these guiding principles. This is why most Americans today, regardless of religious affiliation or background and whether they admit it or not, identify with the Judeo-Christian essence of America; if not consciously then at least through custom, experience and expectations of how they should be treated by their own government and by their neighbors.

As for myself, I belong to no formal or organized religion and follow no religious doctrine. Yet the morals, values and lifestyle I hold and instill in my family closely parallel the values passed on through the American Judeo Christian way. If you were born and raised in the United States, then so do you. Not Judeo Christian theology, but its values and principles as they have been codified in the New and Old Testaments – the Bible as threaded through our entire system from the

Constitution to the Supreme Court and down through our legal and educational system. It may be battered and torn; seriously challenged, even at times scorned by forces wishing to tear it down. Still it is there. The spirit of those principles were breathed as life into the Twelve Step recovery plan in, "Alcoholics Anonymous," and founded upon principles that are clearly Judeo-Christian in nature. These are not principles which come from the Bible, rather they are spiritual principles out of which Bibles derive *their* stories, language and message.

Like the forefathers of our country, the co-founders of the Fellowship of the Spirit were men of faith guided in those principles. They shared a sturdy sense of divine purpose and duty to stand against injustice, to represent good and God through the establishment of Godly laws and to place faith in His protection. There was a belief in forgiveness, in the taking on a mantle of security. They saw themselves as an unified assembly of Gods children, not unlike "We the people" of the United States of America; brotherly sentiments also shared among every Jew of the Old Testament as well as those who live today in Israel or anywhere on earth. There is a strong belief that somehow, "We" have an important message to carry forth to others and "We" have been *Chosen*.

The *Big Book* is replete with monotheistic spiritual principles and anyone adopting its design begins to experience direction and guidance supported by them. You may not identify yourself as Christian, Jew or any denomination. You may not even be American, yet if you are moral, ethical and have a potential for *God-vision* then you are Judeo Christian in spirit. The truth of that spirit has existed long before we ever had a name for it. How can anyone being so affected as virtually each person in good conscience is, fully adopt concepts borne out of polytheistic cultures, without undertaking a major overhaul of their own visceral faith in a God of their understanding? They cannot. Usually they do not.

Here is the crux of the meditation dilemma for Twelve-Steppers. It gets to the heart of just why we resist meditation; how the rub of opposing spiritual beliefs can produce conflict. When this happens, "meditation" becomes a source of new conflicting ideas for our consciences to struggle with—not a remedy for God-separation. Shouldn't meditation serve as a tool to resolve internal conflicts of spirit and not create new ones?

Is it not unreasonable for someone raised from childhood as a Protestant to suddenly be asked to discard their belief in the one God of Christianity and accept Buddhism's doctrine of many gods—just because they need to have a meditation practice in their lives? They could end up being unwittingly indoctrinated into the Buddhist religion or a Buddhist like movement such as Hatha Yoga or Transcendental Meditation—or else abandon their monotheistic faith entirely. Some give up. They just say, "Screw it. Meditation is too hard. Who needs this complication in my life?"

Others are more persistent and look for a watered-down version of Buddhist practices such as can be found in yoga classes at the local YMCA and in adult education courses across the country. I am not saying that all Buddhists principles are bad, or that all yoga is evil. I *am* asking that you be careful.

Nevertheless, despite our experimenting, we do not know how to meditate properly. No one has shown us the ancient spiritual technique for expanding communication with God, or they have shown us techniques that have only pulled us further away from our Creator. *What to do?...What to do?*

So now the hunt is on. You begin investigating. You sniff around the Internet. You check out Amazon. You investigate some spiritual literature. Chances are you already know some people who have told you about some form of meditation that they practice—perhaps some *controlled thinking* technique or a focused *breathing* exercise that some yoga instructor showed them. These are quite ubiquitous. Even the gym I belong to has a resident mystical lady who will massage your back and teach you how to go into a trance designed to induce a relaxed state and feelings of ease and comfort. These can be tempting. After all, folks who practice some of these seem to be doing well with them. Considering your nervous, sensitive state, you might figure "What can I lose?"

The real question is, "Do you really want to get involved in a foreign religious practice or pseudo-spiritual, self-help system?" After all, this Twelve-Step stuff is new enough. It represents a drastic change in your way of life. You have had to throw out many long-held beliefs in order to accommodate this new design for living and believing. The *last* thing you are looking to do is to become caught up in something even more radical, especially something that might contradict your new life.

Yet the temptation to get involved is strong. You are in a quandary, and there is no shortage of appealing meditation's out there.

What about the originators of the Twelve-Step practice—the cofounders of *Alcoholics Anonymous*? It is fair to ask, *"Exactly how did they go about it?"* Seriously, think about this question for a moment. I mean, if Bill W. or Doctor Bob had a specific meditation technique that worked for them, how cool would it be to learn that method? Sadly, if there exists any such information, there is hardly any of it available. In the annals of AA history, there is *some* mention of how early AAs pursued meditation, albeit woefully little. Dick B. (Richard Burns), a well-known, respected AA historian and Christian writer, has published extensively on early AAs and their approaches to meditation. I suggest that you see what he has discovered.[9] In essence, he reveals that these pioneers had very little in the way of practice or experience. Nor did they develop very much.

Now let's not discredit these men and women entirely. It should be remembered that the *Alcoholics Anonymous,* Twelve-Step angle of spiritual living, created *by* alcoholics *for* alcoholics, was still in its infancy, and as apprentices in the fellowship they were just getting started. These were folks who had just gotten onto the spiritual path, not wise old sages with years of experience living spiritual lives, passing on guidance garnered out of a life well lived. These were recently sober, newly awakened dregs, yet toddlers stumbling through their own spiritual kindergarten. After spending their lifetimes immersed in the sick, delusionary, and spiritually void world preoccupied with *defeating* meaningful, *conscious contact* with God, these newly recovered men and women had only barely climbed out of the pits of alcoholic despair and misery. God-consciousness was new to them,

---

[9]http://www.dickb.com/articles/meditation_roots_dsb.shtml

perhaps as new to them as it is to you reading this right now. What little information is available from the early practitioners is so negligible it would hardly qualify as instructional.

So how much life-experience and real-time practice would they have had with the spiritual realm of human existence? Not a whole lot. These were people who, only a few months prior to our coming upon them in our reading, were as crazy as bedbugs, still drunk as skunks, as deep into their cups as they were into their own doo-doo. Their problems had mounted so high, their lives so unmanageable, they could barely hold on to living at all. Not only are we looking at a snapshot of the authors frozen in time—we are seeing only their baby pictures.

Indeed, these *newbies* had something to offer. Even the most recently awakened person can have more *uncommon* sense in their little pinky finger than a thirty-year veteran of sobriety who has managed not to drink, one day at a time, through sheer human willpower and *managed* distraction.

So it is really no surprise that we are left at a loss with regard to obtaining a Twelve-Step-*friendly* meditation. Looking to early AAs to pass on to us a meditation technique is like asking a teenager, just issued a fresh learners' permit, to show us how to drive; or asking a newlywed for marital advice.

So what we end up with is speculation about how early AAs may or may not have meditated and what "materials" they used to assist them.

No matter. You need and want to meditate, and so you give it a whirl in the best way you can with whatever you can find. And why not? There seems to be many people, already into the fray of New-Age, New-Thought mysticism, who certainly appear to be learning so much about spirituality. They have adopted such impressive language, speaking of inner peace, inner transformation, relaxation and calmness—maybe even the ever-coveted "serenity" and "acceptance." These ideas and the prospect of attaining them are just too much to resist. With so much insight into the human condition, sugary spiritual concepts seem to pour from their lips like sweet maple syrup out of the top of Mrs. Butterworth's head. It is really quite amazing.

New doctrines, beliefs, rituals, exotic deities, sometimes even the worship of *multiple* deities can become alluring. The newness of unconventional spiritual pursuits can seem exciting endeavors.

Now through an engaging set of fresh spiritual guidelines, religious in nature, you are unwittingly indoctrinated *into* a religion. Some venerate avatars and incarnations of hundreds of "gods," as well as planets, the sky, the sun, time, weather, rain, thunder, lightning. Even animals are idolized in the search for spiritual fulfillment. Before long new spiritual principles begin to conflict with visceral Judeo-Christian values. Worse, many of these are 180 degrees opposite those proposed by the Twelve Steps. If you are a Twelve Stepper this clash of convictions will pose a problem.

There too are cults and pseudo religions founded upon even more peculiar premises. Self-proclaimed mystics armed with manuscripts and manifestos, allegedly co-authored through extraterrestrials or underworld spirits, regularly garner throngs of susceptible 'seekers'. There are guru, life coaching people, claiming special abilities like psychic channeling to Christ and God Himself issuing directives over the lives of the "faithful." Others gird up their credibility to the gullible by claiming to have powerful 'connections' with alien beings or associations with nature, celestial objects or cosmic events. Calamitous prophesies and end of times scenarios have been old favorites for centuries. These have become absurdly cliché and yet always seem to proliferate.

Then there are exotic movements where the founders themselves serve as the earthy mouthpiece of God or other benevolent "spirits" of the universe. It gets quite bizarre. Particularly disturbing are those "spiritual" leaders who offer *themselves* as ersatz deities or the human embodiment of God. Self appointed spiritual potentates like David Koresh, Jim Jones, Sun Myung Moon are prime examples. Perhaps *exotic* is an understatement. How long from now after reading this book will there be another major news story of some mass suicide committed by cult members taking their lead from a charismatic guru? Our history is tragically spotted with such events.

Like the shopper going to the supermarket for milk and bread and coming home with a cartful of groceries he never intended to buy, you could soon find yourself accepting doctrine and adopting spiritual philosophies and practices you probably would never in a million years have considered. Soon the allure of the shopping trip 'grows' on you because when intellect combines with physical stimulation you risk becoming *addicted* to some new religious doctrine. Relaxation techniques or breathing exercises and mental imagery become ritualistic substitutes for true God consciousness.

This is not to say that all spiritual cultures are so brazenly eccentric. Some are much more subtle and have developed a flair of legitimacy, fitting well into respectable society. It is easy to find yourself involved with a religion or cult encouraging prayer and petitioning God in hopes of affecting outcomes. Who could be faulted for wanting things like happiness and prosperity. Heck, why not take it even higher and nobler: World peace, the cure for cancer, the end of wars; or how about easing the suffering of sick children? Many mainstream religions and spiritual movements do that. Their intentions seem so noble and good.

For the Twelve Stepper, impassioned beseeching toward Heaven is clearly not the kind of prayer spoken of in their *Big Book*, which states to pray "only for knowledge of His will for us and the power to carry that out." Aunt Fannie's goiter is out of the question.

There is a problem with this ambitious business of praying for outcomes, no matter how wonderful we think they are or how vital we see them to be. "Petitioning the Lord with prayer," as our old alcoholic friend Jim Morrison aptly recognized, may be quite common in many religious sects, but it is a spiritual concept that is entirely incompatible with the Twelve-Step practice. The *Big Book*, "Alcoholics Anonymous", quite pointedly tells practicing readers they never ask God for anything unless it bears on a very special kind of usefulness to others. Not merely *things* that are useful to others, like good health or relief from stress—but specifically *the reader's* usefulness to others.

"I'll pray on it," or "I'll meditate on that," with hopes of affecting outcomes or to wrest "answers" or "fixes" out of God for troublesome problems are sure indicators of "these principles" gone rogue—and a return to old ideas that may include *all kinds* of principles instead of "these" principles discussed.

There is conflict that comes out of praying in this manner. It is a clash of intent and purpose that lies in telling God "Thy will, not my will be done" while antithetically proposing, *"OK, God! I am a good and decent fellow so…here is what needs to be done in order for this to be a better world."* Hey, your intentions are good, right? You are only looking out for us all. How could He resist? I mean, *your* will is every bit as benevolent as God's will, is it not? If only He would enact it. He can even take credit for it, right? You don't mind. No one would ever know. (Until you told them, of course, "I was praying for you.") Your humility is heartwarming. Not to mention impressive.

I can guess what you are thinking. "My intentions are good," and "I am only praying for others," as if God could not possibly refuse to go along with your generosity. Perhaps *your* will is every bit as benevolent as the will of God Himself and perhaps, if only He would act upon it all would be well. There would be less unhappiness in the world, no child would suffer at the hands of another, and all the trains would run on time.

As you tell God how things ought to be in His world, you are forgetting one thing. It is something that is so important that if you never rise above it you will never, ever know true spirituality. You are overlooking that your *Big Book*, "Alcoholics Anonymous", is very specific about how the cofounders of *Alcoholics Anonymous* incorporated spiritual ideas into the Twelve-Step lifestyle.

You forgot that the coauthors of the *Big Book* solely accredit only those foreign prayers which "emphasize the principles we have been discussing." They suggest readings recommended by one's own priest, minister, or rabbi—legitimate clerics of established Judeo-Christian religions—and not any gurus, New Age, or pop pseudo-spiritual representatives that make an appeal for followers. I, your "humble narrator"—as Alex in *A Clockwork Orange* might say—and author of this book, should never be viewed as a source of guidance, one's guru, or be put on a pedestal. It is dangerous for all involved and it debases me.

If excuse-making were a sport, most of us would have been forced to turn pro quite early in life. Justifications, excuses, and cop-outs become standard operating procedure as we fool ourselves into thinking that we are making progress. The expression "to the best of my abilities," routinely tacked on to the description of our own spiritually dumbed-down lifestyle, is often the indicator of an underlying unwillingness to abandon old, disingenuous beliefs.

Not willing to go all the way to make the final leap of faith, we find we cannot completely give up the management of our own thought life. We might be willing to give up trying to willfully control the big things—but to stop managing one's own thoughts? *That* seems just too much to surrender. Yet, unless we do, we will never know God's will for us, nor will we ever have the power to carry it forward into the world. We can never experience being the agent of His will on earth *as* it is in heaven. Secret dishonesty and nagging conflicts haunt the inner sanctum of the alcoholic psyche, causing even more pain that needs quenching.

Many of us alcoholics have come to realize that we have always had the *capacity* for honesty, even when we were being dishonest. If you didn't have *any* propensity for truth, it is doubtful that you would even be reading this book.

Confused and conflicted thinking caused by sensing that we are not quite reconciled with our own beliefs can prevent us from fully accepting truth. When we are not 100 percent sure about our own place in the universe, we may doubt truth even if we hear it. The ability to discern the true from the false is dulled. Doubt, lack of faith, is to blame, and seeds of doubt are sown by our own self-centered attempts to *acquire* spirituality instead of *allowing* it to overwhelm and possess us.

What alcoholic has not left in his wake scores of unfinished works, incomplete projects? Our dreams are self-shattered, obliterated by impatience and overreaching ambitions until we feel like failures in life. Ironically, these booby traps destroy all hope of accomplishing the sought-after results by clouding our ability to see what needs to be done in each new moment.

Compromises of truth and inadequate action are earmarks cut into the lifestyle of every drunk. We develop a pattern of settling for less that runs parallel with an unfulfilling, mediocre existence. This behavior develops early in grade school and follows through life, spoiling personal and business relationships, hindering families and careers along the way.

Once an alcoholic stops drinking and pursues a new life that is to be free from this kind of half-assed behavior, he begins to make a conscious devotion toward living a new, improved, sober life, and so the very idea of receiving another incomplete grade in the school of life soon becomes repugnant to him. Cherry-picking through theologies and renovated, exotic religions is no longer an option.

Once we begin to see this, we can also see that "Take what you need and leave the rest" is one of the most self-centered recovery mantras ever conceived. It means dissecting and diluting things to make them fit our level of imperfection, instead of striving for the perfection for which we were created and placed on earth to trudge toward.

When we sober up and commence spiritual growth, we begin to see the incompleteness of our past inadequate life. Embarrassed, we also begin to realize that it does not have to be so any more. We develop an aversion to it. A *half-measured* approach to *anything*, even to alternative religious teachings, seem to sour in the psyche of the earnest person who is now searching for truth. For them, practicing the spiritual principles proposed by the Twelve Steps in *some* affairs is not an option. An earnest effort to practice them in *all* affairs is the only choice, since having so eschewed *half-measured* approaches with regard to their own *Big Book*. The conscience that is inspired through internal, rigorous honesty finds anything less to be too uncomfortable.

"Easy does it" and "Take what you need" These ideas are not deliberately nefarious. Their aim is to give an easygoing, carefree appearance about what might otherwise appear to be a glum matter. No one wants to appear to be a pessimistic, worrisome bore. Nevertheless, being blithe of spirit is a quality we see in secure and confident persons who have earned that security by letting God discipline them. This isn't something that we can *fake* until *we make it*. Self-reliance and dependencies upon people, places, and things is given up. We forget that it is not the step, the book, a sponsor, or a guru that provides us with guidance and direction. It is God.

When we lose our connection with Him we rely upon people, what they say, and what they write to provide us with security and guidance. It is a false security. Why would anyone rely upon someone else's *conscious contact* with God? Why not have it yourself? Get rid of your accountability go-to people. Get rid of your gurus, your dependencies upon rituals and gleaning wisdom from others. We are designed to be the transmitters of *our own* wisdom, which isn't our own since it originates with God, but we can at least be conductors for good—transmitting God's vision—His will, not our own. Again, witness: *His will be done on earth as it is in heaven.*

"God talks through other people" is a copout. It becomes a mantra for those who have not established their own *conscious contact.* It is meant to convey the idea that "I am no longer an egomaniac and playing the God role serving myself." However, transferring the god role onto other humans is not the humble act we imagine it to be. It means we are placing ourselves in the role of creator of little gods—who we then place on pedestals. It is only a matter of time before they fall from their thrones, after which time we resent the sway they have had over us. In our minds, we condemn them to hell for their shortcomings.

Perhaps you have already been *rocketed into the fourth dimension;* if so, then please do not think that you have arrived at your final destination. It is only a beginning. The wonderful ether of this existence is not static, and you are about to begin a journey you did not know you could make, through space and time that you never knew existed.

Like the recipe for the egg cream—specifically, the New York Egg Cream mentioned in the beginning of this chapter, Step Eleven proposes a simple, uncomplicated recipe. Modify the recipe, and we will also modify the result. On their own, each individual Step is a unique portion of the whole plan to be carefully followed. The slightest change, even in the smallest way, will profoundly alter the final product.

You have to decide if you really want to take that chance. Hey, you might end up with a really groovy glass of chocolate soda. Just do not call it a *New York Egg Cream*. Okay, that's it. This chapter's done. . . . now fuggettaboutit!

"As far as we can discern, the sole purpose of human existence is to kindle the light of meaning in the darkness of mere "being." - *Carl Gustav Jung*

2 WHY DO I FEEL LOUSY?

Again

Deep in the hearts of some Twelve-Step practitioners there sometimes lurks a nagging notion. It may not always be a conscious thought, but like one of those splinters that are so small you cannot quite pinpoint its exact location, the irritation begs for some relief nevertheless. Secretly Twelve-Steppers struggle with the idea that by overlooking or skimping on an effective meditation practice, there may also be a nib of personal hypocrisy. The claim of "practicing these principles in all our affairs" is shot through with an irritating thread of dishonesty. It can put a drag on usefulness. We can even resent our own imperfect spirituality, cutting us off even further from experiencing continued growth. It makes the *"skimper"* feel like a fraud.

Let's face it. Many Twelve-Steppers have gotten very good at projecting good cheer to the outside world while inside they remain boiling pots. Because of their ability to act like good God-centered people, what they have managed to do is adopt a script of outward serenity while efficiently suppressing anger. This is why so many Twelve-Steppers continue to be plagued by broken relationships, divorce, wild children and poor health. Illnesses like cancer and heart disease cause untimely suffering and death, many years before their time. Disingenuous attitude, secret lives, if you will, is also why the "enlightened" continue with their food, sex, and chemical obsessions; many of those habits increasing as time goes on.

I know that some who are reading this have learned this role well. I also know that I now risk having you discard this book right here and now. Still, there will be some of you who are ready to get honest enough to admit some horrible truths. For you and your children, I dedicate not only this book but also my life.

Blaming ourselves for our despair and confusion, we get the idea that perhaps the problem is that we are not doing enough. Being far from admitting that we have jumbled and confused our once-simple spirituality, we try to turn up the spiritual juice. "More is better," we think. Now we expect our ramped-up over-involvement with doctrines and spiritually flavored activities to provide relief. It may, but only for a while. Soon we discover even these are not enough, leading us into worse confusion than before. The principles that saved us in the first place seem to be failing us. It's part of the dilemma.

They say that alcoholics are delusional. For me, training in the art of the delusion began early. I was raised in a halfway house. No, not one of those recovery homes or sober-living facilities set up to reintegrate drunks and addicts into society. (Those places are "dry"—our house was anything but dry.) What I mean is a house where nothing was ever done altogether. Most things looking to be *normal* appeared so only out of exaggeration. Maybe half-*assed* house would be a better description. Every screw was only half screwed in. Our car could usually "make it" to most places we needed to go—but it was never fully operational. Everything was half washed, half cooked, half painted. Plans were half baked, accounts were half full, time was cut short, and everyone was in some state of restlessness or discontentment over it all.

It was a fractured family structure—not the spiritual entity that families are designed to be. It had been rendered into a struggling biological unit: a fatherless boy and two girls with a husbandless mother living together without direction, no discipline or guidance other than the criticism and brutality of a drunken, broken interloper—himself addicted to the guiles of Mother. (Mom had an alcoholic, part-time live-in boyfriend with a violent streak, who terrorized us all.)

With such a way of thinking, nothing ever seemed right, and nothing was ever satisfying. There was always a need to find some compensating pleasure to drown out the noise of the ensuing internal discomfort.

For the alcoholic, the home is the training ground for a lifetime of delusion. It starts with perfecting the installation of inflated esteem. For our family, it set in motion a style of self-centered living pitted with unsettling mediocrity, always forced to settle for less while

25

constantly longing for the best of everything. What could not be earned rightly had to be conjured in the mind.

Delusion is mental trickery. It acts as a mental placebo, inciting the false idea that we are better than we really are. Failed human beings would rather feel good than experience the pain of their own failures—despite that the sting of conscience would empower them to straighten out and recover.

They must compensate and they must do it obsessively. First with food, followed by sex, then alcohol and finally, drugs.

Without exception, all of my family members, including myself, have come to destructive ends, with *all* of these factors being chief instigators. In our family we were doing the best we could, but the reality of our station was glossed over with delusional ideas of grandiosity and false self-esteem. We were quick to take our bragging rights to anything and everything we could. It didn't matter what it was.

We were sure that our doctor was better than anyone's. We were convinced that our car ran better, even if it was older, rustier, and noisier than all the other cars on the block. In our minds we were constantly telling ourselves that we made superior choices about anything and everything and that these choices were a direct reflection of our superiority over others. The color of our skin, our heritage, our food preferences—we were better regardless. The whole world was stupid and probably going to hell for it—but not us.

All of this was very far from the truth. All of this was deep, deep denial. The truth is we ate white-trash food and drove a crappy rusted-out white-trash car that blew blue smoke. We siblings were the products of human lust; bastard progeny of adulterous, alcohol-fueled affairs and relationships. Not exactly the royal bluebloods we would have supposed. This may sound like some mere, soured reminiscence, but, having been freed from my "Self," all of these destructive behaviors and attitudes have fallen away with no regret. I have made peace with the past, and it does me no pain to talk about it.

Alcoholics are infamous for their ability to manufacture false impressions *of* themselves *for* themselves and for anyone willing to listen. For those unwilling, "To hell with them," we think. Yet, introduce onlookers, observers in work or social environs, and the actor takes his mark on stage. From there he stands to receive the addictive food of approval upon which *Self* thrives, courtesy of his audience. His dependency upon people, his adoring *fans,* is set.

Bill Wilson, long-time practitioner of the prayer and meditation-intense recovery program (the Twelve Steps), was very familiar with this experience. In a masterful collection of essays, "Twelve Steps and Twelve Traditions" Wilson speaks of combining *contemplative prayer* with a visualization exercise. The unnamed contemplative prayer he opts for is actually *the Prayer of Saint Francis*—a beautiful expression of one man's[10] spiritual experience.

The visualization exercise he recommends suggests common routines to rouse the imagination to tranquility.

Just five years later, Bill presented his report on the practice in an article that he wrote for the January 1958 issue of *A A Grapevine.* The article is titled "The Next Frontier: Emotional Sobriety," and it presents Bill's honest assessment of how much he had progressed since first writing *Step Eleven.* Despite the wholehearted presentation made in his earlier essay, Bill's progress with prayer and meditation took a deadly dive. It was very bad. Contemplating the "Prayer of Saint Francis," by his own admission, "didn't work." Instead of helping Bill, as he had supposed it might, it brought him a great deal of trouble. In the years immediately following the publication of his meditation technique in "Twelve Steps and Twelve Traditions," Bill tells us that "depression, having no really rational cause at all, almost took me to the cleaners."

Bill is not obliquely condemning prayer or meditation, certainly not the spirit of this specific prayer. It is however, a clear indictment that the methods Bill was using at the time that he wrote this chapter had ultimately done him more harm than good. Not only did Bill feel cheated by his willful efforts to install his own peace, but this kind of prayer and meditation was very likely to have triggered his depression. He knew it. He certainly *was* cheated. He was swindled out of maximizing his usefulness in the name of spirituality, for sure.

---

[10]Francis of Assisi

27

As Bill put it, "There wasn't a chance of making the outgoing love of St. Francis a workable and joyous way of life until these fatal and almost absolute dependencies were cut away." Just as my family and I had developed a lifestyle and attitude that nurtured sick dependencies comprising sets of circumstances and people, Bill had turned to others, even to his beloved A A fellowship, for self-esteem, driving his unduly *elevated* personal valuation.

If he could not be freed from those dependencies, then the beauty of the "Prayer of Saint Francis" would never matter—because he would remain spiritually flat-lined.

So much for Bills' experiment with contemplative meditation and visualization. It is good for Bill that he was able to recognize it and that he was able to discover the solution.

So the question remains, "Did Bill have something else to replace his failed 'Twelve and Twelve' meditation experiment?" Yes, he did. And it was effective, powerful and simple. It had been under his nose the whole time, and it lay within the Twelve-Step solution that required losing reliance upon self—not engaging in recitations, contemplation or visualization. Once Bill discovered this truth and began living it, the bipolar condition from which he suffered as the result of his misguided prayer and meditation practice was gone.

He was then free from anger, which meant he was free to love because he had discarded ambition, expectations of outcomes, and, above all, he gave up placing requirements upon God and His world for his "happiness."

Spiritual wellness begins when we can stand free from entanglements with our emotions. This is *exactly* where you will be brought, if you use the meditation I am introducing to you; to *Bill's* place of *no demands*; to that elusive "acceptance"—an idea that is not instilled hypnotically but becomes a *symptom* of spiritual growth. "Acceptance" is not something we *do*. "Accepting" is something we *are* after we finally let go of *self-will* and let *God's will* take over, moment by moment.

We do not transform ourselves, but we are transformed. Sometimes we may encounter attempts to merge religious doctrines with otherwise innocuous methods of producing such feelings of "inner transformation." There are many such movements. These often have an "East meets West" flavor—a forced marriage between scriptural Judeo-Christian theology and mysticism is forged.

A fine example of this is the Santeria religion, a large spiritual movement that combines classic Catholicism with traditional Caribbean-style voodoo and witchcraft. Practitioners perform elaborate rituals, carry talismans and amulets and cast spells *in the name of Jesus* Christ as well as the iconic saints. If that floats your boat, go for it.

Though plentiful, not all movements are as overtly religious as Santeria. Turn on many late-night cable TV shows or your local PBS station, and it is easy enough to find some guru with a correspondence course that will teach you how to meditate. Celebrity-hosts and best-selling authors tout all kinds of pseudo-spiritual philosophies and metaphysically flavored lifestyles—many of which suggest meditation. There is no shortage of these self-help personalities, seminar purveyors, and the like who package and market their custom brands of spirituality "systems," each designed to turn us into happy *followers*.

Nearly all of what a Twelve-Stepping seeker discovers among these are meditation methods that come bundled with religious and spiritual philosophies, most contrary to the basic spiritual principles to which they feel they owe their recovery. The questions to ask are, "Is it appropriate"? and "Is it effective?"

In helping to answer these, it is important to acknowledge that a self-centered mind attaches to ideas passing through it as though they were its own creation. It is gullibility masquerading as open-mindedness. It allows diametrically opposed ideas to dictate how we live. Such attachment could eventually lead to dissatisfaction with the Twelve-Step recovery process and the very fellowship responsible for first delivering the message—while we slip into unmanageability, depression, anxiety, restlessness, and perhaps even relapse back into drinking.

In most cases we find that religious and philosophical contradictions to the principles of the Twelve-Step program run deep and can be so severe that great irreconcilable rifts in faith develop. Many of the basic tenets of the organizations and movements promoting meditation shake hard at the foundation of some highly cherished Judeo-Christian principles—in particular those proposed in "Alcoholics Anonymous". In the search for meditation, we can find ourselves indoctrinated to accept religious dogma and spiritual concepts that go to war with what we already intuitively know to be *truth*.

Many alcoholics discover that while they are grateful for a newfound relationship with the Creator through the Twelve-Step solution, there is a conflict causing great internal dissonance experienced as anger, fear and disillusionment. They wonder what went wrong with their wonderful spirituality. "Where are 'the promises?'" they ask. "Is God still there?" "Does God want me to suffer or is the 'happy, joyous and free' idea a lie?" After all, "aren't I pursuing a spiritual life 'to the best of my abilities'?"

This is not an indictment of any particular religion. I say if you want to become a Buddhist then be a Buddhist. If you want to become a Catholic or a Jew, or a *Santero*—then be one of those. These established religions are supposed to lead us to God; putting some of what they offer to good use has helped many find the elusive, narrow path to Him.

The *ego* tries to associate tranquility and stillness with spiritual enlightenment, but that is a lie. It is not stillness that feeds the searching soul with God's will, but understanding. Understanding only *comes through* stillness—stillness is not the objective. It is one of the characterizing effects of God consciousness. Seeking first enlightenment, knowledge, doctrine and "wisdom" is a widespread practice and a futile exercise; often associated with pantheistic religions and pagan mysticism. If practiced individually, either of these alone would be mesmerizing, producing some short-term effect. In the long term, each can lead only to undesirable ends.

Combining the hypnotic focusing of attention with imagery is simply a one-two sucker punch. These seductive practices can easily lead to depression and eventually to suicide. This is why so many Twelve-Steppers continue to experience bedeviling emotional states with continual need to revisit inventories *after* incorporating such practices into their *Step Eleven* life. If you continue reading this book and practice the meditation I use, the precise reason for this will become clear to you.[11]

Bill W. gave up hypnotically injecting himself with spirituality through seductive mind games. Once he did, he felt emotional stability as his mind quieted down. It allowed him to let go of the deadly emotion—anger. This is all we have to do. This is the true meaning of the familiar expression, "Let Go." This is what the meditation will show you. It will show you how to go about finding what Bill finally discovered and of which he wrote in his wonderful article.

At the time that he wrote the aforementioned article, Bill had obviously found the remedy for his bipolar state. The highs were gone. The lows were gone. He existed in that "quiet place in bright sunshine" that all of us aspire to reach. Yet, even after arriving there, Bill Wilson was not able to stay. Later he developed physical ailments, in part due to his continued addiction to nicotine, and died tragically from pulmonary complications usually associated with such drug addiction. Had Bill used the meditation proposed in this book, it is not likely that he would have suffered so. I have sometimes pondered, *"If only."* *If only* I had access to this wonderfully inspired and spiritual man. Not to selfishly tap Bill dry of his knowledge and understanding, but to express my gratitude to him for his work by presenting to him the keys to a kingdom that he somehow missed. It would have given him and AA many more years together.

Just because something seems to us to be *new* and therefore exciting, does not automatically means it is good and right—although *newness* can help a delusional mind create an illusion that it is right. (The same way rearranging furniture in a room—or moving to a new region—can create a temporary false sense of new hopes and lift spirits.) This is a very common misapplication of *change.* A mind that

---

[11] Please visit the "How To Get There," page in the back of this book for fast access to the meditation exercise. It is available for streaming or download. It is free and always will be.

is inspired and discerning is not necessarily *closed-minded* just because it has come to a conclusion—not when it has recognized the need for selectivity. Theologically flavored themes that have been inserted into a "meditation" practice (or meditation practices "inserted" into religions) can be downright offensive to some, or are at the very least uncomfortable.

This is another way so many people *default* into practicing only *half* of Step eleven—the "seek through prayer" half—and so they miss out on much of the spiritual growth and maximization of usefulness that they might otherwise experience through the inclusion of the second half of Step Eleven: an effective meditation practice. They cut themselves off from truly maximizing their usefulness and their *total* Twelve-Step experience. This meditation removes this hindrance to growth.

It is merely an exercise. In itself, it holds no power. Yet it serves as the single key that will unlock the gates to growth by permitting an experience not produced by any other technique. It gently brings us to a quiet place where we will continually experience *conscious contact* with God.

If you see this as a rather bold idea, rest assured I know well it will seem so. I will stick to it however, and defend its validity to the end. For *conscious contact* with *Self,* or with *Self as* God, often mimics contact with *God,* placing spiritual growth beyond the grasp of even the most dedicated Twelve-Step practitioner. It can be frustrating to be "practicing these principles in all my affairs" and yet still suffer from mental and emotional disruption, becoming physically unhealthy and haunted by the nagging sense that we are dying. You can avoid this through using *this* meditation exercise.

I can't tell you how many times I have run into folks who are apparently living a Twelve-Step lifestyle that eschews praying for anything *not* bearing on their usefulness to others and yet continue to pray to God in order to affect outcomes. These are two opposing views which cancel each other out! No wonder they are still miserable.

The meditation I propose in this book has no religious affiliation at all. It will work for you whether you are a denominational Christian or a Jew or have no denomination at all. For Twelve-Step practitioners who have shied away from meditation for fear of religious implication, it *is* the answer.[12] It is a way to *access* truth, and since any truth is universal, it has no allegiances to any specific philosophy or any established religion. It is not allied with any theological organization or school of philosophy.

We are coming up on the end of these first two chapters delineating the dilemma. I have been trying my darndest to articulate the predicament and convince you that there is a solution to it. If you move forward through this book, you will be directed to it. But I have not completed my job just yet; there is a whole bunch more to go. So far all I have really done is attempt getting you to identify *with* the problem in hopes that you will be intrigued enough to continue. If I have failed; if the problem has not been enumerated for you; if you share no such dilemma, then this book, this meditation is probably not for you—you probably don't need it because you have already discovered it.

Nevertheless, I hope I have begun to make my case well. This meditation will bring you to a spontaneous state of conscious awareness. I am excited for you. As you extend this awareness throughout your day, you will discover a completely new way of living that is effortless. You will find that your struggles with life are now gone as people and circumstances that used to baffle and upset you to the point of misery, depression, and sickness no longer have a stranglehold over you. The exercise presented imparts the most perfect alignment of *your* vision with that of God's you will ever know. You will intuitively be able to do what you know is right without receiving any direction from any other human being. Not from any sponsor, pastor, guru, or advisor.

Through the awareness which comes as you use this exercise, you will realize the true *knowledge* spoken of by all the "ancients" that you have ever read about, that perhaps you thought was reserved solely for the spiritually studied or accredited. There is no such spiritually

---

[12]Please visit the "How To Get There," page in the back of this book for fast access to the meditation exercise. It is available for streaming or download. It is free and always will be.

elite class. There is only *God-consciousness* or *God-unconsciousness*—awakened or asleep, light or darkness. Intellectual *knowing* and rote, book knowledge will take a backseat to spiritual understanding. If you subscribe to the principles expounded upon through the "Alcoholics Anonymous" *Big Book* or Judeo-Christian scripture, those will now begin to come alive as never before—without anyone having to explain them to you. Instead, you will be able to explain it to *them*—when appropriate, and if they have ears to hear. You will no longer need to agree with your *Big Book*, but the *Big Book* will agree with you.

You will become free from all of the subjective and prejudiced entanglements of spoken language. As your faith strengthens, you will gain true humility and have unwavering *understanding* that cannot be disturbed. This technique is a wakeful, psychically stimulating practice whereby we can initiate and maintain an ongoing growth phase of *conscious contact with* God. It continues for a lifetime—for as long as you continue to practice living in the aware state.

This meditation exercise establishes our inner guidance system, a kind of spiritual GPS that not only awakens us to our present location on the path to God, but also helps maintain our heading —as we move in the direction toward Him. No longer will you be dependent upon faulty outside guidance from prejudiced and tainted sources. The effect doesn't clear out the mind entirely. It is an emptying of thought from the subconscious mind into the conscious mind, where God consciousness is automatic, independent of any human being. This is not simply some nice thought I came up with one day or which I gleaned from reading or heard from a preacher. I have all of these things. My family enjoys these things. We live a life that if free from anger, fear, illnesses, emotional or mental disease and is full of peace and ease. This is no ploy or spiritual ruse. Anyone who lives this way has all of these things.

The next chapter really begins the get into the crux of the matter for all alcoholics, so you may want to protect your thinking cap with a crash helmet. I am not kidding.

"It is the mark of an educated mind to be able to entertain a thought without accepting it." – *Aristotle*

3 THE STREAM OF LIFE

Good Times, Bad Times

"I wanna Coke," said Gary.

"Egg creams!" Betty smiled.

"Chocolate." Willie assumed.

"Yes, two." Her smile widened and she ignored Gary.

"He doesn't want a Coke," she thought.

Gary's mouth snapped shut as if his jawbone was hinged by rubber bands. He thought of sweet acidy cola bubbling down the back of his throat. In his head the vision of a full frosty Coca Cola glass appeared, cold condensation dripping down its sides. It was there for a moment, then shifted from the front of his skull to the back – like an image in a slide projector. Now, a new slide clicked into place. It was a picture of Betty's face.

Her smile . . . . her skin . . . her hair . . . her eyes . . . . looking at him.

Like it was on the silver screen at Square Movies, the brain-side of Gary's forehead reflected the close-up. He could see clear into her expression, that inside the girl resided an undiscovered personality, some intelligence looking back at him, peering into his soul. It knew him. It wasn't scary. He stared back at 'the Betty' on the skull-screen sensing a little bit of himself melting. It didn't matter. Whatever it was that laid behind those eyes, it was oddly comforting. Gary felt soothed, sliding into a warm, wet, velvety glove. "Beautiful," he thought.

Betty curved her head and looked over at Willie.

"Well? Chocolate...right?" Willie was being as patient as a gentle stream.

Inside Gary's skull the slide with her smile remained, watching him—frozen, clear and sharp as real life. He would have the egg cream. "Yes. Two," he thought to 'the Betty'.

"How much are they?" Gary asked aloud. He felt in control.

"Ten cents, or twelve cents for a large," Willies cigar bounced wildly from his teeth as he spoke. The ash stayed.

"My mom used to pay two cents." Betty had heard her mother say that once.

"That was a hundred years ago. This is 1968, not 1950," Gary said.

"You're so stupid. 1950 was not a hundred years ago."

"I already know that!" Gary did not like when the question of his intelligence arose. He didn't like it when Sister Loretta did it, especially when it was in front of the other students; he didn't like it when his father would scream, "What are you a moron?" any time he left the kitchen cabinet door half-way opened; when he got a C minus in History; when he didn't come home in time for dinner; when covering centerfield for the Chatterton Avenue Chargers he missed a pop fly ball to center. Gary was used to it, and you could hardly notice him wince anytime he heard it, but no, he did not like it at all.

"I'm not stupid. You're stupid."

"No, Gary, I'm not, I got all A's in everything, even Science... and besides, two cents is for a two-cent plain—not for a real soda. Not for an egg cream."

Betty's javelin gaze plunged through the boy's eye sockets. He sensed it penetrating his head. Without blinking, without budging, looking straight into Gary Greengrass, Betty Wilson ordered, "Two large ones, Willie."

"Life is a carnival, believe it or not," as the Levon Helm song goes—and we all have ringside seats in the circus that is our lives. It can be a spectacular show. Some of it isn't very funny. Each of us moves forward through time and space experiencing a continuous stream of performances. We make observations and have experiences with whatever we encounter.

Over the course of our lifetime lots of stuff happens *to* us— *because* of us, and despite us too. Not all of what occurs in the world falls within our immediate field of vision. Some events that touch us and shape our lives originate well beyond the reach of our line of sight. Much of the time we are not aware of causes even though their effects may impact us in powerful ways. The effects of all cause appear as events we think of as *our lives.* Weddings, births, relationships, divorces, good times, bad times—*Lord, we've had our share.* Not everything going on in the world around us falls into the "good-times" category. Quite a bit of it could only be termed as bad—cruel and unfair. As we view these inequities, we watch through our own personal looking-glass that we can call *awareness.* Through this *conscious lens* we get to view the good and the bad together. As images of the world form, they become our reality.

Discounting the *good,* for the moment (after all, it isn't the wonderful things in the world that cause us grief, is it?) we are going to look at some of the *bad stuff.* Let me be more specific about what I mean by *bad stuff.* It is just this: People are unthinking. They step on our toes causing us harms—real or imagined. They lie. They cheat. They steal. They are rude. They make mistakes—even as *we* make mistakes—unintentionally, and sometimes they even do it on purpose.

The quality of life we live—emotionally, mentally, and physically—depends on our spiritual fitness—how we meet each of life's irritations as each encounter passes under our conscious looking-glass. It is a moment-by-moment affair. Meeting cruelty, injustice, and the "stupid human tricks" of our fellows each day with assurance is something that is necessary in order for us to grow spiritually.

We do not grow merely by merit of experiencing a negative encounter. Growth occurs when we meet each event, each irritation, and each emotional moment with grace and dignity through dispassionate awareness.

As we observe, taking it all in, we begin to process this information, so that we may somehow respond to elements in the Stream of Life. Events, many of them offensive to our senses as well as our sensibilities, come delivered to us through sight, sound, smell, touch—even our imagination conjures up objectionable events that may not have actually happened. Recollections out of the past emanating from stores of memory are presented to haunt us. It seems our existence runs like some filmstrip: frames of events, situations, and encounters with people strung together, forming our own personal Fellini production. It goes on each day beginning the moment our feet hit the floor in the morning until the second we fall sleep at night—and even after *that*, we dream. We are organic computers processing our experiences, never really seeming to shut down for a moment. The human psyche never sleeps.

In "Alcoholics Anonymous", the co-authors[13] tell readers that practitioners of the Twelve-Step lifestyle should continuously be on the lookout for the effects that worldly, negative forces impart. They specifically mention selfishness, dishonesty, resentment, and fear. Interestingly, it is not suggested that we *fight* these forces. They wisely propose quite the contrary. "Watch," they tell us.

Watching, seeing, and being aware—all suggest that the temptation to concede to our negative emotions needs constructive attention. When we willfully shut off awareness of anger or in any way suppress the inevitable encroaching bitterness and hatred the world throws our way, we are caught unaware and become entangled in that struggle. We end up allowing these harmful forces to enter, to crop up "inside" us where they overwhelm us. We let the boogiemen of negative emotions inside and get caught up in a futile struggle against our own bitterness. This makes us even bitterer. When this happens, we know what it is to be cut off from the Sunlight of the Spirit. This is the first sprig of major depression.

We are urged to observe. This means that it is okay to acknowledge these negative emotions. They *are* there. Ignoring negative emotional forces is foolish. That is why this meditation never suggests that thoughts, even unpleasant ones, be supplanted or replaced with "better," less objectionable ones. This is a harmful practice.

The meditation exercise to which you are being introduced will allow you to remain on the lookout for these things—*with purpose*. Whereas previously you had been subjected to negative emotions, as being attacked in your sleep, now you will remain in the conscious,

---

[13] Not coincidentally, also the co-founders of the spiritual fellowship *Alcoholics Anonymous*, named after the book.

aware state as these forces wax and wane, around you —never overtaking you. You will become fearlessly aware of their presence; realizing that these forces will always be on the doorstep to your psyche. That consciousness will increasingly prevent them from cropping up inside, on *your* side of the threshold, just as long as you remain aware.

With practice, your new consciousness will cultivate more and more resiliency to the negative forces cast upon you by daily living. Those who instigate the attacks lose their grip over you and their power to control you diminishes. You will be able to intuitively discern who your real friends are and the positions they hold in your life will take on new significance. Do not be surprised to lose some "friends" as your new strength makes you incompatible with their selfish need to dominate and posses you.

Awareness becomes our armor. It is the effortless protector allowing us to bounce back from the barrage of psychic attack that is immanent to daily living. We can live unscathed by the intelligent adversity trying to kill us through spreading It's confusion. When we have the protective shield of awareness, we find that we do not fear these forces. The foundation of courage is *faith* through awareness. It displaces all fear.

So we are to *watch* and we are to see with objective presence. As we do we can begin to see resentment and *all* forms of negative thought and emotion for the foreign substances they are.

It's true that many horrible unfair things happen to us, some large and some small. It is also true that we are more inclined to recall only the most traumatic of them; those that cause us the greatest emotional distress. It is also the *little* things that, unless properly met, cause as much collective trouble as do the big things.

Repressed memories of the little, embarrassing *trespasses* of others against us accumulates inside. Eventually emotionality amasses tremendous power. It overtakes us all at once, washing over like a deadly tsunami wave. We are drowning in a sea of emotionality. *Those with panic and anxiety disorders can relate.*

It is not the *seeing* that is the problem; it is *what we do* with what we see that gets us into trouble. We should never turn a blind eye to the enemy. The world you were born into is imperfect. And so are you. Both facts much be faced.

As you read this, there is injustice on a global scale—and there are things wrong right in front of you too. As I write this, a crumb fallen off a breakfast biscuit I ate this morning lies on the desk next to the keyboard. For some reason the optical mouse keeps finding it. Each time it does, there is an annoyance threatening my serenity. If this emotion overwhelms me, I will no longer be able to write anything worthwhile. I'll be a hypocrite.

Meanwhile,

- A tornado has wiped out a town and killed scores of innocent *people and the paint in the kitchen has not dried properly. The drips are visible. It's terrible!*
- Right now, genocide is being perpetrated upon innocent children somewhere in the world, *and a hair on the head of a soccer mom has just fallen out of place. She must brush it back for the umpteenth time. It's that damned careless stylist's fault. Mom is infuriated.*
- A high school girl who will die from an overdose before her twentieth birthday, bangs a needle full of heroin into a vein for the very first time; encouraged by her own drug-addicted *dad and someone has selfishly left a dirty glass on a counter. How dare they? "If I've told them once, I have told them a thousand times not to do that!" thinks Dad. His face tightens with rage he will shove deep into his soul. No one will see.*

Obviously, these examples cannot come *close* to depicting even a fraction of the injustices in the world. Even so, when considering our own personal problems within our own imperfectly annoying world, a complete picture must include the full injuriousness of them. This means acknowledging *how* we *relate* to these injustices.

As our sensitivity to the negative force of resentment increases, it takes less and less outside pressure to upset us. Our behaviors and our responses to even the smallest infringement on our comforts brought about by others are often embarrassing, especially for those of us who would much prefer to project a more respectable spiritual image for the world to see.

Resentment is specifically designed to throw us off balance and to block us from the Sunlight of the Spirit. Reacting poorly, with emotion and with resentment, causes us to regress spiritually, while becoming more and more conditioned to respond with even more emotion. This happens in each moment we fail to forgive and let go. Spiritual illness—spiritual malady in regression, is like a decay growing inside us. If we live in the present moment, awake and aware, we are okay; protected from the mean-spirited forces that exist through others.

Once sensitized, even the tiniest infraction that others commit can set us off. Until we find our ground of inner being—a strength to place us on a firm foundational base through unemotional detachment—we cannot help but respond.[14]

Barry, the man who first introduced me to the Twelve Steps, used to say, "I am either moving away from a drink or moving toward a drink." This is more than a trite recovery expression. It is a reference to the spread between spiritual wellness and illness. Somewhere in that spread is where we live at any given moment. Our position is not static. We are either progressing or regressing spiritually. The *regression* of our spiritual health spells the *progression* of spiritual illness. Our tendency toward dishonesty and internal excuse making causes us to repress the little things—stuffing ill will deep so it remains far and away from our conscious awareness. There it will sit to fester—infecting our psyche—twisting our minds, our behaviors, and finally mangling our bodies with emotionally caused diseases until we are at last dead.

Therefore it is preferable to handle those seemingly inconsequential events *in the moment*, as they happen, in *real-time*—while they are still current. Since such occurrences are the food for *ego*,

---

[14]This 'crumb' story was written many months ago. I recall that immediately afterwards I got up, went upstairs and returned with a sponge and a pot of water. I washed down my entire desk. Problem solved. The resentment temptation never got inside and I never thought about it again until just now. Isn't that cool? It's a great way to live, with regard to all emotional temptation.

and *ego* seeks to draw them in; repression only leads to a miserable lifetime of fighting against the *self* for domination. Strangely, we become addicted to the struggle. Fighting *self* becomes our new obsession.

Let's see now just what is beginning to happen to us as we process the brutal and objectionable "data" that surround us.

The old axiom that, "Life is five percent what you *make* it and ninety-five percent *how* you take it" is true. Short of dropping out of the stream of life to become hermits, we cannot place any physical insulation between us and the events we encounter, no matter how pleasant or objectionable, how slight or foreboding. We must still live and suffer them all. Just *how* we do this will greatly affect the quality of our lives and how we affect others, and so none are insignificant. Subsequently, each encounter holds either the power to set us up to fail—or else to guarantee our success. Whichever it is depends upon *how* we respond.

Failure is automatic every time any affair upsets us. Fortunately, we have a *first line* of defense against all cruelty. The ability to discern *without* entanglement with emotion is our natural birthright. It is through being upset, through emotional response to cruelty, that we lose it. Yes, resentment is at the cause of all our problems—bar none.

Success is equally automatic whenever we maintain balance and neutrality through *not* being upset by the things we see. This happens automatically after we learn to make allowances for those responsible for rocking the boat. *This* in turn becomes possible once we realize that others are not so much deserving of condemnation as they are of forgiveness. Being unthinking and reactionary themselves when *they* are being cruel, they are not even aware of the harms they do to us and to others. They are just as asleep as you have been. They have been subjected to the same causes that influence you to do the harms unto them. It is a diabolical quid pro quo system of cruelty—an exchange of negative energy between human beings. The exchange is tantamount to an alien invasion. It is an evil reciprocity.

✌○✍

The intrusion into your psyche began in the crib at the hands of your parents. This is an unfortunate fact. *I understand some readers may be shocked to hear this said, but please do not be overly offended.*

Through the impatience of whoever was responsible for your upbringing, a train of consequences was set in motion that set you up for a life of bedeviling failure. This is true of all alcoholics. There are no exceptions. You could never have helped it.

Your mother or father may not have been bad people; still, their inexperience and inability to exhibit tolerance under the strain of the inconveniences in their Stream of Life caused them to turn cruel. That cruelty was an expression of the resentment that had infected *them* through the sick relationships *they* had with their own parents—your grandparents. They were no more born that way than you were. This is why you must learn to forgive them, just as you would want to be forgiven.

The venomous nature of their own impatience was injected into your tiny yet innocent baby psyche. You had no defense whatsoever against its toxic effects. Now you can see why people are led to believe that alcoholism is genetic. It is not alcoholism that is genetic; it is the spiritual infection that gets passed on through the generations.

There are alcoholic families, fat families, cancer families—all with a direct lineage stemming back to spiritual sickness and disconnect from God through anger.

A three-legged dog does not know or care that he does not have all his limbs. He lives a perfectly normal dog-life hopping around, balancing on his three legs, physically compensated for the handicap. But the dynamics of human handicap are far more perplexing than this. That is because humans are not merely animals. We are animal and we are spiritual. We straddle two worlds. One is spiritually ethereal, the other sensual and earthly.

As humans, we have the same ability to compensate that animals have. A deaf man can develop other physical senses to make up for his lack of hearing. Likewise, we can develop compensations for spiritual shortcomings. That is something animals cannot do, because animals do not have spiritual shortcomings. They do not have spirit.

What psychologists call *coping skills*, naturally developed in response to trauma, are cover-ups. When we cannot develop these fast enough to keep up with our inability to stand up to stress, we may have to seek counseling to help us develop artificial mechanisms. These may be useful in making us appear well on the outside; however, they are merely mental placebos that conceal our emotional disturbance and therefore are not permanent solutions. They are *compensations* for spiritual failure—a counterbalancing in response to our ancient predisposition toward egotistical (animal) indulgences.

These compensations assist us in developing personal, phony fixes that psychologists call *repression*. "Stuffing it" is another popular term for these smokescreens. The more and longer we do this, the more sophisticated we will need to get in developing compensation. Eventually we begin to run out of them and life begins to get really awkward as we become more and more anti-social. Of course, few alcoholics would ever admit it.

Later in life, these repressed negative emotions, resentments, will be the cause of the troubles we will hope to resolve—purchasing the services of, *guess who?*—the very psychologists and counselors who have encouraged us to adopt phony coping skills in the first place. Really, these "skills" are nothing more than acknowledging our suppressed emotions and exchanging old repression devices with newer ones. Modern-day psychologists are in the business of teaching us how to hide from the horrible truth that we have failed to respond to evil with love.

What some call *anger management* does not amount to much more than human-guided, systematic applications that can sometimes offer a temporary cover-up of symptoms—but always ends up producing disastrous results, since it allows resentments to continue accruing under the radar. It is the study and application of systematic repression. It is also an extremely dangerous practice. There really is no way to manage anger.

Effective meditation does not manage thoughts and emotions but instead separates them from the spiritual *you*. They are ironically "managed" by *not managing* them. Thoughts simply melt away out of the lens of our vision *before* they can cause the harms for which they are intended. It is that simple.

"Selfish" is not some hackneyed human characterization reserved for the kid who took the last cookie on the plate, the boor who failed to signal a right turn at an intersection or the vacant girl who skipped wiping down the equipment at the gym. The length and breadth of the selfish roots of man go deep and long. All evil perpetrated by humankind begins with the infectious nature of resentment fueling *self* toward heinous acts. Some obviously big, others seemingly inconsequential.

Each year it seems we are following another horrific story on cable news about a mother *suspected* of killing her own child. We wonder how a mother, even the stone-coldest narcissistic bitch, could defy the natural laws of maternity, carry a baby inside of her belly for nine months, experience the miracle of birth, take on the role of nurturer—then kill her young. The key to that answer lies in the word *selfish*. It was not the mother who killed the babies, it was her *Self* who committed the deed. Under the lash of emotional slavery, even the sound of a crying baby can incite annoyance in an edgy, irritable mom as she becomes restless and eager for change. Her inability to maintain composure spawns a seed of anger and becomes a gateway to violence and abusiveness. She doesn't mean to do it. She doesn't want to do it. And yet how many parents find themselves remorsefully comforting the baby they have just smacked out of their own nervous and abusive haste, as if coerced while lost in some strange mental blank spot?

If you are an alcoholic then you will undoubtedly recognize some of this disturbing impatience in your own early development. For whatever unpleasantness such memories of your childhood anxieties this may dredge up, I apologize. Some of you may even feel shame for intolerance you have directed at your own children in the past. It is only right that you feel guilt. Be assured that this meditation exercise will help you with it.

Impatient parents usually find some relief once they send their child off to school. Here, impetuous teachers, many of whom themselves have similarly ruined even their own children, can take over the task in the classroom where Mom has left off at home.

Then it is out of the frying pan and into the fire. Schools can also be a breeding ground of resentment and future troubles. Very often problems for the child only intensify.

Just about the time I was finishing this book, I made a decision to pull our sixteen-year-old son out of the public school system. Do my wife and I both feel that the school's academics are derelict? Yes. Are the teachers pushing social agendas and revisionist history theories that we find objectionable? Absolutely. But these played only a minor role in the decision to scrap the public halls in favor of a private secondary school for Danny. Neither of these were problems we felt we could not somehow get around. There was something else, something far more significant.

Schools are supposed to be a place for young minds to blossom and grow through learning. But there is much more going on in schools than academics. In reality, the school is place where future terrors are refined. There is an unseen, secret spirituality that operates under the radar.

I know parents who absolutely refuse to put their children into a religious private school because they are troubled by the religious teaching in those institutions. Fair enough. Believing they are avoiding spiritual contamination, they are unknowingly tossing their kids into a deep pool of it and often without the benefit of even rudimentary spiritual swimming skills. The spirituality of the public schools, the unseen forces that transpire between students and teachers can be even more harmful than outright disagreeable religious instruction. A brain can be freed from brainwashing by a skilled deprogrammer but an infected spirit can only be refurbished by God.

Public schools are riddled with spiritual indoctrination and influence and the worst fears of parents are happening right under their noses. If you haven't the desire to raise your children inside a particular religion that is certainly understandable. That is exactly how I feel about educating my own children. But if you think you are keeping spirituality out of the socialization of your child by enrolling him in non-religious schools, think again, please. Because boy are you mistaken.

There is no spiritual neutrality in the public schools, in fact unbridled spirituality runs so strongly there it will knock your socks off. They do not have the catechism and they do not have the bells, whistles (or incense and prayers or hymns) that religiously administered educational facilities typically have, but their spiritual undercurrents hold enormous power over our children. There are some powers that love secrecy. (Isn't this the case with all things sinister?)

It is not the obvious stuff that first comes to mind like drugs, alcohol and promiscuity. Although these do play large roles. Hell, smoking in the boys room has been an iconic American adolescent rite of passage into adulthood since the demise of the little red schoolhouse.

What I am referring to is, for the most part, a nefarious, hidden agenda that very few can see. There is another scheme of spiritual forces operating through the social currents running the lives and actions of children and teachers.

I pulled my son out of the public school system because its student body was so spiritually corrupt, the dangers so severe that at sixteen, as spiritually fit as he was, there would be little chance my son could survive it.

I went to a Catholic elementary and High School for Boys, in the Bronx, Saint Raymond's. The High School was administered by an order of religious men called the Lasallian Brothers of the Christian Schools. These wonderful men truly loved kids. These guys knew how to teach and for the most part were positive, powerful examples to many of us young Christian adolescent boys. Up the street, at the elementary school and church, there was different story. There were problems. Big ones.

What went on in the Parish of Saint Raymond's made life for some a living hell on earth. What should have been a path to heaven was really a peek into darkest hell. From the fifth grade through the eighth, the Parochial school served as a veritable hotbed of abuse—some of it sexual but much of it also emotional and mental; all directed toward young children. To date several of the priests who abused

3 The Stream of Life

children have been identified and either convicted or in some way punished; even the Monsignor was convicted and publicly disgraced; just one of several high profile priest-to-boy molestation cases out of Saint Raymonds in the Bronx. Unfortunately any lay teachers involved, and there was at least one I can recall, have gotten away with it.

These days "Raymonds" has repented and changed its ways, from what I understand. But back in the 60s and 70s when I attended, well put it this way, I have many stories to tell. (And I probably will.)

Father Eremito,[15] the director and "lover" of Saint Raymond's altar boys, didn't start out with the hope of becoming sexual predator. First he hated somebody. I guarantee it. Monsignor Schultiess, drunk as a skunk much of the time that I ever saw him, harbored anger. Sister Anne, Sister Emmaline, two of the nastiest women I have ever met probably started out playing hopscotch, Jacks, and dressing little dolls. Then at some point in their lives became unwitting inoculants of hate. Mr. Lee, the *friendly* pedophiliac sixth grade history teacher, liked to play 'stick shift' with the penises of twelve year old boys—these were all victims of some horrors themselves. To hate them for what they did is to *become* them.

Each of these trusted servants made a decision to join the community of Christian spiritual leadership in a wealthy, widely respected Catholic parish, yet look at what happened to them. They turned into monsters. Sister Anne was a monster, Sarah Hatton was a monster, Ronald Lee, the list goes on—each one the carriers of an infection they had no idea had gotten inside them.

Sister Emmaline was certainly no sexual predator. She was just an old woman. A classic, aged black-habited nun who rattled rosary beads and a crucifix from her hip and kept Kleenex stuffed up her sleeves. She hated Johnny Carson, loved Edgar Allen Poe, grew up on the Bronx Grand Concourse and came from Kingston, New York. At least once a day she reminded us Bronx kids that we were "city

[15]http://www.votfnj.org/page.cfm?Web_ID=24 from a New York Times, THE NEW YORK TIMES July 7, 2002 METROPOLITAN DESK "Priest Who Saw Abuse From Other Side Becomes Watchdog" By RICHARD LEZIN JONES (NYT); http://www.bishop-accountability.org/news3/2002_06_17_Saul_APriests_Anthony_Eremito_4.htm

slickers." "Emmy" we called her. Sister Emmy had the reputation of being…let's say, *off her rocker.*

I always got along with her well enough. I thought she was smart if not a little loony. Not so some of the other kids. It was clear that some children just bothered Emmy. She picked on them with regularity. Michael Murphy for his shirttail always sticking out from the back of his pants and for eating pancakes for breakfast. "You'll be a fat pig unable to walk by the time you're twenty." She told him. "You're a slob. Don't your parents even care about you?"

One afternoon, right after lunch time, I had Emmy for Reading and English Composition. It was the first class right after the break.

I used to walk home for lunch. The cafeteria food was gross. Catholic School cafeteria lunches; now that is child abuse for sure. One time I found a green worm inside my Friday fish stick. After that, I just could not bring myself to ever eat the school fare again.

The school bell rang. I was still in the hall. That definitely meant getting *marked down* "LATE" for Emmy's class.

"Maybe she'll be late too." I hoped. Or if she was setting up our lesson on the blackboard with her back to the room, I might be able to slip in the back door unnoticed and slink into my seat unchallenged.

That was not about to happen.

I stopped short of the doorway and peered in. With a quick path scoped up the isle to my seat I made my move. I was going in. In the half second it took for my attention to slip so did my giant math textbook, right out from under my arm. The book headed straight for the floor and could only slap the floor with a loud thud. I was sure of that. I glanced up toward Sister Emmaline. She had not noticed me yet. She was about to.

BANG! Contact.

Emmy jumped as if a safety pin under her holy underskirts had just sprung and pricked her blessed butt. She hurled a holy scowl across the room at me. I ducked. Then another up to the clock above the door. Then one back at me. I ducked again. This time I was nearly hit.

"Oh shit," I thought. "She's about to scream."

Instead, she picked up a book, and proceeded to open the class. I was getting away with it.

"Thank God." I was relieved.

Still there was a niggling thought that she would somehow get even.

"She'll call on me first. I just know it." Still too shaken from dropping the book and arriving late, I was not ready for anything.

"Mr. . ." She scanned the classroom, "Mr. Lavin." I let out a sigh. Again relieved.

Unfortunately, Tommy Lavin was going to pay the price for me.

Every kid in that room knew what was about to happen. We also knew there wasn't a dammed thing we could do about it.

Tommy Lavin had a more-than-moderate case of stuttering. To this day, the worst I have ever witnessed.

Tommy leapt up from his seat and snapped to attention next to his desk. He looked up to the front of the room waiting for the next command.

"Mr. Lavin would you please read starting at chapter five."

" Ye-yes Si-Sis-Sis-Si-Ssss..."

"Yes Sister Emmaline!" She barked. " I know my name." The nun surveyed the class as if we might mimic an incredulous look. We did not.

Just read it!" She ordered. My chest vibrated. I looked over at Warren Mula. Hunched over in his seat, Warren's eyes were fixed on the floor tiles, he looked nervous.

Tommy fumbled for his copy of Red Badge of Courage for a moment, thumbed some pages, cleared his throat and began, "Suh-suh-some-wuh, someone cuh-cuh cried." This was truly a fantastic start.

"Here here he-he-here they cuh-come," and there he stopped. He stared at the book as if he would restart. He wanted to. But he didn't. He was frozen stiff.

"Are you going to read?" The nuns voice was oddly sweet and demanding at the same time. I looked up from my own book at her. Her face was not sweet. It looked knotted and disturbed. I watched as she looked back at me and twisted her face, like I might gesture an agreement back. I didn't. I wouldn't. I hated Emmy.

Emmy looked back over at the curly haired eleven year old boy standing in the center of the classroom, "Well...keep going." She said.

"Ye-yes Si-Sis-Sister," he held the book up close to his face and put a finger on the page.

"Here they come. He-he-here they cuh-cuh come! Here they come. Here they come. Here they cuh-come."

The harder poor Tommy tried, the worse it got. His face reddened but he continued. "He-here they come. Here here they come!"

Some of the kids muffled giggles. A few smirked. Most managed neither. Instead, blank looks of horror drew across wan faces. This was nothing new to us. Yet no matter how familiar, it wasn't the kind of thing with which you ever became comfortable. It was always disturbing.

"Oh, sit down, you ninny!" Emmy shrieked.

Tommy sat down and blew a loud stream of relieving air from his lungs.

"You made it through Tommy," I thought. *"When she calls on me I am going to do real good."*

Afterward, several of us kids gathered outside the school across the street to smoke cigarettes. Smoking cigarettes helped. Though he wasn't even a teenager yet Tommy was a pack-a-day Marlboro man. How could he *not* be. As we were commiserating Tommy's horrible treatment, I had to wonder if there was not some way we might report Sister Emmaline. I never actually suggested it. I suppose I was too fearful. I don't think anything was ever done about it.

What I would not give today to go back to stand up for young Tommy!

Graduating from the eighth grade was a big deal. There was not one kid, with whom I hung out, who did not harbor a plan to get rip roaring drunk immediately following commencement exercises. On graduation day, about 100 of us, dressed as little business people in suit jackets, ties and dresses, filed into the school auditorium to accept our initiation into the future. One by one, we would each march across the auditorium stage, shake hands with principle, Sister Helen Mary and English teacher, Ms. Sweeney. Monsignor Schultiess, aka "Schultz" would bless us with a sign of the cross over the head and hand us our *Saint Raymond's Elementary School Diploma*. We would sing, The

Carpenters, "We've Only Just Begun," while our parents, spectators at the edges of auditorium seats, would well up with tears.

"A kiss for luck and we're on our way, We've only begun,"[16] and it was off to the races. Boones Farm Apple Wine, Ripples, Budweiser, rooftop cocktails of Bacardi's Rum or cheap vodka mixed with orange juice; maybe some grab-ass with a local girl and some puking over the fence railing of the shuffleboard court on Purdy Street. Looking at that today, and considering that we were all barely teens, just 13 and 14-year-olds, it is hard to wrap my head around how it was.

My son Danny is sixteen and he has never so much as tasted beer, smoked a cigarette or had a single swig of Red Bull, let alone gotten drunk or high on alcohol or drugs. Not because we are some strict tea totaling nuts, but because none of us, not even our kids have the need, nor the desire, to engage in that kind of distraction. The "highest" buzz anyone in our house ever gets is the giddiness following an inadvertently-on-purpose dark chocolate Mini Milky Way binge on Halloween night or a slice of homemade Birthday cake. Even then the sugar rush is due to our lack of sweet indulgences the year round. There's no sugar rule, there just is no sugar need.

For eight graders, some of us were becoming quite daring. Some kind of adolescent vertigo kicked in with the realization that finally, we were getting out of this school. At last we would no longer be subjected to these nuns. Accordingly, as the end of the school year approached, some of us were becoming increasingly lax with our studies and coquet in behavior. John Silverberg, just grinned at Mr. *Falchier*, saying, "So?" after being reminded that he had failed to answer so much as a single question on his weekly Science quiz.

Thomas Palladino, smacked away Sister Anne's Fulffs hand in the school library after she had pinched her boney fingers onto one of his ears for whispering to me in the stacks. So when Donna Piri stood up at her desk, looked Sister Anne in the eye and told her, "Fuck you Anne!" It amazed, but did not come as a complete shock. Yes it was vulgar. It was disrespectful. And though certainly not acceptable, it

---

[16]We've Only Just Begun lyrics © Universal Music Publishing Group, EMI Music Publishing

was perfectly understandable. Having already been corrupted we now could champion the obscene.

Sister Anne Fulffs moved out from behind her oversized wooden desk and charged like a raging rhinoceros, and went to right smack her face. Donna ducked but got hit with Anne's left. She grabbed at the nuns next right but Sister Anne clenched a fist onto the students hair and shook. Donna's head flailed back and forth. Her face widened and flushed in shock and surprise. The nun yanked out a clump—a whole handful of brown hair. "Hey look. It's a Tribble," said Silverberg. He was grinning. I was horrified. The children gasped. Several began to cry. Marie Bucci stood up from her seat up and screamed at Fulffs.

"You can't do that," yelled Marie. "We're reporting you."

The kids were rebelling—young, courageous, if not indignant girls, began shouting, in fear and anger, at the nun. A hateful cloud of negative energy filled the air like a plume of electricity. It was magnetic and warm and slow as time could not wait for these moments to catch up. I could feel it.

Maybe I should go for help" I thought, "Mr. Stewart's class is right across the hall". I thought if he would come see what was going on he would make us safe.

So who was this Donna Piri and why is she important in this scenario? It has to do with adolescent, puppy love crushes.

I had infatuations before. At Holy Family in the second grade there was Nancy Brown, Virginia Bart in the third. Then in the fourth grade Doreen Heinz was the new object of attention. Nothing in fifth, sixth or seventh because we had no girls in those grades. In the eighth grade, Donna Piri became the very first girl to ever give me cause to drool. This was more than just a classic crush. This was hormonal. Even Elke Somer, Barbra Eden and Jill St John took a back seat to this new call of the wild. Donna was no sexy celluloid sweetie. Donna was a real girl. My heart would just about pop out of my chest at the sound of her name. We were classmates in the fourth grade, but rarely spoke. I really didn't even notice her then, but by the eighth grade, she had blossomed into a living, breathing pharmacy of relief, and I was drawn to her like a fly to honey—as if my life depended on getting her.

She lived a short walk from the school, just half a block off Castle Hill Avenue. Altering my route for the purpose, I would escort her to the front of her apartment building every day. I know it sounds corny...I even carried her books.

Donna was not a good girl. She was a bad girl. Donna cursed, smoked Newports, grass, had tripped once, popped downers regularly and was reported to have already had sex. This is not that big of a deal in today's junior high schools, but in the '60s and '70s, especially in Parochial school, it was huge. It was revolutionary. Revolutionary meant hip. If you were hip then you were important. The sexual and drug revolution was in full swing in the East Bronx as it was everywhere else in the United States and anyone who was anything took part in it. I wanted *in*. I needed *in*. I needed to be important.

Pressure mounted. It approached unmanageable levels. I had tapped the booze, there was no money for drugs, but sex was absolutely free. It was also important. Bad Donna, the Bronx Borinquen beauty, held the key that could unlock a solution to what had been ailing me for a long time: *lack of importance.*

Fortunately I did not possess the social guts and I was not to have sex until meeting my wife Nancy, years later. And so Donna remained just as beyond reach as would any Hollywood hottie appearing in the fantasies of an adolescent boy. Oh yea, and there was also another rather inconvenient little matter, a steady boyfriend—another panting dog, like me, except who was getting some of her—the poor son-of-a-bitch. I was jealous.

The faceoff at the head of the room continued. Donna held her head with two hands and cried; Fulffs stood looking blankly at the nest of hair suspending from her fist. She snapped her fingers open and she let it drop. Donna watched in horror realizing the Tribble was a piece of her falling into the floor and let out a shriek.

The nun knew what she had done.

"You shut up, you fresh things!" The nun was shouting at the infidel girls, now standing at their seats, tears rolling down defiant, frightened faces.

Then Sister Anne fled out of the room.

She was gone.

We were stunned.

The wordless aftermath was numbing. Tears streaked down some cheeks. There was an occasional sob, some from Donna and some out of the rows of children; in between sporadic whimpers there was quiet. Not a peaceful silence but an empty hole in the universe where the din of young life used to be. It was like that moment in the Wizard of Oz, just after the wicked witch had been doused with water, melted away and was no more. We who remained were not quite sure if what we had just witnessed was real or even right. We were in shock. Finally safe, but stunned. No one spoke a word. Like dust settling over a demolished building a cloud of anger hovered over the classroom; it descending like a soft blanket onto us all, its essence bled into our young spirits. Not one child would go home clean today.

Sister Helen Mary came into the still silent room several minutes later to begin damage control, to close the hole. Not to soothe the damage done to us, but like a painter might spackle over a hole punched into a wall by an angry drunk, she came to smooth it over; to mitigate any possible harm to the reputation of the school administration, to the parish or to Sister Anne Fulffs.

I was head over heels in love with Donna Piri and so, boy, did this piss me off. It seemed to me that these nuns were women who had taken vows of dedication to Christianity. They had declared that they were mystically betrothed to Jesus Christ and in fact wore gold wedding bands symbolizing as much. If your husband is Christ Himself you would think one would have a better handle on one's own meanness and anger issues.

Hypocrisy exists to be hated so that it can sow the seeds of anger. The way that authorities handled problems like this was to take measures designed to cover-up. Damage control protocols help dodge scandalous publicity and such efforts would effectively stave off a bad public image for decades to come. No one is ever going to investigate the "mean nuns" of Saint Raymond Elementary School; not when priests have finally been caught getting their jollies playing with alter-boys in the same parish. Still, the damages done eventually became legend and the PTSD of children unwittingly placed into the hands of some very wicked people would carry forward.

All resentment, all negative emotions are deadly, whether they are cast onto an America GI placed into a bamboo cage or into children in a neat, inner city classroom with a crucifix hanging over the door. It is all the same.

As most preteen infatuations are apt to do, mine with Donna broke my heart. By the time eighth grade had come to a finish and Saint Raymond's High School for Boys beckoned, I was a lovesick and broken young man, a casualty of unrequited love. But I could consciously acknowledge *that* damage and within weeks of beginning High School, it was forgotten. Remembered, but not regretted.

These days there is not one twinge of grudge in my body for the Catholic educational institutions. I went on to receive superior handling and education by Christian Brothers. Today my own son is enrolled in a private Catholic education system staffed by wonderful, caring and able administrators and teachers. Beyond the watchful eye that any parent ought to have we have no qualms or reservations concerning the safety and wellbeing of our children.

As for Donna Piri, I have no idea if she is even still alive. I assume she is. I am sure she went on with life not even aware of the role she played in mine. Heck, I didn't even know, how could either of us?

We rarely know for sure how the things we do and say, how we are, may affect others. I later learned that the outburst between Sister Anne, Donna and her supporters was not as spontaneous as it seemed; that she and a few of the girls had prescripted the event. Yelling, "FU," at Sister Anne before leaving Saint Raymond's was an accomplishment she did not want to leave behind. She did get her way, but surely it would have been more healthy to yearn and earn good grades or scholarships; but there just are some environments that are not conducive to that kind of wholesomeness. Saint Raymond's grade school, and Saint Raymond's Parish in the 60s and 70 in the Bronx was like that. The disgrace was no secret. It made the newswires across the country.

Not only did my heart break for Donna Piri but she also played a much more enduring role shattering another part of me; the vestiges of religious faith there may have been left inside. Just as broken as my heart, was my belief that clergy could have anything to do with God, goodness, or Heaven.

Undoubtedly, when some of the kids walked across that stage to receive their diplomas there were hopes and dreams for the future, moving on to High School and growing up through their teens. The anticipated life was exciting and new. For me there was that, but there was also another hope—even more exhilarating than growing up. Eagerness hinged on knowing that within hours of the juvenile pomp and circumstance that on Greg Gilligan's roof, just a block away, there awaited a brown paper bag containing a half-pint of vodka and a 25 cent waxed cardboard container of *Sundew* orange drink. I had set it up the night before. With the contents of that bag I could forget about Donna, nuns, schools and all my fears of the present and future. Most of all, I would not *feel* the anger anymore. The numbing had "Only just begun".

Schoolchildren do not get the hair yanked out of their heads or their butts paddled for misbehaving much anymore. I suspect because of the outrage of good parents and the installation of new laws more than the spiritual progress made by the average teacher—is to be credited. Today we have more *civil* methods of controlling and manipulating young students.

The school bullies were not only those who donned religious habits; they had the standard American uniforms of authority and knowledge: ties and dresses. Being derided in front of the class and public flogging with paddles were common practices back in those days.

It is ironic that the self-appointed champions of anti-bullying in our educational system today are themselves employing the heavy guns in the bully wars. There is the power of words and their commanding vitriol, artificially sweetened and dissolved into the Facebook and schoolyard Kool-Aid. Like any verbal abuse, it is always rooted in impatience. It is that angry mother of a teacher by whom he or she has been similarly groomed and trained in the inhumane art of behavior modification.

Still, whether you were a victim of such abuse at the hands of trusted servants, a teacher, or by stimulating positive and negative reinforcements in an attempt to manipulate your behavior, you were trained, like an animal is trained; you were treated like a dog.

Parents, relatives, and teachers were not the only culprits. There were other instigators too. You also developed relationships outside of the home, accruing friendships among schoolmates and within other communities as you became more and more socialized.

Their negative emotionality traveled across the plasma of environments through words and deeds. Your involvement in those cliques exposed you to violence and abusive behaviors that were born out of the very same parentally inflicted impatience that you experienced in your own home; except now, they were joined by horrible forces carried out of other dysfunctional homes and into the schoolyard.

Bullying on the Internet has become a big concern in the media—and therefore among parents. Kids have always had negative and immature things to say to each other, and since social networks like Facebook create textual trails, what was once secret schoolyard nastiness has become more evident.

Bullying can always be traced back to a secret, tragic home life; a negatively charged force gains its power to harm others long before it ever becomes an apparent problem broadcast over Facebook or in any social network. By the time they become visible to the naked eye, it is too late. The disease has already gone viral.

The infection is not limited to online communities. The more traditional breeding grounds are still around. Scout troops, little league teams, karate classes—literally *any* social community can become a petri dish for spiritual disease. This is where the horror of one family enters into another to reproduce and spread infectious spiritual blight. If you think about it a bit, it should not be too difficult to recall this effect in your own past.

Make no mistake; bullies on the Internet, in the schoolyard, and at the summer camp are created in the home by parents. The blame falls on the parents. Facebook bullies are the alcoholics, drug addicts, and food abusers of the future—for some, the not-so-distant future. For them, the impatience of the parents is projected onto the children and carried into the community.

Poet W. H. Auden once wrote, "Perhaps there is only one cardinal sin: impatience. Because of impatience we were driven out of Paradise, because of impatience we cannot return." There is an amazing implication in Auden's words for any alcoholic holding hope for recovery.

Learning the means for acquiring patience through practicing and living through *conscious contact* with God, we experience a return to our original Paradise; the way it was prior to mankind's setting in motion his current mode of existence where he attempts to play God. What a world it would be if this were this to come about!

Lack of patience is one of those symptoms of continuing spiritual disease; eventually disaster. It is my greatest hope that the information in this book may cause many to consider the solution to their problems presented through the meditation practice I have discovered. They might also experience a reentry to Paradise and know victory over their troubles from within.

As you saw your world becoming more and more contaminated by injustice, cruelty, and just plain old *wrongdoing,* you became agitated. Illicit authorities, government workers, and organizations—all kinds of human entities, people and institutions both—became sources of annoyance. I know how morose this all sounds. I am not trying to infer that there have been absolutely no positive influences in your world at all.

I hope that you will recall the earlier warning I made in the introduction. The information presented in this book is not for the fainthearted. So I will offer a wisp of fresh air here just for a moment. Yes, of course there probably were some wonderfully positive role models and good times in your life too. But we do not need to be freed from those, do we?

OK. Remember, this is a book about alcoholism; that means it is a book about spiritual dysfunction. No one ever found himself or herself emotionally broken, beaten, or scarred by the acts of love in their lives. Nevertheless, they sure have experienced distress through separation from God and by diving headfirst into excessively dangerous and deadly behaviors.

The Stream of Life includes the good *and* the bad; the true *and* the false; positive and negative; light and dark. Unless we learn to distinguish right from wrong; to discern without hating (or elation) we will never survive life. This is a book concerning matters of life and death. One day perhaps I will scribe a delightfully cheery little recovery book of sappy spiritual affirmations meant to uplift. This isn't it. (But please come find and shoot me to put me out of my misery if I do. Promise?)

World affairs, news stories, family troubles, relationship difficulties—sometimes it seems that there is nothing but negativity afoot. It feels as if there is a dark veil of gloom over the head of the alcoholic, even one who doesn't drink anymore—often *especially* the alcoholic who doesn't drink anymore.

Alcoholism and depression is a combination of maladies that can be even more deadly than either of the two standing alone. This is common comorbidity that kills millions each year. Never mind what your therapist has told you. The cause for *all* post-recovery depression has but one root that taps down into the sickened mind. It originates out of forces that the alcoholic does not understand.

Natural disasters, 9/11, serial killers, criminals getting away with abominable crimes—all such atrocities seem to exist for no other reason than to cause worry and spread resentment. That they do. They serve as food and fuel to the collective egos in the matrix of all humanity. Lack of resiliency against these forces is the reason for depression.

As observed by Dr. William D. Silkworth, medical director of the renowned Townes Hospital made famous by the *Alcoholics Anonymous* story and historically one of the most highly regarded hospitals in the world to treat alcoholic and drug addiction:

"They are restless, irritable and discontented, unless they can again experience the sense of ease and comfort which comes at once by taking a few drinks"[17]

---

[17]"Alcoholics Anonymous", 4th edition, Alcoholics Anonymous World Services, "The Doctors Opinion," p. xxvii

The classic alcoholic never seems pleased with what he has. He always wants more. Constantly on the lookout for a *change for the better*, he really seems forever agitated and dispirited. He is excessively sensitive and readily provoked to temper. Despite what he says, his peevish and transparent personality projects a stubborn unwillingness to *ever be* happy. The only thing worse than *being* an alcoholic is trying to live with one. (And being set on fire. That sucks too.)

I grew up in the Bronx in an alcoholically charged environment. It was a broken home, and my mother's part-time, live-in boyfriend an ex-NYPD cop, was the dominating influential personality in the home. Of course, he was a violent, raging alcoholic, so there was this cloud of fear, terror, and embarrassment constantly hovering over us, even when he was not directly under the influence of the sauce.

It's funny how some alcoholics think that when they are not drunk, they are okay. They just never seem to realize that their drinking is merely a symptom and that their overall demeanor, even without the booze, can be just as foul. Being in constant conflict with his own conscience, my mother's boyfriend was horribly negative in his outlook of just about everything.

Everything was broken. Everything was wrong. Nothing worked—not the world, not us, not his job. He hated ginnys and queers, niggers and spics, hippies and commies, fat broads, skinny skanks— you name it, and he had a derogatory, negative word for anyone with two legs, and if you were missing a limb you were a "goddamned misfit" too. The food we ate was horrible. Anyone who was not a white, Catholic, Irish male was going to hell, and even then, if you were not 100 percent thoroughbred, you would be denied Heaven.

The slightest tinge of non-Irish blood in your veins put you immediately onto his "shit-list". The people running the country were crooks. The government was wrong. Everyone was a fool, a thief or a sinner. The teachers were wrong. My mother was wrong. We were wrong. Nothing was ever right. And the only time the world was okay was after he had a few drinks—or at least a solid plan for a spree. Of course, we totally ignored that he was an obese, chain-smoking, wife-cheating drunk (he had a wife and kids living on the other side of the Bronx) who we never once saw on the inside of our church.

You can just imagine the resentments and suppressed anger and loathing my sisters and I developed under such conditions.

We were not atypical. If you are an alcoholic, then you will likely see much of your own upbringing in my brief description. Any of us who have grown up in an alcoholic household know what it is like to live under a constant cloud of pessimism, negativity, irritability, discontentment, and depression. That is because a key personality in the household is playing God—usually a father. But mother herself, or a boyfriend, will do in the absence of one.

An optimist is someone who has faith that things are going to turn out well. He has learned that he is not in charge of world events; nor can he control the future, as it becomes the present. He realizes that the present belongs to God alone. The pessimist is full of doubt and can see only negative outcomes. That is because he has become attached to his own thinking; his own thinking is sourced from a negative place, not a place of this world. The pessimist is plagued by the pain of his own judgment.

By expressing negativity, the pessimist is only expressing emotional attachments as he feeds his ego with the food it needs to inflate and play God. A pessimistic person has already been overrun by bitterness and has judged his tormentors as unworthy.

You don't *have* to be a real alcoholic to be a real royal asshole, but it sure helps. The aforementioned are just *some* of the typical signposts, not only of alcoholism but also of depression. In short form, this classic idea in Silkworth's discomforting triplet, "restless, irritable, and discontent" describes very well how an alcoholic feels. These feelings are symptoms; mere effects of the underlying spiritual problem and are only a small part of the *entire* picture—not the causes of them.

Just as when the Add Oil "idiot light" goes off on the dashboard, the problem is not that an annoying light that keeps going off, it is what that light indicates. Likewise, *feelings* are never the causes of problems. They should be considered the warning, indicating unseen spiritual disturbances.

Filling in around all of these pockets of despair are the inane, personally irritating incidents that each of us experience privately: the untimely glob of mustard dripping off a corned beef sandwich onto the floor, a mosquito bite, an itch, an ache, a pain, an up-close subway straphanger with salami breath; all of the unpleasantries that each of us encounters every day come in a continuous stream of personal affronts. They are indignities that never seem to stop. They never will. The age old idea that "this too shall pass" may not be as sage and axiomatic as we had hoped.

Most alcoholics don't fall asleep at night. They pass out. Even the sober ones—that is, unless they have a way of dealing with this din of negativity that is simply life as we know it.

Each day that we go to bed at night we fall asleep having repressed a day's worth of resentments. No wonder we are so tired and worn. The onslaught is relentless as we stuff the charge of bitter negativity deep into our craw—into our psyche. This is where *Step Eleven* comes to the rescue. It can save the practitioner from the imperfect handling of stresses throughout the day.

Twelve steppers are supposed to remain continually vigilant throughout the day, maintaining watchfulness for the looming negative emotions that threaten to crop up at any moment. This real-time course of conscious awareness is a major component of the Twelve Stepper's Tenth step practice—but how many execute even *near*-perfect adherence to their daily practice? Precious few. "We are not saints," as the co-authors of "Alcoholics Anonymous" admit.

Twelve-Step practitioners who don't have an effective way of dealing with the stresses of daily life, who let up on the spiritual program, head straight into trouble.

The first sign of difficulty will be expressed in *a very busy Step Eleven* review at night. You would be lucky to stay awake long enough to complete such a task. It could more resemble a Step Four style exhaustive inventory list, than the more general, nightly consideration proposed by the "Big Book" co-authors.

An eye for an eye, it's dog-eat-dog world, quid pro quo, karma—call it what you like, a lifetime participating in a tit-for-tat world is slavery. It is a *bondage of self* that includes not only you but also armies of other slaves. You are no longer the individual child of God but one of many soldiers: a collective brood of pawns in a hellish regime that is bent on subtle domination and control. *Hell on earth* is the goal.

Until you can tolerate the trespasses of others, you can never hope to survive.

Then what is tolerance? How can we get it? In the study of electricity, electrical charges of varying strengths are objectively compared with each other based upon measurable, allowable variations. We can perceive and make the comparison without being electrocuted or burning out the wiring of a circuit. We can see which charges are negative and which ones are positive without prejudice, making allowances for and recording whatever fluctuating variances we assess. The measure of variances between these positive and negative charges is called tolerance.

Likewise, when we are centered and objective we can dispassionately distinguish positive events from negative events. Then we are distinguishing right from wrong, establishing a tolerance level for any variance without being affected by *either* charge. We are naturally insulated, remaining neutral, without judgment—without playing God. Our neutrality is our natural insulation from emotional shock, and we develop a natural capacity for love.

Whenever we make allowances for the negatively charged events around us, we are exercising a choice. Either we tolerate the cruel, unfair and offensive situations and the people who cause them, so they no longer affect us negatively—or we succumb to anger and *become* what we have hated.

The simple attitude of neutrality prevents resentment from getting inside us. *That* is true tolerance.

Resentment, bitterness, and anger all remain on the doorstep to our psyche, never gaining entry to serve as food for the judgment-hungry ego-self. We remain neutral and unmoved. We are shielded and free to use our impartial vision to move naturally, without struggling to make ego-feeding decisions. With such protection, ego cannot be fed and it remains hungry, subdued, and right-sized. There ought to be a sign on our backs, which reads, "Please Do Not Feed the Ego."

If you could just starve the "Self" of anger-food, you would live long and well. Your obsessions would fall away. You would be permanently straightened both mentally and physically for as long as you maintained your disconnected existence. The exercise I have been showing alcoholics over the last decade brings you to this state. All you have to do is try it for yourself to see. If you do, life will never be the same.[18]

Most of us like to think that we are as calm as this. I mean, how cool would it be to be as collected as James Bond? Bombs explode all around him, as he's falling out of an airplane. A beckoning woman in a string bikini flies past in a glider. Meanwhile James's leg is caught in a rope while a countdown is in progress that will end with the planet exploding into nuclear oblivion; James keeps his composure and somehow has the presence of mind to offer us a smarmy quip.

We may put on an outward display of serenity and calmness, yet, because of repressed resentments, very few of us ever truly experience life as the person we are pretending to be. We may *think* we have been tolerant and forgiving, when in reality we are harboring secret hostilities and disapproving emotions. You may have done well to project such an image to the world. Yet anger and bitterness got stuffed deep down into your being. Hoping no one would notice, you may have compensated with well-honed acts, oozing self-manufactured serenity, happiness, and altruism. Some of us get away with this kind of overcompensated lifestyle for a very long time.

Many people think tolerance means, "You must agree with me"—if not, then you are not being tolerant. If I do not resent your errors, then I am being tolerant. In the spiritual realm, intolerance and judgment are one and the same.

True tolerance, exemplified by patience, is a demonstration of non-response to pressure—stresses that would otherwise inject us with

---

[18]Please visit the "How To Get There," page in the back of this book for fast access to the meditation exercise. It is available for streaming or download. It is free and always will be.

the poisonous venom of resentment. In Scriptural terms, this is what temptation[19] is all about. The moment that pressure takes a run at us is the very moment we have to exercise tolerance and patience. If we miss it, the negative charge of resentment enters to cloud our clear vision and evolve into thoughts—thoughts we *think* are our own and represent us.

Do you ever get lost in your thoughts? This is exactly how it has happened, and each time you allow it, you feed it, identifying even more resolutely with it than you did before the attack. When instead we exhibit grace through the natural light of awareness, we remain undisturbed by stress, living in that moment. In that moment is the only place where we can have such clear vision and discernment. We can discern the true from the false and displace doubt with faith.

Going forward now into the next chapter, please keep these ideas fresh in your mind:

There always is a "now" moment. Another way to put this might be, "It is never *not* now." As sure as the sun is always shining somewhere on earth, its heat, light, and energy is perpetual and never ceases. Now is eternal and it never goes away. It is always *now*.

Here-and-now is the place in time and space—in our consciousness—where we review the events we have been observing. It is the place where we process and experience both the good and the bad—in a place that goes beyond mere eyesight and human vision. It is the conscious place where we can either feel emotional about these events or not feel them; to be at one with the world, *which is death*—or separated from the world, living in it but unaffected, *which is life.*

In the moment when we simply discern, we do not feel. This is an unfettered vision and ability to distinguish danger from benefit—to dispassionately tell right from wrong. This moment is entirely unencumbered by emotion and is pure vision without any self-will injected into it. This kind of detached vision happens in a moment, in a twinkling of the eye, *in the now*, if you prefer. This is the exact moment that we exert our free choice to either properly relate to cruelty and injustice or improperly react to them. It is through

---

[19]The true meaning of temptation has been stripped out of most religious teachings.

responding that the alcoholic sets himself up to be violated further, and so failing to make the choice to be awake is also failing at being human—failing at life. To be a success we must not run from our negative thoughts but turn *all* thinking over to God, relating properly to cruelty and injustice, or else risk ultimate failure.

That is a single choice, the only one mankind has ever had, from Adam to now. It is a choice that is beyond intellect and knowledge, delicately balanced on a precarious line separating two paralleled universes, one in which God is king, and the other in which man plays God. It is the choice to be awake and aware or asleep and numb. When one chooses incorrectly, as all alcoholics do, this violation is imminent, and it happens in the manner described in the next chapter. This ride will get even bumpier, so please remain calm.

"The best way to make your dreams come true is to wake up."
- *Paul Valery*

4 THERE'S A WOLF IN THE FOLD

A Case of Mistaken Identity

Do you like action films? If so, think of the last one you saw. No doubt it was full of intrigue, action, and suspense—all arced into a sexy, flashy story line designed to draw you in and take you somewhere else. Your heart raced while James Bond dangled by a rope hanging from a helicopter skid. You got excited as "the spy who loved me" allowed himself to be seduced by a pretty woman. You saw the 007 character on the silver screen, and, for that brief time in that theater, you became the suave, sophisticated secret agent—well, in your head, anyway. Ladies, you too. If you are a woman then you identified with the sexy seductress taking advantage of James's weakness for sex. *Of course once James gets his 'fix' he's back to his ruthless ways. Too bad for you girls!*

Your imagination fired, and in your stimulated state a strange phenomenon occurred; you became oblivious to your physical environment. As if disappearing into thin air, you were absorbed into the cinematic experience. Forgetting that you were in a theater, you began to feel what James feels in your thoughts and in your body. You entered a dream world.

It's great fun, but make no mistake. In those moment, *you are out of your mind.*

You are but a single observer in a room full of temporarily insane moviegoers, as you, along with the entire audience, succumb to a subtle pressure being exerted through the field of vision. You have surrendered your will.

Like Malcolm McDowell's character, Alex, in *A Clockwork Orange*, your thoughts and your behaviors are being modified by images you see on the giant screen before you. In time, you begin to act compulsively, perhaps smoking, overeating, abusing substances, against your well-being. You have been reconditioned. However, unlike Alex, perhaps you have welcomed it—even sought it out.

68

Let's be frank about this, shall we? Sex, violence, and celluloid chicanery are attractive. We love it. Within minutes of the start of a film, a dark room full of people have become entangled in the intrigue of the film's plot. The scenery and characters parading onscreen become objects of a controlled mental obsession that crowds out all thoughts of anything else. All you need to do is sit and watch.

The filmmaker takes control of both mind and body while you and the viewing audience responds in unison. With your heart racing and your blood pressure spiking, you can *try* to remind yourself, "It's only a movie.... It's only a movie," but your body doesn't believe you, and so your breathing becomes shallow and rapid while beaucoup oxygen floods into your bloodstream. Glucose levels leap. Muscles tense. Your body becomes stoked, preparing itself to do whatever it has to do in order to endure whatever imminent danger or excitement it has been fooled into thinking exists. Even in a brief moment of clarity all you can think of is, "Honey, do you want more popcorn?" or "Do you think it's okay to go pee now?"

This auto-responsiveness is part of our natural human-animal conditioning. It is something that begins when some initial excitement leads to an increased sensitivity to surrounding sights and sounds. Our perceptions affect us more deeply than we realize as we unite with our environment, leaving reality behind.

After a time we can no longer safely watch any scene without becoming what we experience in the theater. Imagine the power held by any person or entity having access to our minds while we are lost inside those sensitive, vulnerable moments.

As a brief, entertaining interlude to temporarily take us away from the world, this is fine. A Saturday night out at the local cinema is a kind of mini vacation. But what about after we leave the theater? What about real life—in the real world? If the scenes in a movie can so dramatically affect the thoughts in your mind, even so far as to cause an automatic physical response in your body, then what is to prevent the same kind of involuntary action from happening *after* you leave the theater? What if once you venture out into the real world, real people (not scripted characters) hate you, point pistols at you, love you, or caress you? Are not those real world characters also as controlling of your responses as the moviemakers? You bet they are! It is a little scary, wouldn't you say?

For the purposes of this book, I am not referring to those social influences stemming out of Madison-Avenue-style marketing and media. What I am really talking about is *life*: the flawed, irritating people in your world, those who are as much a part of your environment as you are theirs. All around is the imperfect cast of actors performing in the cavalcade of events that flow through and around all of human existence. This is the Stream of Life. It is packed solidly with all that we know to be our universe—its people, places, and things. Do we run away from it all? Do we allow it to wash over and drown us? Or do we impact it? More importantly, is the effect it has on *us*, and *we* on *it*, positive—or is it negative? Just how we respond holds the key to answering that question. It will be the major influence over our actions. The people who control our responses also control our actions—how we behave.

Within this reality is the entire world, and although creation can be a remarkable sight, it is still a fallen Paradise where cruelty and injustice are rampant. Yes, amid the wonders of creation thrives the teaming broods of human beings, all of whom seem forever up to their old stupid human tricks: selfish, self-absorbed, and frightened, gracelessly stumbling and bumbling their way around and stepping on the toes of anyone who happens to get in their way. Most are not even aware of their own inelegance or the harms they spread through their self-centered existence.

Even when we live a good life and manage to evade much of what is wrong with the world, isn't is also possible to find that at certain times you live as an actor, playing out scenes in some nightmarish false-reality play you only *think* of as real life?

What if instead you could perceive the brutally unfair and nasty state of affairs in the world and process what you see *without* being affected by it? Then, your reaction would be one of *no response*. With your emotions no longer unchecked, the people who tempt you to respond to their cruelties would lose the control they have over you. Instead of living through a vision that is blurred by the inferior lens of emotionality that always leads to willful decision-making, you would be free to make effortless choices based upon clear vision.

But this has not been the case all of your life.

You see, you didn't not know it, but while your mind was busy processing what your eyes were seeing, something else was happening— like a program running on your laptop, except in the background. Malware. A force, like some cosmic energy, came along to contaminate what would otherwise have been your natural power of discernment. It dampened intuition. It spoiled your healthy ability to distinguish the true from the false. It infused you with a negative energy, an alien force we call *resentment*.

Has it ever bothered you that it is so easy for others to piss you off? Have you ever cringed at a memory or thought to yourself that the very sound of a person's voice makes your skin crawl?

That is because responding with bitterness, even just once—even the tiniest bit—allows ego to feast on the force of anger. The moment this happens, we automatically lose emotional stability. From then on we become increasingly sensitized and progressively more subject to our surroundings and memories. We can become ruled by our past.

Once the train of emotional responses is set in motion, we lose the ability to make right choices. What appears to be a *right* choice will eventually prove to be wrong. Someone or something has taken control of us. It could be a boss or a spouse. It might be a parent. It might even be person we call "friend", someone we think of as a trusted confidant. Seeing our error, resenting our own resentment, serves only to drive us into depression as we become increasingly angry with our own "self" for gorging on bitter impatience.

It is exactly what happens with food. I recall in the past when I had a problem with obesity and would try various diets. If I faltered just once, that single failing could easily result in tossing all healthy eating aside in frustration. Once that happened, I had condemned myself to being as fat and (resentful) as ever.

Do *that*, and you will know dread. What is frustration but one more flavor of resentment?

There is hardly a person or object in existence that cannot serve as a source of stress, betraying us, tempting us to fall away from consciousness through indulging in emotional ego-food.

This secret, embarrassing sensitivity to others will eventually kill you.

To survive this, you must find the way to immunity—a daily centering that quiets the thought-addicted mind and protects against the infectious effect resentment has on you. That centering is not an ordinary quietness. It is the original stillness you had when you were a little child—before the pull of the world and the cruelties in it took its toll on you. It is a very special stillness to be rediscovered through a very special kind of meditation which automatically brings you to a resilient condition, a *state of grace* that is a shield against all negative emotional energies just waiting to crop up inside your psyche.

To the degree that you recoup this protection will you live a long, happy and healthy life – a reflection of wellness upon you and your family. If not, you continue projecting resentment onto those to whom you might otherwise show love—even your children.

The moment we accept the negative charge of anger, the ego-self gorges on its bitter energy. It comes alive, nourishing on resentment and enlarging until it becomes gross and unwieldy—unmanageable. Each time this happens, our response becomes a precondition for the next time, as we set ourselves up for failure after failure. No matter how hard we try to break free of this ever-increasing sensitivity, we remain bound. We become addicted to our own bitterness while exhibiting impatience to others—including those we purport to love— doing *unto others as was done onto us.* We would not wish such horror unto ourselves, would we? Why then do we put others through it?

Eventually even innocents become a threat to us, because their innocence exposes us by contrast. We respond with anger to those who mean us no harm at all, who do not deserve our inner wrath and secret judgment.

Repressed, secret anger stuffed away and covered up with phony goodness causes more heart disease and cancer than any of the environmental causes to which society wants us to redirect our attentions.

Repressed resentments will kill you. Each year in the United States, over four hundred thousand folks die from sudden cardiac arrest. In a recent (2009) study published in the March 3 issue of the *Journal of the American College of Cardiology*, researchers demonstrate a clear link between mental stress and heart disease.

In the study, anger produced ventricular tachycardia (V-tach), which is just an egghead's way of saying, when you get mad your heart beats rapidly. The problem however is that over sustained periods of time, say years, this constant V-tach condition prevents the ventricles in the heart from filling adequately so the heart cannot pump at its full potential. When this happens, there can be a sticky plaque buildup inside the coronary arteries and coronary artery disease (CAD) occurs.[20] This is a hideous precursor to a heart attack, and sudden death is the concern. I think you will agree that risk of "sudden death" is a pretty serious problem, one most of us would like to avoid. Many of us will not avoid it.[21]

It is sort of like if you do not use a toilet often enough. When we first moved from New York City to Cape Cod, we went shopping for a home. One house we viewed was somebody's vacation place. They had not been there in quite a while—several months, I am guessing—and the toilets were cruddy and full of nasty-looking brown deposits and rust. Even a couple of flushes did not seem to help. When water does not flush through the tank and the bowl, clearing itself out of minerals and other stuff dissolved into the water, calcium, metals, and oxidation deposits build up on the porcelain and begin to encrust what was once a nice, smooth, sleek, shiny surface. It is nasty. Well, the same things can happen in the heart chambers if they are not sufficiently flushed through with fresh blood.

If anger can cause the heart to beat irregularly or dangerously fast, as this study suggests, then such emotions can also be associated with sudden cardiac death (SCD). This kind of instant death accounts for half of all heart disease deaths in the US. It can happen even without any history of heart disease. In SCD, excitement such as anger causes the heart's electrical system to go haywire, and, instead of pumping blood through the body as it normally would, the heart begins to quiver. Death can occur in minutes.

Death always has a cause, but there is something particularly sinister about dying by way of emotional stress, especially repressed,

---

[20]http://www.webmd.com/heart-disease/ss/slideshow-visual-guide-to-heart-disease.

[21]JACC article, along with updated information and services, is located on the World Wide Web at http://www.nlm.nih.gov/medlineplus/coronaryarterydisease.html

negative emotions abetted by the ego-self. The graveyards are full of folks who on the surface appeared placid, serene and centered, but who were really emotionally repressed, resentfully harboring secret devils that lurked deep inside and fed on hate and anger floating in the Stream of Life.

Instead of relying upon *spiritually* powered intuition and inspiration, we rely more and more upon *sensually* powered instinct and the nervous energy it generates for us—like animals in the wild. The longer this goes on, the *less human* we become.

The question is how to break free. Severing a sick reliance upon self-will through the sheer *force of will* is a spiritual oxymoron. Still, we need a way.

The answer comes if we develop a loyalty to our God-vision and live from that dispassionate, quiet place in the Sunlight of the Spirit—where grace is. When we truly know what it means to be freed from the bondage of "self," then we might *unhitch* from the wagon of the inferior "self" and reconnect to something far *superior*—a star—a divine source of power. It is not a power that is *us*, nor does it originate inside us.

We have been given a way to do just that. It comes through separating from the alien, false self (ego) and seeing "It" for what it is.

When we do that simple thing and nothing more, "It" flees, and we are free. That simple thing is what we practice by meditating. Any other goal in meditation is counterproductive to this kind of spiritual growth.

You have an inner motivation that yearns for this freedom. You feel it as unsettled discontentment accompanying your response to tormentors. This is an indicator that on some deep level, you do not enjoy living in an excited unstable state. That anxiety is your personal living proof that a loving God beckons for you.

If you would just sit still long enough for that *call* to save you, it would.

Do that, and you can receive your daily bread; that is to say, *strength and protection from the forces that seek your response,* through separating from your internal tyrant that you think of as your *self*.

Simple pure meditation—such as the exercise, detailed on my website, that I am attempting to convince you to try—will help you separate from that *self*. *It will do it safely without inserting* anything else into your thinking, with no new thoughts to replace old ones: no doctrine, no suggestions, no positive affirmations—just objective awareness permitting spiritual, emotional, mental, and physical health. Free at last!

You have probably heard of the fight-or-flight response in animals. The sight or scent of the lion triggers the body of the zebra to flee and save its life. The grizzly bear, cornered by a hunter, ceases running only to turn on its pursuer in attack. There is no decision-making involved. This is automated, animal behavior, and it conveys animal responsiveness to situations not involving consciousness or conscience. In fight or flight, the body's primitive automatic systems respond and prepare the body to protect itself from harm or any threat to its survival.

Anything that stresses the animal, whether that pressure is real or perceived, instigates the inborn response, setting off a sequence of nerve-cell firings and a release of chemicals in the hypothalamus area of the brain that physically and mentally prepares the body. It is either "run away" or "stand and fight," and is a *no-brainer*—in the intellectual sense, anyway. Its sole purpose is to get the body ramped up with the boost of fuel and energy it needs to meet the situation. Who needs those little five-hour energy drink bottles or Red Bull? We are all already carrying around our own natural, built-in energy pack. The spontaneity of animal fight-or-flight response works in the forests, under the sea, and on the plains of Africa. It also plays a major role for the two-legged animals lurking on Main Street.

Animals need to cope with the stresses of their environment—humans need solutions to their problems.

Well, there is a fight-or-flight mechanism in human beings too. Because humans are both animal and spirit, this response does something to humans that it does not do to animals. Pressure affects not only the human body but also the human spirit—the life force that animals do not possess. In humans this fight-flight response has evolved into a stress regulation system—a snap coping mechanism for processing whatever resentment has penetrated the human psyche. It regulates it. It does not prevent it. Coping with problems is not the same as answering them. "Coping" only leads to developing compensations that later turn out to be obsessions. The more animal we become, the more obsessions we cultivate. The more spiritual we become, the more of those obsessions fall away.

Once the lion has captured its prey, the rest of the zebra herd resumes grazing—right in full view and reach of the lion, unfettered by the loss of one of their own to the beast. They are not upset. They do not grieve.

Similarly, the grizzly bear will never feel remorse for having killed the hunter. Even the most sinister psychotic killer rotting away in death row may never come to regret his murderous acts, for he has transcended his humanness by identifying fully with the ego-self within. Biologically he appears to be a human being, but he is not. He has turned into something inhuman.

Unlike animals, we humans are partly spirit, bestowed with conscience, that internal guidance system that knows right from wrong without being told what is right or wrong. We enjoy a balance of modalities not shared with animals. It is a balance we can ill afford to ignore and still hope to survive as spiritual human beings. Among us, such ignorance becomes dangerous. We ignore spiritual/animal equilibrium and allow animal instinct to outweigh the spiritually intuitive side of our humanness. It betrays life, giving away human spirit in favor of animal death. Sensing our own demise, we scramble for even more "pleasures" and escapes.

The more instinctual we become, the less inspirational we are. As we trade our spiritual life for an animal life, we embrace sensuality, moving *away* from God-consciousness in favor of ego-*self*-consciousness. The impenitent murderer's thoughts and behavior have been overtaken entirely by that dark nature. He has *gone rogue.*

All of this is meant to show you that what is quite natural for animals is very unnatural for human beings. For this reason, it is never good to embrace our animal instincts. There are many pseudo-spiritual philosophies that do. However, to do so justifies your transference of allegiance *away* from God-consciousness and toward animal unconsciousness, where you can exist as an agnostic organism. We humans, although physically constructed of bone and flesh, are not meant to behave *entirely* like those conscienceless animals.

We can actually wish to switch back and forth between animal and spiritual modalities without regret. This idea is the appeal behind the *Twilight* series romanticizing sexual vampires, as well as H. G. Well's story of Jekyll and Hyde; even werewolf stories have a strange, prurient appeal to something inside us. The ego conjures the fantasy, allowing fans to fantasize about a vicariously animalistic existence— giving in to sensual instincts and getting away with it. Something deep down inside empathizes with the werewolf and grieves his demise. In real life, we never seem to be able to manage traversing two worlds— for us it is either one or the other. That is because resentment puts us to sleep, causing us to turn away from our natural ability to discern without emotion.

Once that happens, we judge, giving up the conscious ability to see the difference between the two states. When we are *not conscious,* it is not possible for us to see that we are *un*conscious. (Please feel free to read that again.) Connecting with our animal side, we lose the spiritual vision meant to serve as our guiding eye. Meditation breaks us out of the emotional spell. As we awaken, we recover God-vision immediately. Life changes in that very instant.

It takes a capacity for honesty to see this in ourselves, and for the alcoholic who has cut his teeth on dishonesty, attaining such truthfulness can seem an insurmountable task. Simple but not easy, this force takes many recognizable forms, and any alcoholic, if he is honest, can identify with them.

Have you ever been pissed off? *That's resentment.* Have you ever huffed in frustration at a missed traffic signal? *Bingo.* Have you ever snapped at someone in conversation or attacked another bitterly in an argument, hoping to hurt his or her feelings or reputation—only later to regret the acerbic outburst? That was the force of resentment getting inside and overpowering you. Even your regret was more likely to have been resentment for your own impatience than it was true repentance. Every time you have ever been upset, annoyed, irritated, or angry, or felt the pangs of outrage, indignation, or frustration—any of these emotions were a sure sign that the electric-like force of resentment had overwhelmed you in that moment.

Anger, whether it comes as a justifiable, petty annoyance, as a wave of irrational rage, or anything in between, is the pervading force of your entire life. It has unseated you from the foundation of your humanity. Even after pursuing a recovery-oriented lifestyle based on spiritual tenets, you have sometimes found yourself basking in ensuing self-righteousness. Through self-searching and personal inventories, you may find yourself startled to realize how destructive your emotions have been. They became harmful to you and to those around you and so have found this inclination toward anger to be objectionable.

As you willfully tried to fix yourself, you repressed your negative emotions, pushing both the memories of resentment-causing events and the bitterness they evoked as deep as you could into your subconscious mind. By doing so, you have maintained a good self-image—by your own view. The stores of emotions and memories—the accumulated debris of the past—may be enumerated in fourth-step inventories. Or you may have found other emotional outlets; you might have spilled your guts out. "A problem shared is a problem halved," as the expression goes. This is the kind of relief gotten through counseling or a chat with a good friend over a cup of coffee or even alone, penning a memoir. Even "sharing" in support groups or at AA meetings can serve this purpose.

We sometimes hear the phrase "ratted myself out" from those looking for relief by publicly admitting to have harbored negativity. "Talking cure" exercises such as these have value, as they release some of the repressed emotional energy stored inside, but the fact remains that, in the absence of true clear vision, the great bulk of your negative emotions, all those secret, bitter flashes of irritation, never make it to the floor of consciousness. They are too embarrassing—even to you.

So you hide them. You might even unwittingly leave them out of a fourth-step inventory. This repression and suppression only covers up the effects without addressing and resolving the causes. The source of troubles remains.

This is exactly why you feel conflict today—from a lifetime of repressing every little flicker and flash of negative emotion we call resentment. Leaving its vitriol intact while ignoring the resentments eventually resulted in mounting guilt, compelling you into exhibits of impatient behaviors that caused harm to others while wreaking havoc in your own life. Obviously, *repression* is not an effective solution. It is typical, but it certainly is not desirable.

Now this unmanageability of life while living under such pressure further demoralized you.

Acknowledging your errors and making amends *seemed* to make life more bearable, for a while. For one thing, it allowed you to repair the damages of the past and to restart living from a clean slate. The relief was a gift. It was good for your conscience. It is a highly recommended practice, especially when starting out on the spiritual journey. Then the same mistakes of the past were repeated.

As you continued to indulge ego food, disenchantment with your new life emerged, and you began to chase the pleasurable feelings that "soul-searching" efforts had earlier afforded you. It was much like hitting your head on the wall in order to feel the relief of stopping. Abusing *amends* ought to be classified along with all other human abusiveness; it seems to do more damage operating under a veil of good intentions.

Man is not meant to spend his life continually repeating his old mistakes, with his blundering missteps continually harming others, and then apologizing and repairing the damages over and over all throughout his life. He is *supposed* to experience *some* spiritual growth over the course of his lifetime as this kind of aberrant behavior lessens. Slowly and steadily he grows closer to, and in the direction of, human perfection. He moves closer to his God.

On the other hand, if you progress in your defects, you move *away* from that perfection, necessitating the making of more and more amends in noble response to the harms you have caused. Making sport of fixing errors in this way becomes a crutch, allowing more and more errors followed still by more *fixing*.

The dirty little secret of every amends-addicted Twelve-Stepper is the selfish motivation to *feel* better for having made the repairs. It's like the firefighter who starts the fire so he can become the hero and extinguish it.

Firefighters who start fires have long been part of an American obsession with true crime, and psychologists have studied the phenomenon for years in attempt to profile potential firefighter arsonists.[22] As you can imagine, it is a complicated issue. The motivation of a firefighter arsonist runs the gamut from revenge to profit, but one very common element is that, in many cases, the firefighter arsonist yearns to become the hero. He is addicted to homage. He craves honor and goes to any lengths to get it. It gets him high, in compensatory response to internal pain.

Similarly we can become addicted to making amends, bowing and scraping before others, getting *high* off their forgiveness.

If we were truly interested in bringing good to the world, we would find a way to cease doing harm to others in the first place. Still under the lash of obsessive behaviors, this is not possible until we are fully aligned with God's vision and can see clearly the true and the false and act out His will from that divinely inspired perspective.

Until then, the pressure created by your secret, recidivist life mounts. It reaches bedeviling degrees and with each occurrence reinforces internal uneasiness. The most severe of these pressures can get so bad the increasing anxiety can move men and woman to violence against each other, their children, and eventually against themselves. This is why alcoholically charged families are so frequently plagued by physical violence. There is always an out-of-control, impatient member to blame. The realization of this can compel a sufferer to take his own life rather than continue to harm innocent loved ones.

Effective meditation will lift the shroud of darkness caused by your own inattentiveness. It will unveil within you the state of personal

---

[22]U.S. Fire Administration/Technical Report Series Special Report: Firefighter Arson USFA-TR-141/January 2003 http://www.usfa.fema.gov/downloads/pdf/publications/tr-141.pdf

awareness, a private affair between you and God that *is* the much-coveted increasing of *conscious contact* with God. The exercise I teach and distribute freely from my website will be your "gimmick" to show you *how* to stay awake during the movie and allow you to see that in the Stream of Life, you are *not* James Bond, and that the girl in the bikini is just another actor. You are only a spectator to the production, meant to get in and out of the theater of life and retain your human dignity as a person. If you do, you do so as one who is awake, happy, whole, and useful. That awareness and objectivity will illuminate the truth about the principalities and powers that override all effects. It narrows them down to the *one big cause.* It is resentment—or more precisely, your lack of protection *from* it.

If you are an alcoholic, then by now you might be feeling a bit disturbed by some of what is being presented in this book. That is because much of the information presented here applies directly to you. It is making sense to you in light of your own experience. That is perfectly fine.

Well, here we are nearing the end of another chapter, and you are still with me. Although the truth about your condition can be painful to hear, you may also feel a sense of relief. If you are a real alcoholic, these ideas about your condition are likely to be making more sense to you than anything else you may have been told before. Substance abuse counselors, clerics, spiritual guides, even those nice folks in the alcoholic support group have not come this close to describing your situation. I know that.

Although some of these may have provided you with a few tricks of the recovery trade to obtain some much-needed respite from your problems, the reprieve had not lasted. That is because their understanding as passed onto them has not been this complete. They just don't talk this way. From now on, at some level there will be a much deeper sense of relief within. Perhaps by now you are beginning to understand what I mean by the term "Mistaken Identity".

For those of you involved in a Twelve Step fellowship, and have been moved to follow the spiritual side of that fellowship then you will be happy to discover nothing here which is at disparity with the Judeo-Christian principles contained in "Alcoholics Anonymous". It is unlikely that you have ever heard alcoholism presented in quite this fashion. It can be disturbing to learn that (1) something has invaded the sanctity of your God-based humanity, (2) this is true in all alcoholics, and that (3) you are yourself responsible for unwittingly allowing this inhuman occupation to happen.

You have lost your true self and traded your birthright God-awareness for a corrupted self-awareness. That Self speaks to you as if it is you. This is the identity; the imposter you mistakenly *thought* was you. (*Many alcoholics hear voices inside their heads. This is exactly why.*) Yet it has been you who has encouraged this violation vis-à-vis identification with your lower Self. *It's* thoughts seemed to be *your* thoughts and then those thoughts became *your* actions. You have been out of control, with something else thinking and controlling your life and will.

This is why you must now turn those both over to God. Begin to realize that by being free from your connection to this impostor "Self" you can also finally be free of your slavery to the people, places and things; even alcohol—that your dependency upon these has been a form of human slavery. You can do so without struggle, without hardly any effort. You can find true peace with the world and with your Creator by doing one extremely simple thing. Separate from this *thing* inside. The meditation will be the device to help you do that. Nothing more than that is required.

The difference between this book and other spiritual works is that this does not merely talk about it. If you take my recommendation, you are going to have a solution to the problem. I direct you to the meditation exercise which is free.[23]

But before you do that—we are not done yet. The situation gets even more heated as we proceed. Let the sticker shock of the first of truths about your condition fade into the background a bit now as you stick with me a little longer, please. You will not regret it if you do.

---

[23]Please visit the "How To Get There," page in the back of this book for fast access to the meditation exercise. It is available for streaming or download. It is free and always will be.

This is not a book about astrophysics, but you will notice that I have been referring to resentment as if it were some universal cosmic *force of energy*. This is not metaphoric. I mean it in every sense of the term. I am not saying we should go back and change all the high-school physics textbooks to accommodate this single idea. But at least we can acknowledge that our emotions, particularly the forces of *love* and *hate*—expressed as *patience* and *resentment*—do fit somewhere into the scheme of man's ever-changing fundamental understanding of the universe.

Science pretty much agrees that the function of gravity and other nuclear forces is to hold time, light, and matter together, forming an entire universe, and that all of these energies are inevitable and ubiquitous and are pushing with purpose through space. What science is supposed to do it does well enough, and it is adaptive, if nothing else. Science really does not know, and may never fully know, what exactly is happening at atomic and subatomic levels and what is holding everything, the seen *and* the unseen, into a presence so that it exists. What science has a hard time doing is acknowledging spiritual principles and allowing for them as influences in the universe. Just as sure as there are light, gamma rays, and time flowing through and around us—so do emotional energies.

Scientific discovery will forever fail to approach a full understanding of existence because of this omission. Always erring on the side of agnosticism, scientists can only avoid acknowledging the roles played by energies relating to much higher powers than those governing mere galaxies of stars or the formations of solar systems. Perhaps it is not their job to consider the immense powers and vital roles that love and hate play in the universe. We need not join them in their spiritual bigotry.

All energetic stresses that exist, forces like gravity and light, exist for intelligently directed purposes; including the forces of love and hate. Resentment *is* hate and like many other cosmic forces it is every bit as predictable as the other energies moving through the universe. Yes, spirituality and materialism do meet—somewhere. Rather than being two worlds colliding, they form a seamless union we experience as *now*.

Sometimes fiction depicts real life with alarming clarity and realism. I love Hollywood and TV examples, so let me give you one to show you what I mean. In the famous 1967 *Star Trek* episode "Wolf in the Fold," Kirk and crew try to solve a rash of murders, but they are unable to find the killer. Kirk and McCoy decide to take Scotty, who is recovering from a head wound accidentally caused by a female crew member, to a nightclub on the recreational planet Argelius II, a popular shore-leave destination for Federation starship crews. They hit the bars, and, despite suffering from a mild concussion, Scotty gets hooked up with a hot nightclub dancer. They take off, paired for some, shall we say, consensual "companionship." (It is network TV in the '60s, after all.)

The next thing we know, the dancer is dead, and Scotty stands holding the bloody knife. Obviously, he is the murderer.

He has of course no memory of his actions whatsoever. Some strange mental blank spot has overridden any recall of what he has done. Doctor McCoy's quick Freudian analysis theorizes that Scotty has been harboring suppressed resentment for the woman who accidentally injured his head back on the *Enterprise* and suggests that Scotty has projected that hatred onto all women. Now his bitterness has manifested in murder. It is very realistic.

Scotty tells of feeling a presence of a cold, evil creature.

That creature is Redjac, an incorporeal, formless electromagnetic impulse with an insatiable hunger and hatred of women that feeds on the emotions of others. Even fear itself serves as its food. It has no personality of its own except that it assumes the identity of those it inhabits—of those from whom it derives life and form: in this case, poor Scotty, Starfleet's intergalactic Scottish lush. It exploits his lust for hot space chicks. It turns out that this ethereal spirit entity has been doing this stuff all throughout the galaxies, leaving behind a bloody wake of hatred and murder. As Spock and Kirk continue their investigation, it is finally revealed that the name *Redjac* is a homophone for none other than *Red Jack*, the nickname used in the 1800s for the infamous serial killer none other than Jack the Ripper.

But watch this: Jack the Ripper is not just some elusive figure with a broken brain that slashes the throats and guts the bellies of hookers in the Whitechapel slums of nineteenth-century London. Disguised in the human personage of Ripper is just *one* of its many personifications, as it makes one of many stops along the way, blazing a trail of hatred and fear across the universe.

Just like the murderous Redjac force in the episode, resentment energy is sourced through an intelligence that seeks entry into our psyches. Once inside it alters our own natures and therefore our behaviors. We will take on a mistaken identity believing that the things we do are of our own design as we identify with this invading alien within, more and more – acting less and less our true selves.

We are no longer acting on behalf of our original "Self" but are bound to this false alien Self we *think* is us and isn't. We become oblivious to why we do the things we do, acting out the will of something that is *not* us. When we do this – we become sick; spiritually, mentally, and then physically until we finally hand our physical lives over to evil. That is the day we die—some of us sooner than necessary.

Before we can ever hope to address this problem, we must first distinguish the causes from the effects or else be doomed to spend our lives trying to fix effects—those defects of character over which we have no control and which are mere symptoms. The question must be asked, "Which came first? Was it spiritual illness or was it resentment?" The answer is resentment!

If you never see this, then you will never get well. So I will try my darnedest to convince you that this is the case.

"Whenever, therefore, people are deceived and form opinions wide of the truth, it is clear that the error has slid into their minds through the medium of certain resemblances to that truth." – Socrates

5 DOUBLE CROSSED

Enter The Traitor

*B*etty looked directly at him, into his eyes, into his head and without blinking, without budging her stare, she ordered, "Two large ones, Willie."

She had set the deal and knew it. "See?" a voice told her. It was Betty's own. "Yes, I do," she thought. "Wow."

"That's twenty-four cents for the egg creams, plus two cents for the jelly ring, two for the marshmallow twist, and two for the pretzel rod . . . thirty cents total." Willie looked down at the quarter on the counter. "I'll tell you what"—he leaned over and glanced down the length of the store in both directions—"make it an even twenty-five,"

He snapped up the coin and finger-pitched it into a cigar box on the shelf behind. It jangled into a bed of silver change just as the door-top bell jingled once again. This time Marshall Smith walked in.

"Howdy, Marshall. Will it be the usual?"

"Yup."

"The next thing you know he'll call me 'pardner'" Marshall thought. "What an asshole."

The two looked on as Willie froze. Then he turned and scurried down to the cigarette rack behind the counter where Marshall stood.

"Hey... what are we...chopped liver?" Gary did not like the slight.

"Shhhhh." Betty said. She noticed Marshall's hair. It was greasy blond. It reminded her of someone. She fixed her gape on him.

"Make it two."

"Two packs of Marlboro. Gotcha."

Willie stuck one hand under the counter and pulled out two packs of cigarettes and two books of matches and smacked them together on top. He took a dollar from Marshall and gave him his change. All very official-like. Willie was wary of Marshall. There was something that lay behind Marshall's eyes that was unsettling.

Only thirteen years old and the boy already wore a kind of stare on his face. It was a particular look, the same one the older kids brought with them to Westchester Square when they got back from Vietnam—at least the ones who came back alive. He had the look that he knew something you didn't know. Marshall had seen something. Willie couldn't be sure what it was, but knew it was something bad.

"Marlboro? Marshall smokes!" Gary said.

Betty again looked admiringly over at the tall, slim, light-haired boy buying cigarettes just in time to see him walk out the door. Her eyes followed him through the store display window, and in a second he had passed completely out of sight.

"Didn't stunt his growth any," she thought.

If the spiritual illness that infects the soul of every alcoholic spawns out of resentment, then how could this succession of disease have started in the first place? Surely, you were not born this way, were you?

The answer to this question is key in understanding the solution to an infinitely grave human dilemma. This is fair to ask, for if we could just get to that crux, then perhaps we could stop it for future generations, for our children, your children.

Remember that resentment is an emotional state. It is a negatively charged power that is just as real and ubiquitous a force in the universe as is gravity or light. It is here and it isn't going anywhere.

No one comes sliding out of the womb full of anger—physically stimulated, certainly—but not bitter and vitriolic. You no more came into the world preloaded with resentment than you did afflicted with the drinking obsession. We may surmise that a newborn baby is quite shocked and surprised by his rather abrupt change of scenery, but full of anger? It is not possible.

There is no such thing as being born an alcoholic, a drug addict, a sex addict, a gambler or even a foodaholic. You enter this world with a spiritually flawed predilection toward playing God. Human-spirit and animal-body unite forming a human being who inherits not only his physical form and spiritual substance, but a *lower* self. This *inferior nature* expresses in self-centered traits that all of us must rise above in order to do God's *will*, or else the will of another. Call it Self. Call it Ego. Call it Dark Side or even Lower Nature[24] if you wish, just as long as you acknowledge It's existence. Then at least awareness can empower you to challenge It's call.

This *other will* comes through your Lower Nature with which every human being since the first man, the exception being just One, was born.

As much as conjecture and junk science may suggest to the contrary, there is no alcoholic "gene." There is no anger "gene." You cannot "catch" alcoholism. But you can become contaminated by negative energy transferred from person to person and therefore from generation to generation. This is the alien force that we have been talking about in this book: Resentment.

Hate is contagious and although not born with it inside you, it soon entered after birth; through injection administered by the very people who were *supposed* to love you and didn't. (They didn't know how.) That's right; you did not do it to yourself. It was done to you after you were born, by someone.

This is not a blame game. This is not to exonerate you for your part. You had one. A starring role, in fact. This is a deadly serious look at how spiritual disease is passed on through families; from parent to child, from generation to generation. This idea requires some careful consideration and a look at what really happened to you, the alcoholic. We need to look further into your need to play God. This is not easy to face.

If you have been involved in a recovery program or fellowship, then you have probably been told the importance of honesty when perceiving this dark side to your makeup. Many alcoholics in recovery have been taught to consider this *lower nature*. It is good to awaken to this reality, to concede to the flaws within. Even so, your honesty will

---

[24] I refer to It using all of these terms throughout this book and when speaking with alcoholics.

need to go a bit further than you may have been willing to go in the past; despite an honest approach such as you may have taken through a written inventory.[25]

During this kind of fact finding mission, there are revelations that occur, "Aha" moments, the result of a thorough and searching fourth step inventory, deeply personal disclosures prompted by what *has* been written and analyzed but contain spiritual code beyond what appears in paper and ink.

The fourth step as it turns out is really just a collection of revealing talking points leading to even deeper understanding as we begin to see for the first time, very objectionable traits about ourselves. Being as thorough and searching as we can, a fourth Step inventory still barely scratches the psychic surface of our past behaviors. Each person's past contains individualized "tip-offs" as to the nature of Self which reveals a truth that can be hard to face; that somewhere lurking inside resides something unwholesome.

Many of us are conditioned to think of this dark *nature* as a part of ourselves—as just another aspect of our complex human personality. The truth is that this nature is not *us* at all. It is a parasitical foreigner—an intrusive intelligence. It is an alien with which we incorrectly identify. We believe It to be us. As we carry on, experiencing the Stream of Life, we become increasingly desensitized to its presence, until we are not able to distinguish where *we* begin and *it* ends. *Insane asylums and prisons are full of highly perceptive people who have seen this but have not been able to break free of it.*

It is as though we are asleep. As we go about our business in this stupor, the entity continues to nourish itself on the resentments that we have unwittingly fed it by allowing them to crop up inside us. This is where the alcoholics full culpability lies.

In order to conjure an inflated self-image of *it*self, now *you*rself, it must engorge on the negative energy of resentment—the universal force mentioned previously. As each new temptation in the Stream of Life comes along, stresses often succeed in overwhelming us with anger, manifesting in a prideful condition.

---

[25] A Step-Four, written inventory of resentments, fears, and harms. See "Alcoholics Anonymous", 4th edition, Alcoholics Anonymous World Services, 64:2

Yes, *pride* has been your downfall. It has caused you to manufacture and shape an unearned, undeserved image of yourself that you have cherished and protected. The world calls it "self-esteem." Being convinced that this unmerited and elevated "Self" esteem is a good and necessary part of your personality, society has encouraged you to cultivate it. It cajoled you into developing a lifestyle that supports and maintains your own creation of the *you* that you want others to see. It is easy to do. It is easy to play Creator in this manner.

Then you were able to fit right in with the rest of the world, which similarly pursues activities, people, and situations that help build false and exaggerated personal icons of *Self.* The world populates with legions of people who have no real idea of who they are or what they have become. They are not who they think they are and do not even know it.

This charade is the divisive double-cross. The false self has played the double agent to a true, spiritual person that is you. Masquerading as you, the ego identity was a traitor to your true self, that child of God. It betrayed you, your neutrality and your wellness. It robbed you of original, natural and discerning vision so that It could live and use you as host to its pathetic parasitical existence.

If this sounds like some scene out of a science fiction movie, I assure you, it is not. This is real. A disturbing picture to paint indeed; yet, if you are an alcoholic with a capacity for some honesty then you will be able to see some of yourself in this nightmarish picture.

This brings us back to the original question posed at the beginning of this chapter, "How did this come to be?" There must have been a "first" to set the ball rolling. The answer lies in trauma. It was your first upset; the first time you ever became resentful. Was it the first smack on the bottom by the delivering physician? Did the doctor grab you by the ankles, dangle you in mid air like a Peking duck and whack your *tuchas* and make you cry? That might do the trick, I suppose, but today a newborn infant receives a gentle clearing of the airway through suctioning, not a spanking.

Was it the first time Mommy raised her voice? Was it the first reprimand? For each person there will be an individual answer to this question. But there are some first times for everyone. Whenever it was, the parent to whom you were closest is the person who likely delivered it. This first contact is our initial exposure to the enemy; the betrayer; the Thing that wants, more than anything else, to be God. In Its betrayal *of* God, it also betrays us through lie and deceit. It happened to you when you were very young.

Contrary to what some psychologists teach, it is not important to identify the specific event. While it can be helpful, certainly interesting, too much focus on events of the past can end up an endless exercise in speculation and error at best; at worst, one more distracting activity to dull your present awareness through intellectual involvement. What is more important is recognizing that there is a *not you*. It rose to the occasion to hate, established It's hold on you and It has been doing this ever since. You will never as long as you live be free of this lower nature, but there are things you can do to stop feeding it – get free from its anger food. It is possible to break the anger addiction. The chief mission of this book is to show this so that the importance of becoming free from your anger will become clear; then to show you exactly how this is done.[26]

For all of your life, each time you have become entangled in irritation, restlessness, annoyance and frustration you may have also noticed a strange satisfaction while some dark *thing* greedily gobbled resentment. As it came to life, you became uncomfortable. A growing sense of impending doom arose, and this frightened you. That fear is the dread for what you are becoming. Rather than face your fate, you futilely compensated for your discontentment, cultivating a lifestyle that supports the self-image that your ego has manufactured. We have all lived in a lying world that tells us lies. In order to maintain Its existence, ego self must feed and enlarge with resentment to fuel and nurture its growth. It begins to rule. That kind of life needs to end, if you are to live.

At first, It exerts dominion individually, only over *us*, but It has bigger plans. It is only in order to eventually rule the world. We change

---

[26]Please visit the "How To Get There," page in the back of this book for fast access to the meditation exercise. It is available for streaming or download. It is free and always will be.

91

for the worse as we fall in line with the diabolic scheme. Attitudes and behaviors are altered while we transform into hapless mutants. Thus, the development of ambition begins. We soon become bossy and demanding to those around us. We become mini-potentates in our own mind.

This ghastly scenario doesn't need be. There is another way. We can choose not to participate. By denying Self the judgment-food it needs to overinflate its *self-worth*, the ego cannot help but shrink to its proper size. This is one of the most vital precepts of the spiritual life—the kind that is laid out in the blueprint for daily living proposed by the co-founders of *Alcoholics Anonymous*.

These recovered, spiritually awakened men and women suggest that the alcoholic needs to experience a "deflation of ego"—a deep leveling of pride in order to awaken and be placed in a position of neutrality that has become known as being a "recovered alcoholic." This is a safe place from where the alcoholic should not sit in admiration of his accomplishment, but rather it is a starting platform from where he first begins his spiritual growth toward perfection.

NOTE: As the author of this book and later as the teacher of meditation, I am not the one to deflate your ego. I am not the one to level your pride. God forbid anyone ought to be elevated to that position. There is something else that will do this. It is called divine understanding, and this comes from a place that is well beyond the abilities of any human effort. It comes from God.

But beware. While God is perfectly capable of doing all the deflating of ego necessary, there are plenty of people who are only too happy to take on His job. There are husbands, wives, ministers, counselors, Life Coaches and yes, even cranky, controlling recovery sponsors, all eager to become surrogate Gods, dispensing direction and wresting control from others.

In order to satisfy their own inner, self-centered lust for power and control, they will exploit the need for deflation of others, taking advantage of the spiritually ailing, creating a host of minion-clients and staunch followers. The devout are happy to put their tyrant on the pedestal, where he can serve them from his perch of undeserved, false authority. The unwary become god-makers, creating phony authorities while humiliating and debasing themselves in the process. Sometimes people mistake humiliation for humility. They are not the same.

The inability to distinguish true from false is one of the most infamously baffling characteristics of the alcoholic. Seriously now, is there any other creature besides the functioning alcoholic, more prone to futilely clinging to the hope that his own bullshale is true? There may be—but if there is, I assure you, either he is a potential alcoholic or otherwise heavily involved in some kind of abuse. Overeating, sexual extravagances or abuse of other substances are just as likely candidates as is drinking.

Most of us will simply set out to "fix" ourselves. Ego loves to take credit for having taken action. Hypnotic stresses press us through emotional involvement and egocentric prodding, often masquerading as self-actuating motives. Actually, such pressures are outward motivations that originate from somewhere outside us and somehow have gotten inside. These are not part of true self, and they gain access to us through ego. Under this regime we have no real motive of our own.

Convinced that the "not-you" *is* you, you cling to the false belief that your motivation originates from within. You think that your good ideas and actions are motivated by some benevolent self that dwells within, when the actual source has been from with-*out*. Sometimes these motivations seem fortuitous and profitable.

There is no good luck here, only chance and subjection to kismet. You are no longer behaving as a child of God, but you are a victim: a humanoid organism with no more spiritual existence than a mosquito forever in danger of smacking right into the windshield of the next speeding car on the highway. You *can* sense the danger in the stream of traffic.

Right before the *splat* on the glass, there is an odd sense of impending doom that you cannot quite place; and so you wake up each morning, reverently get on your knees, and give the Wheel of Fortune yet another spin, hoping God does *your* will, which of course just happens to include *your* serenity and acceptance—for yourself.

After all, how can you carry a beneficial message, unless you are the perfect picture you paint of serenity and well-being, free from fear and troubles, right?

There is hope.

Now, if you meditate ardently, using the exercise I propose, not only will you find yourself the observer of your thoughts, you will also begin to see that you are not the originator of thoughts. Not even the *happy* ones. Your new state of awareness will also show you the futility of living attached to your thinking. To see others continue to go about their affairs as zombies, living as you once did, can be disconcerting. You will see that your ego is an imposter—that it has been tricking you for a long time, just as it has fooled us all. This is a horrible truth to learn.

This is why I suggested early on practicing the meditation exercise on my website before reading this book. If you have already done that, then welcome to the land of the living. You are soon coming to be able to forgive those still lost.[27]

When I show alcoholics how to meditate, the first thing we do is get into a discussion about this human condition that is characterized by the term *alcoholic*. Once having been shown the mental and physical conditions—how they have combined to create the alcoholic syndrome—and having experienced the hopelessness these symptoms yield, the alcoholic cries to his Creator for the way out, a solution neither he nor any human being can offer. Until then, there is really not much that can be done. Without true understanding of our hopelessness, seeing that *of ourselves we can do nothing*, ego still thrives. We, as hosts in this parasitical bond, remain convinced of our (really It's) false power—that of ourselves, *we can do anything. It* will fix us! *Sure it will.*

Hope arrives upon seeing that the root of our problems has been our own self-centeredness—our dedication to *Self*—helping *Self* find

---

[27]Please visit the "How To Get There," page in the back of this book for fast access to the meditation exercise. It is available for streaming or download. It is free and always will be.

nourishment through resentment. Through completing a thorough and searching inventory of a lifelong accumulation of resentful repression, you can clearly see that it has been your resentment of others—expressed through envy, jealousy, annoyance and irritation, that has been the single largest cause of your tormented, spiritually suffering mind and malfunctioning body. It has been the pain of the separation you have experienced that created the need for alcohol to obtain relief. Drinking became the solution, not the problem. A Godless existence made you into the pained human wretch we know to be *the alcoholic.* There is no other reason. None. *All* alcoholics become ill exactly this way. There has never been a single exception—not since the first grape turned bad, and the caveman farmer drank its juice, rolled his eyes up into his head, and said, "Ahhhh."

What good does it do to see this?

Once the alcoholic sees why it is he became one, that alcoholism has been the least of his issues, only a symptom of his real problem, he can yield to the gravity of his situation, gently compelled toward accepting a new lifestyle. What moves him is a goodly pressure.

He can allow a new attitude in his thinking to prevail. It is an outlook that comes upon him, not only bringing him to a full recovery but also allowing for the effortless maintenance of an anger-free, spiritual condition sufficient to stave off virtually any assault on his spiritual psyche that comes along. It is his protection.

The attacks *will* come.

There can be no life or growth unless they do. All those wishing to get well must arrive at a willingness to endure so that they can begin to develop increasing, personal resilience to negative, emotion-laden ego-food threatening to crop up before it overwhelms. The meditation exercise on my website will show you exactly how that is done.

But beware. There are appealing meditation techniques that promote pleasant and highly desirable results and sensations like *floating*—"out of body" experiences, feelings of empowerment, relaxation, and other sensual effects that easily addict the *results-oriented* ego to such gratifying experiences. Even the seemingly innocuous act of trying to breathe in a certain way or to affect our heart rate injects just enough ambition to ensure that we go deeper into sleep instead of becoming more aware. These can also be very hypnotic as rhythmic fixations such as music, sound effects; even the constant sound of one's own breath will tend to suspend awareness rather than increase it. Through this kind of subtle, sensory seduction, we are easily subjected to suggestions.

Once planted into our subconscious, these can actually cause us to begin living *inside* of a waking dream. The suggestion is planted— and we can actually *dream* that we are becoming aware. This is not genuine awareness. It becomes an addictive meditative association. Now our addiction becomes the energy that motivates us to into re-experiencing those ego-inflating sensations.

To be motivated in this manner—to be encouraged by a self-centered need to "feel spiritual" or to acquire some imagined spiritual credentials that can be lauded over others—means a lack of sincerity. It *feels* like a search for truth, when it neatly avoids it. Rather than sharpening awareness and honing an honestly acquired *conscious contact with* God, it results in the exact opposite. It dulls consciousness.

A sleepwalker dreams that he has awoken. Unaware that he is really sleeping, he dreams that he rises up from bed and proceeds with what he believes to be his daytime affairs. His mind runs a dream-tape that he is awake.

Likewise, believing we are awake does not necessarily means that we are also aware. It is possible for the ego to create an illusion that we are awake when we are not aware. *Awake* and *aware* are not the same things.

As alcoholics, when we see the length and breadth of the dilemma—its enormously universal ramifications, not only on our own lives but also on the entire human race—and we can see just how important it is to finally want to do something about it. With no real will of our own, we may be powerless to *fix* the world, but at least we can yearn to receive inspired reasoning and open a personal commitment toward contributing toward God's plan.

Intuitive direction can outweigh our own ambitiously guided self-will in favor of a God-inspired will, a Power that will light and love the world instead of contributing to darkening and destroying it. It becomes apparent to the alcoholic that his condition is not so much about his own well-being and enriching his life as it is about the well-being of his fellows. It is about the struggle for human existence.

The recovered, spiritually awakened alcoholic finally sees that his place in God's world and how he lives has an impact on the future of his children and his loved ones—not only now but also for generations to come. He understands that maybe he has real purpose in this world after all, and that just maybe God has some really big plans for him. Life is important and has much more intrinsic value than the worldly pleasures it provides us. He begins to *get* that his life is a mission.

The next chapter is brief, but it will get to the essence of why alcoholism even exists and even more succinctly uncover how is it that you became one. I want you to say, "HOLY MACKEREL! So that's how it happened!" So, hold on to your hat. The ride gets even bumpier.

"Reinforced by what grace I could secure in prayer, I found I had to exert every ounce of will and action to cut off these faulty emotional dependencies upon people, upon AA, indeed upon any set of circumstances whatsoever." - *Bill Wilson*

6 SPIRITUAL AMALGAMATION

The Ancient Error of Judgment

If you squeeze a little lemon juice into a saucer of milk and let it stand, within minutes you will no longer recognize the saucer's contents. It isn't milk anymore. It will have turned into a thick gooey glob of something that is more akin to a runny cottage cheese than to whole milk. A transformation will have taken place—a conversion that Food Network star Alton Brown could better explain than I could. The remaining viscous liquid is something that bakers call buttermilk. We make this ersatz buttermilk all the time at our house for use in biscuits and muffins—even for the infrequent pancake party (an indulgence usually reserved for kiddie-sleepovers). Making your own is a lot cheaper than buying the store-pack version, and there's no waste because we make only as much as we need.

The world is full of instances like this, when the blending of two ingredients, events, or ideas works to form brand-new substances— even new designs or plans. In metallurgy, alloys usually have different properties from those of their component elements. Combine tin with iron, for example, and we will have a new metal called steel. Copper and tin unite to cast bronze.

Did you know that the "silver" filling the dentist placed in your tooth is not as *silvery* as you may have believed? It is likely to be an amalgam material that is half mercury—*yes, that's right; poisonous mercury*—plus fifteen percent tin. Only the remaining third of the metallic mixture in a typical silver dental filing is created using genuine silver.

Like homemade buttermilk or bronze, alcoholism cannot exist without first combining two indispensable components, jointly forging the binary malady into existence.

This well-known phenomenon is masterfully delineated in the book "Alcoholics Anonymous". The volume reveals that alcoholism is not so much a *disease* as it is a *syndrome;* an amalgam, not of substances, but of *mental* and *physical* phenomena. Those phenomena are *obsession* and *craving.* Standing alone, either of these individual elements in the two-fold description would not complete the formation of the final composite—the one that the coauthors of the volume describe as *"real alcoholism."* Just as tin and iron mix to form steel, combining *obsession* with *craving* creates alcoholism. You simply cannot have alcoholism without both ingredients present.

Let's look at another kind of amalgam—one that is more within the spiritual realm. It is a unification of two common anomalies of human concern: *resentment* mixed with *discernment*—God's *patient will* exchanged with the *impatient will* of something sinister that *wishes* to become God. The ensuing fusion is called "judgment."

Let's look at *how* alcoholics *become* judgmental.

If you are alcoholic, then what follows is exactly what happened to you: The original, discerning ability you were born with became infected by an emotion, such as anger. This contamination translated into an emotional unhinging from truth. Your God-given vision—the ability to see clearly—clouded, and scales of prejudice formed over your eyes. Anytime in the past when you have become upset, the negative charge of resentment violated the sanctity of your innermost self. It combined with your vision to form this new substance. It never failed. Judgment is a *spiritual amalgam.* This new "product" is as ancient as recorded time.

Now, look what you have done. Having identified with the false, alien Self, you have abandoned your ability to discern God's will and have begun to think and act as an agent for the inferior *lower nature.* Now you are *self*-motivated instead of *God*-motivated. You no longer use your God-based *inner* vision but instead begin placing more and more reliance upon *outward* stimuli. A conversion from inspirational to instinctual—spiritual to animal—has taken place. The biased, extremely gullible human intellect adores its own power of reasoning and believes it has a handle on its animal drives. It believes it can indulge in lower impulses and somehow not get as burned as the rest of the world does—or as it has in the past. This is the very same mechanism that writes the inner script that says "this time it will be different." This happens with eating, in relationships, when drinking—

you name it! *(This mechanism is the number-one factor in all failed sexual relationships that begin without life-commitment.)* It happens all the time. Does it not?

Ego self would rather *manage* life on its own terms than hand the reigns over to a superior guidance; direction that would otherwise come by way of original *inward* inspiration. In this self-deluded state of reliance upon the imposter-self within, you began allowing the alien to play God *through* you. As you identified with it, your new amalgamated *self-identity* is one of *Judge*—making decisions and passing verdicts and sentences on those who are to be condemned and those who are to be saved. You are playing God. Whenever we are conjoined this way with the lower, dark invader, we feel as though *we are* God, just as the alien feels like it is God *through* us. We feel the same as *it* feels when we are so identified.

There was a time long ago, when you were still a child, when you had a certain potential for a very special spiritual existence. It was a time *before* your corruption—*before* anger entered—while your uninterrupted supply of Power still flowed. You enjoyed a birthright connectivity that equipped you with divine, fatherly inspiration and intuition. You were *truly* a child of God. That was the time you intuitively knew the difference between right and wrong, left from right, true from false—without anyone *telling* you. You needed no minster, rabbi, guru, or self-help apostle. You needed no Scriptures, theologies, or rote learning of any kind. The discipline needed for living, and getting along with others—be they similarly inclined or opposed to such *in*-dependence—*that is to say, your spiritually inspired guidance,* came directly from your Creator.

Then, all hell broke loose. You saw injustice and cruelty and you were violated by anger—and so you judged. You were born with a heavenly connection, but that relationship with God's will was severed. You were set adrift. Disconnected from your *spiritually informed* sense of direction, you were forced into making *self*-willful decisions based upon an inferior, self-absorbed vision. You traded your *uncommon* spiritual sense for a sensual, *common* sense. Anytime a man rejects God's vision, replacing it with his own, that man carries inferiority into his daily life and remains cut off from natural, heavenly guidance. That is exactly what you did. That is exactly what *all* alcoholics do.

Heirloom vegetables all come from the same garden and have been around forever. Likewise, all garden-variety alkies have the same genetic lineage going back to the beginning. There is nothing really special about them. Being an *heirloom alcoholic*, you are not about to betray your spiritual genetics. Now you also become arbiter of what *you* believe is right or wrong with the world. You pay special attention to *your* judgment of *"the dammed,"* often the very people to whom you suppose you hold great love, affection, and caring. Now instead of being aligned with God's will, you are allied with the will of the alien invader. Your will cannot be trusted, because it is not your own will. It is the will of an alien-self, a self also known as *ego.*

A simple example makes the point. Let's say you are walking along a roadway and the pavement abruptly ends. You stand at the precipice of a deep gorge cut into the earth where the road has been washed out by a recent flood. The deep split across the roadway has rendered it impassable. Assuming the best—*that you do not simply walk off the edge of the cliff to your death*—you can have one of two possible reactions.

The first is to respond with resentment for having been inconvenienced. *"Oh, great! Look at this! Now we shall be late. The road ends here, and all because of the flooding. Someone should have built this road better or repaired it by now. Or at least have warned me, so I could have planned better."* You might even pat yourself on the back for being so alert and being able to save yourself from harm. *"Thank goodness I saw this and stopped to save myself."* You might even plan revenge, plotting a scheme to locate the person responsible: *"I'll sue."* Now you make a decision to turn left or turn right in order to *indignantly* pass around the gorge to continue on your journey. Fuming, yes—but onward you trudge, sour puss and all. (Or grinning like an idiot to compensate.)

Eventually the memory of the aggravation and your negative emotional response will fade from consciousness into subconsciousness.

Your grin will fade—or your scowl, whichever—as you believe that you have successfully gotten over the incident. With the passage of time, it seems that you have managed to righteously rise above, and you think your outburst—or 'in'-burst—of rage is gone. That negative resentment energy that violated you has dissipated but the memory is there. It has been neatly tucked away, out of consciousness and into your psychic store of grudges and suppressed negative thoughts; the vitriolic potential for rancor remains ready and waiting for Self to draw upon, maybe years later. It will cause great discomfort and problems down the road. *Confronting these resentments in order to reduce obsessive behaviors such as alcohol abuse is the Twelve-Step basis for a fourth-step inventory process as well as the kinds of analytical therapies used in modern psychoanalysis.*

Now let's look at our cliff example from a different perspective. Do you remember that *uncharged,* neutral "discernment" I spoke of in Chapter Three? Suppose if, instead of responding with emotion, you had met the situation with no emotion at all, without the dulling entanglement of furious thought. In that case you might have seen the cliff, become aware of the danger and met that hazard without the addition of hate or the desire to confront *"whoever is responsible for this"* Then, with a clear head, absent from judgment, you could have automatically and serenely assessed what your next action should have been. Who knows? Perhaps without your vision being distorted by emotion, you would have noticed a bridge across the precipice—a solution to your problem you had not noticed before. Instead, you stormed off in a huff, your life clearly on a different path.

Or perhaps, being clear and perceptive, you might even have seen that your trip ought to be redirected altogether, or that you ought to continue the journey alongside the cliff's edge for a while, or maybe that you might need to climb down into the gorge in order to get to the other side. These are options that you always had at your disposal but could not see when your irritation was blocking your outlook.

Fear, or, more precisely, worries about things that have not happened yet can actually guarantee that they will happen. There is a perspective about depression that no psychologist is likely to tell you. Do you remember Job in the Bible? How his worst fears came upon him? There is an enormously profound spiritual lesson in his plight—as well as the solution he finally found.

Job was a worrier. It was only his good fortune and materially abundant station in life that made it easy for him to appear humble. But ol' Job harbored secret doubts, worries that Satan was able to bring out of him, and so suffering and misery came upon him. Besieged by the fears in his head, he became depressed and negative, wishing for death to relieve him. Job is a biblical example of someone suffering from major depression. He is also a good lesson on how to get out of it.

That mystical axiom, that we become what we hate, is as true for us today is it was then for Job when he succumbed to doubt. As with Job, our fears for the future always become the reality of our present when we lose faith. We end up hating God and ourselves for expectations unsatisfied. It is a selfish, self-centered existence from which so few of us ever escape. The only way to be liberated from a fear plagued existence is through awareness that permits living in the present moment without fear of what is to come.

Accepting that something is going to happen, and we don't know what it is, without being upset, is the life lesson of humility and faith. This is a spiritual reality about events yet to pass that many have seen but few have ever understood. They know man is not alone in the universe, that there are forces and principalities afoot. They know something is there—something very powerful. They feel that if they can harness that Power, they can make it their own. They try to harness the very will of God, wresting it from Him through positive thinking; ironically sometimes even in His name. Man cannot own the will of God nor manipulate it. Man can only allow it to flow into him or not.

Yes, denying God's will, replacing it with the spirit of another will, is possible. It is in denying Him that man steps out of the neutrality of his safe-alignment with God—or, as the co-authors of the *Big Book,* "Alcoholic Anonymous," called it, "The Sunlight of the Spirit." Christianity that is more formal often calls it "grace".

If you have been the type of person who is consumed with the future—in other words, a worrier—then perhaps you can now see how the possibilities for your entire future change for the worse in the exact moment that you allow the negative energy of resentment to pollute and spoil your *now* perception.

When I was a stockbroker on Wall Street, there was a period of time when a group of other brokers with whom I worked seemed to be doing so much better financially than I was doing. I mean, these guys routinely had thirty and forty-thousand-dollar monthly paychecks while I was struggling to make barely a few thousand. They drove brand-new Porsche 911 Turbo S's, lived in million-dollar homes, regularly had sex liaisons with hot, young girls; and seemed so much better at closing deals than I was. I lived in a three-bedroom rental in Queens and drove a Ford LTD station wagon, bought secondhand from a Long Island funeral home. (For some reason the interior reeked something that smelled like formaldehyde. *You don't think...nah!*)

Coincidently, these high "achievers" were advocates of a book titled *Think and Grow Rich*, by Napoleon Hill. At first, I thought it was just some harmless, self-help narrative that offered encouraging words for success. Years earlier I had been thoroughly entertained by *Winning through Intimidation* written by Robert J. Ringer, who became one of my heroes of the '70s and '80s. I estimated Hill's work to be just more of the same. Looking at the lifestyles of the nouveau riche twenty-four-year-old securities salesmen around me, I could say, "This stuff works!" Oh, man did it ever.

For them it did. For me...not so much.

I don't mean to pick on the *Think and Grow Rich* philosophy exclusively. There are many disciplines, both secular and spiritual in nature, advocating a school of thought that implies that if you are in pain, if you are stuck and can't seem to change, it is no one's fault but your own, and if you will follow particular doctrines and live within the dictates of some special system, you will become empowered to get the things you want out of life. "Follow the directions in this book, and you can be what you want to be," they say.

It isn't true. The book you hold in your hands at the moment makes a distinctly opposing point. It proposes that if you are in pain, if you are stuck and can't seem to change, then the only solution is to *stop trying*. You cannot install your own happiness, and only by separating from the willful self that *thinks* it can change will there ever be any true change in your life. And therein lies the resistance for many people who are so attached to their ego that they cannot help but shoot themselves in the foot by continuing to try and to struggle for change and happiness. It doesn't work.

Over the years, hundreds of such books, pamphlets, and guides have been successfully published, and spiritual movements established surrounding this idea. There are correspondence courses, psychologies, and "spiritual" movements, some packaged as "self-help" systems, that play upon such fears and the desire to control. Solutions for worry, which provide false hope that our worst fears shall be somehow managed and controlled through our own efforts, is a marketable commodity.

Surely, you have noticed how often purveyors of positive possibilities, prosperity preachers, "abundance" gurus and other vendors of bliss use the word *abundance* and other words connoting material gain and comfort. Phrases craftily peppered with words like *gratitude, empowerment, money, health, manifest, abundance,* and so on are prolific among the "self-help" cult sets. Haven't you noticed how so many phony preachers "spiritual" messages can be boiled down to one simple "Get Rich with Jesus" but "only if you send me money"? I mean, *really!*

It is this simplicity of spiritual dynamics, this battle of wills, Good vs. Evil, that existence is validated, revealing that human purpose is to be based upon God's will instead of any *other will*, and that there is a clear-cut distinction between the will of God and the will of any other. Those who cannot comprehend this (yet) have suggested the use of will to force positive events. They only make matters worse for themselves. Only letting go of *will*fulness (and gently so, without struggle) checks fate, because there is no future until the future happens—then it is gone.

Therefore, the only hope for the future is that it becomes *now.* That is why we must live in the *now*—in the present moment—because it is where we receive our wordless God-consciousness and alignment with God's will (whatever His will is). We secure our humbled position, eschewing judgment, and instead gracefully play our God-directed role in the flow of events comprising the Stream of Life.

Originally, we were created in God's image, but when we judge, we recreate Him in our image. It severs our relationship with Him.

How dark it is when the power goes out.

Judgment, or playing God, affects lives—not only yours but the lives of those around you, in ways that you may never know. Fortunately for us, this goes the other way too, because the example also shows how the simple act of giving up judging through accepting that you are *not* God affects the journey in positive ways. Life simply seems charmed by the good fortune of living in grace.

This judgment phenomenon happens in that single corrupting moment when we exercise our freedom of choice either to admit we are not God or to play God. This is the only choice any of us have ever really had. Playing God—*judging*—is the ancient error of Heaven itself, a blight of spirit passed on through Creation as a cursed legacy to us all, and we have all participated in this corruption of mankind. It is our mission as human beings to each, individually, rise above it. Humanity can be saved in the collective.

It is my hope that you are beginning to see the enormity of the situation. It can be mind-blowing to think that we could bring a plague of the generations upon ourselves and into the world, causing not only alcoholism and other obsessions but also every problem we have ever had, just by being resentful.

It's not as if we are always conscious of the gravity of this situation as it plays out. For as long as we continue our existence in a somnambulant state, our *God-play* doesn't seem so epic. Yet just the slightest awareness at once reveals even the most mundane of the affairs of daily living that lead us to so much misery and pain. Realize that an answer to this is in your hands right now. It lies in the meditation exercise I will show you on my website.[28]

While caught in the resentment-judgment trap, if asked, you would not admit that you were judgmental, because it is not likely that you would even be aware that you were. You might grudgingly admit

---

[28]Please visit the "How To Get There," page in the back of this book for fast access to the meditation exercise. It is available for streaming or download. It is free and always will be.

to the negative emotion of resentment, once shown how to identify it, but play God? You are marching in a procession that will send you careening off a cliff and into the obsessive abyss of compensatory addiction and misery. This ancient sequence is the drawback to resentment, but without it, there would never be enough desperation to give it up.

The deep ramifications of judging are not always apparent. It is not merely pissing off other people or using criticism and disapproval or controlling others by instilling fear and insecurity in them. To be damaging, judgment does not need to be all that obvious. It doesn't need a conscious voice at all. It works best when concealed deep in the crevices of our inner being, invisible to the world and out of reach from our own awareness. Most often it can remain our own dark little secret, hidden deep inside while still playing its role in our destruction, causing all its collateral damage through our hollowness and dishonesty. Just like its cause, *resentment*, judgment is merely a conversion from *enlightened reason* to *darkened reasoning*, and, just like all forms of hate, it occurs mostly deep down in the inner recesses of our subconscious. It is one more *cause* in a train of *effects* that ultimately and progressively brings every alcoholic to his knees or else to his death.

This progression is not something you can simply turn off and on. You cannot wish and *will* it away. When we resent, the creation of judgment is automatic. You have no control over it. It is only the willful ego that *thinks* it does, and will react through suppression and denial. It may do so systematically, with mantras, positive affirmations, and all kinds of distractions, taking credit for its concealment, but denial and glossing over the truth about itself is still the game ego always plays.

Review the order: Injustice causes us to resent. *Resentment* morphs into *judgment*. Judgment means playing God.

You will see that prior to judgment comes the *now* moment. It is the moment of truth, and it exists only in the present, in the human psyche of us all. Here, in a solitary moment, where the innermost *true* Self exists, our psyche becomes like a mixing bowl. One moment there is clarity and dispassionate vision, clear discernment of what is right and wrong; then, with the addition of resentment, comes the forging of the brand-new substance called *judgment*.

Now instead of being naturally moved through God-inspired discipline and direction, life becomes subject to chance—a coin toss. We become entirely subjected to random fate. We w*illfully* decide between right and wrong, but, unable to effect real lasting change, we are rudderless existentialists, set adrift with only our ego-self as a guide. We become frustrated because Its decisions are self-centered, always leading us toward some destructive end.

This is how agnosticism takes hold and how lack of faith leaves us with no real direction other than any way the wind blows. This idea ought to scare the Bejeebers out of anyone.

All of this decision-making is a hell of a lot of work. The emotional poison of hostility ensures that we will rarely make the right decision about anything. Life becomes incredibly unmanageable as our problems mount and our bitterness grows. We become unlovely creatures who must contain and conceal our problems as best as we can, lest anyone see how sick we really are. We develop façades to obstruct the view to the outside world. Sometimes these are spiritual façades; religions or movements, even cults help us develop extensive displays of outward benevolence and portray an "enlightened" deportment.

The goody-two-shoes lifestyle is only a smokescreen to camouflage the mounting negativity of emotional turmoil. Sensing that something is wrong, we become more and more efficient and "saintly" by trying to ease that feeling of discomfort. Meanwhile, stores of emotional pressure build, twisting the mind and body. Even physical health and appearance will be gravely affected by this inner deceit. By all outward appearances, we are getting *better* and *higher* spiritually, while in reality we are sinking deeper and deeper into the hole of faithlessness, self-reliance, and fear. Suppressed anger is a chief cause of heart disease in the United States today. It is why seemingly placid and "together" folks, perhaps even spiritual and genteel in their outward demeanor, end up hypertensive and dying from heart disease, strokes, and aneurysms. Show me a cool, calm, smiling Cheshire cat of a person, and I will show you a boiling human cauldron of repression—a pressure cooker of concealed anger that must one day explode—or implode. What a dilemma!

Some people believe it is normal and right to be resentful. Psychologists actually teach their patients how to use will to control their anger, convincing them that emotions, even when they are negative ones such as anger, can be a rightful, natural condition and an acceptable validation of their humanness. They will teach *(sell)* theories and systems designed to manage anger.

The theory is that successful anger management will result in a better life. It does not. That is because anger is not human. It is subhuman. I can hear the howls now. When humans try to manage anger, life will only get worse in the struggle. This sort of self-discipline avoids the spiritual side of humanness and addresses only the animal side of our existence. It ignores the spiritual side of every man or woman's humanity, where we are not *self*-disciplined but instead allow God to do the disciplining. Simply letting go of resentments, as they occur, is all that it takes. Not management.

It is extremely dangerous to learn tricks to conceal anger. Any ploy to do so is merely another form of suppression and serves only to help maintain outward appearances and sociability, a façade we have maintained all throughout our spiritually sick lives. Meanwhile, something dark and sinister takes root inside, continuing to grow. It is our lower nature.

The first time you ever caved in to your lower nature, allowing the negative charge of resentment or hate to permeate your psyche, you set yourself up as a hapless target for *a hostile takeover*. Then, you were in effect *born again*—not as a superior being, but as an inferior slave serving something sinister residing inside you. Now with your new identity, your lower self was free to pass a sentence of damnation upon those who dare to *trespass against us*. And so you proceeded on with your life—playing the judge.

The problem with living this way is that such adjudication is the privilege of a God and reserved for the One and only. We are *not* God, although there is something in us that would like to think so, and that *something* plays the role in this manner.

It should be no wonder then that in the book "Alcoholics Anonymous", the coauthors propose the very Judeo Christian precept that "either God is everything or else He is nothing".[29]

If it is true that He is *everything*, then that hardly leaves room for *us* to be *anything*, especially not to be God. The spot is already taken, and by default we are nothing. Ego-self might jump in and tell us, "Well, since this says that God is everything, and we are part of 'everything' then we must be God too," but whenever ego-self speaks, it is lying. This is a "me too" philosophy that has gotten many a seeker into deep spiritual conflict.

This meddling with matters of Heaven and Hell is not our privilege. Playing God through judging causes an automatic separation from Him. *Ouch.* There is no human suffering as painful, enduring, or as damaging as this one, for it has plagued mankind since Adam first ate of the tree, against God's will, a long, long time ago.

Seeing the wrong in others makes us seem right by comparison. It ensures that we remain unable to forgive others and therefore never experience any forgiveness ourselves, feeling only guilt as we continue in our wrongs. Something willful lives deep down inside us and wants more than anything to feel right about itself. It will do anything to feel it is becoming God.

It is not the offensive behaviors of others or the objectionable turns of events in the world that causes our separation from God. To believe so would be placing blame upon others. Culpability falls back onto us. It is always our *reaction* to the offenses that is the problem that harms us much more than the incidental cause. *That* is our downfall. Through meditation, we sit still to face the shame of this. It is a correcting shame; it is God's corrective love, that discipline we have never been able to give to ourselves.

We accept the poison of hate and anger that converts us into judgmental little gods in our own right. No tormentor can break us off from *conscious contact* with God, but we do it ourselves by playing Him, judging our enemies, those who tempt us to hate them, through our unconscious acceptance of hate. Remove *righteous* from

---

[29]"Alcoholics Anonymous", 4th edition, Alcoholics Anonymous World Services, 53:2

indignation and what is left is truly undignified. Not humbled, but humiliated.

I have just given you a ton of stuff to consider. The truth is not always easy to take. If you have not yet begun the meditation exercise on my website, it can be even more difficult to swallow, as you may still be asleep. If this is the case, then I ask you to please seek out and try the meditation exercise I teach my alcoholic protégées. It will lift the scales off your eyes, and, as some of what is written here comes into clear vision, it will begin to make better sense to you. Once awakened, you will see how judgment is not what you once *thought* it was. You will see how it is more often something done subconsciously—that once resentment had cropped up inside, you really had no control over your actions. Lost control over their drinking is the hallmark of a *real alcoholic*. That being the case, you can see how God's forgiveness is already yours, without your begging.

In the new light of awareness, you will be able to see just what you have done. By separating from your thoughts the way I will teach you in the meditation, you will gain the clarity of vision to see that although you may have been an unwilling participant, you have been doing this your whole life. From now on be free to short-circuit *God-playing* judgment by going *before* the judgment and experiencing resiliency to the resentments that always trigger it. Then the gap of your separation from Him will become narrower and narrower as you draw closer and closer, and His presence becomes more and more clear. As you can see, this is no ordinary book about alcoholism, spirituality, and meditation. It is quite special.

"... he was the first living human with whom I had ever talked, who knew what he was talking about in regard to alcoholism from actual experience. In other words, he talked my language. He knew all the answers, and certainly not because he had picked them up in his reading." - *Dr. Robert Smith (Dr. Bob)*

7 INSTANT AGNOSTIC

The Mechanics of Spiritual Sickness

*B*etty watched. Her eyes followed the tall, slim, light-haired boy with the two packs of Marlboros as he walked out the door, past the store display window and passed of sight. The cigarettes, "sure didn't stunt his growth any," she was thinking.

Willie slammed the register drawer shut and headed back up to his soda station. The floorboards creaked under his feet and he scuttled along behind the counter.

With two hands, he snatched up a pair of squeaky-clean glasses out of perhaps twenty identical ones – all parked upside down in rows. Willie's already rolled up sleeves tugged back revealing two muscular forearms. For a fifty-three year old, Willie was in excellent shape. Wednesdays and Saturdays the soda delivery truck came. He never missed an opportunity to stack wooden soda trays when they arrived and twenty years of delivery days, twice a week, showed.

Gary looked over at Willie's arms, then down at his own, then back to the soda man's.

"Man, those are hairy." He said.

The wiry black and grey bramble over Willie's arms barely concealed a…"What the heck is that?" Gary strained his neck and peered over the counter as nonchalantly as he could, trying not to appear too obvious.

"My dad has one of those." He saw a vestige of some faded, hardly visible image on Willie's skin. Another picture arose in his head. He recalled the American bald eagle his father proudly wore over his right bicep; inked during a Navy tour in the South Pacific. It was a work of art, courtesy of a three-day Kava spree.

"Got it on Santo," he always said whenever anyone asked him about it. Gary had no idea where Santo was. He just figured it was some island somewhere in some far away tropical ocean. *A place like Hawaii.*

"Don't you ever get one. You can get hepatitis and die." Gary's dad would warn.

"A tattoo" Gary thought. "Willie must have been in the Navy." He thought of his friend Richie's father. He had one too. A rose. From the Philippines.

*The mark on Willie's arm was different. This was no bald eagle. It was not a flower or some whimsical sketch. This wasn't artwork at all. The turquoise stain looked crude, as if etched freehand by someone who had lost his patience. "What does that say?" Gary wondered. But these were no letters. He saw what looked like a **2** . . . and a **4** . . . the string of hand-drawn digits trailed up and then disappeared under the roll of Willie's shirt.*

"Numbers!" he said. "I'll bet that's some kind of military ID or something," Gary's mind meandered. "Or maybe some hot Asian girl's phone number" He imagined it may have been drawn on him to prove his undying love. Whatever it was, "At least Dad's tattoo showed some creativity," he thought.

"I'll bet Willie could tell some real wild stories."

Willie up-righted the two glasses together onto the Formica counter along the wall. Gary watched through the reflection in the long wood framed mirror mounted above.

"Look. He's making four egg creams!" Gary was pointing at the glasses and their reflections.

"It's just an illusion!" Betty said. "Things aren't always as they appear Gary! That's a mirror."

"I know that," Now it was obvious to him. Did she really think he didn't know it was a mirror? Did she think he was dumb or something? He felt small. And a little sore. "Why would she say that?"

"It's only two egg creams!" she said.

"Bitch." He thought.

Oh, so you don't think you are agnostic? When was the last time you became upset, annoyed, or irritated? Was it yesterday? An hour ago? Was it while reading the last chapter? Did a dog bark in the distance? Did a baby cry next door? Did a child break your precious concentration with a cough? *"Whose cell phone is that going off, anyway?"*

Here are two even more important questions: "What did you feel when you last experienced that emotional twinge? " and "Were you even aware of it as it was happening?"

Whether he knows it or not, whether he is recovered or not, every alcoholic is in a constant battle for his life, enduring (or failing to endure) a seemingly endless torrent of irritation, anger, or bitterness of one kind or another. After a while, it seems he has become overly sensitive to those who *trespass against* him. People who are often characterized as being "very emotional" are those plagued by this oversensitivity. Even if our walking on eggshells is well hidden to the outside world, we remain nervous, boiling pots of tension and unease inside, our fight or flight mechanism constantly on alert. We are tired and worn out and depleted halfway through the day, from all of the energy-draining inner emotional excitement we repress.

There always seems to be someone or some *thing* in the wrong, and this pisses us off, to some degree. It could be the simplest irritation or the vilest eruption of anger and rage—negative emotion is resentment, and, depending upon how sensitive we have become, is a measure of wellness or sickness. The old AA axiom that "some are sicker than others" is a clear reference to the spiritual condition. If this is true, then it is also true that *some are more well* than others.

Either way, "Welcome to the Stream of Life." You are in it; and in the moment that it gets in you, you resent, immediately invoking judgment—this is the when you become the *instant agnostic*. That is because discernment tainted by anger produces *immediate* God-separateness.

If you meditate the way I propose you will automatically endure. A spiritual stamina will take the place of intolerance and judgment as you will increasingly gain patience.

Agnosticism is being in the judgmental state. Just as it is not possible to resent without judging, it is not possible to be playing the god-judge role without also being agnostic. Many of us are taught that *agnostic* means "without knowledge of God," and while literally that is correct, this translation has lost much of its original meaning. It is not mere rote knowledge about God that is missing from the agnostic. Just because someone does not buy a particular religious sect or speak a special doctrinal lingo has nothing to do with agnosticism. It is a lack of awareness that if *only God is God* then *I must not be Him.*

The AA proposal that *God is everything* doesn't leave any room for us to be God too. *God is everything* tells us that the job is already filled, and that we, therefore, must be *nothing.* That hurts and threatens the ego, and so the ego, desperate to justify his *"me too"* to the original "know that I am God" idea, must revise his thinking. And that means reading into prophetic texts meanings that do not exist. Within the context of all the principles conveyed by "Alcoholics Anonymous", the "God is everything" idea is meant to *exclude* us from the role—not *include* us.

We can *say* "God," speak in terms of "God," and read and preach to others what data we have amassed *about* "God." Not all of the intellectually stimulated awareness in the world can provide an effective defense against our agnosticism. As long as we remain without the spiritually inspired awareness of God, we will find it difficult to see much beyond the limits of our own thinking. There is more to understanding than that. That is because when we play God, in other words, judge, we are now knowing *ourselves* to be god. We might even boast of having made *conscious contact* with God, except from our point of view, God is *us.* We delve more and more into ourselves in order to experience ourselves and become more and more conscious of the illusion that we are God.

This is a moment of both doubt and faith. The instant we doubt that only God is judge, we also have faith that *we* are judge. Yeah, it's a dirty job. Someone's got to do it; it may as well be us, right? It is quite a large role to play, filling the shoes of God. Wellness, the result of natural union with God, is interrupted as we are instantly separated from Him and afflicted with spiritual illness.

To discover that resentment and its unholy scion, judgment, has separated you from Him can be alarming—especially if you have ever taken the view that resentment is natural and acceptable. It would mean that you have accepted as *normal* a way of life that is disconnected from God—an idea abhorrent to just about anyone who considers himself a candidate for a spiritual design of living.

Don't be offended to learn that every time you are angry, resentful, irritated, or annoyed, you are rejecting God (and playing God). This stewing in emotion symbolizes a lack of faith. We have developed lifelong associations with our negative emotions. We detest the very idea of negative emotions because they happen so embarrassingly often. It is an unpleasant thought to consider, that we may be spending so many of our days in a God-disconnected state. In doing this we subject ourselves to emotional entanglements, amassing more and more intellectual panacea to problems and avoiding real solutions.

Even the slightest impatience or disdain for being inconvenienced is a real *god-play* event. Most of us are familiar with the often quoted "Don't they know who I am?" It is usually a self-deprecating reference; the idea of playing God is repulsive to anyone seeking a spiritual existence; it is at least on an *intellectual* level. On a *spiritual* level, it has been accurate, and anyone who fancies himself or herself on a spiritual path would find this revelation objectionable.

It is rarely heard anymore, but old-timers in AA use to tell newcomers, "Have any concept of God you want—as long as it is not you." It is an adage we hear less these days. This is due to a postmodern-AA membership that has allowed a spiritual degradation of Judeo-Christian principles inherent in the Twelve-Steps. When we backtrack spiritually, we develop an addiction to our own judging. Judge just once and that sage advice is out the window. It takes only one resentment to take us from humility.

"Ye are Gods" is a favorite scriptural clip often extrapolated for misuse among religious and cult leaders. Removed from its context, this classic Bible-byte allows for a scriptural agreement of what the follower has suspected and hoped for a long time: proof that he is God. After all, he has played the role secretly, judging and basking in that self-glorification for most of his life. The irony is that, within context, this passage actually discredits the theory entirely, as do all the rest of the Scriptural teachings. Leave it to the desperate to cling to such isolated nuggets of anti-theist theory. The alcoholic may not go to such lengths, but isn't that what is happening anyway, deep inside the psyche of the self-centered, self-absorbed, narcissistically degenerated and judgmental alcoholic?

The bleakness of the picture I paint for the spiritually diseased alcoholic is not lost on me. If it were not for a solution it might all be too much to swallow and this book too depressing. What good would it do for any alcoholic to toss this book away in disgust without accessing the entire presentation; and so this chapter does contain some relief. It also explains *God-separation* in terms that clearly remind that a person's spiritual dysfunction is not exclusive to them—or unique to alcoholics.

It is axiomatic throughout all mankind and plays a terrible role over the course of human evolution—a part each of us plays in our own life. It is not something we originate within ourselves but rather the inheritance of a horrific legacy that is spiritually viral in all humanity, through all generations. In explaining this separation, we can pay tribute to the very first incident of this ever happening. The story of Adam and Eve, often viewed as mere allegory, may contain more practically useful information than we have ever before dreamed; certainly more than Sunday morning preachers ever convey.

You may notice a trend here, leading you to wonder, "Why so much attention to resentments and judgment?" That is because when we play God through judgment, we automatically experience separateness from God. There can be only one God, and if we play God, we prevent admitting the first truth—that *He* was there first.

Sorry. The position has been already filled. This is what is meant by the idea that God is everything. It is only the egotistic applicant applying for the position who deludes himself into thinking he might actually get the job, and then he further convinces himself he's *got* it.

Judgment, that word for "playing God," is set in motion the instant we feed *Self* with the negative energy force called *resentment,* because resentment fuels judgment and separates us all from God. It is an energy—an alien force, if you will—as real and omnipresent as gravity, light, or love, and it must be acknowledged.

Twelve-Step practitioners have at their fingertips a method that assists in neutralizing past resentments and honing a new way of life. It includes a divine, protective element that doesn't allow new resentments to come along and destroy us as the old ones had. That is Twelve-Step practice and living in its totality. It's that simple.

So if it's all about resentments, old ones *and* current ones, and how to live life in spite of them flying in our faces all the time, why don't we just pray to God? Have Him make us well and *then* we can deal with resentments? Isn't that all we should do? We can get that from church. No? Join a church, just don't drink, pray to God, praise Jesus, and obey the Ten Commandments. Right? Isn't that keeping it simple?

Actually, no, it isn't, not simple enough. Religions can be *way* too complex—not insofar as intent and purpose, but *as practiced*. When religions pervert their original propose, they always complicate matters as they evolve into unwieldy institutions.

That is because even the most sincere practice or study of religious doctrine and principles is not worth Jack's crap as long as they skirt this issue of resentment and playing God, leaving us to remain resentful, angry, and irritable. It would be nice if such religious affiliations and their practices worked and had convincing legacy of efficacy to which they could point. They would hold irreproachable authority and power to teach us the secret to finding God, but bitter experience shows that most spiritual organizations haven't got any secrets to give.

If they did have the answer, then there never would have been a need for Twelve-Step Fellowship movement in the United States. All the alkies would have probably just signed up for their tour with the Oxford Group, stuck with it, and that would have sufficed.

If you are not yet familiar with the Oxford Group, it was a evangelical Christian movement derived out of the "First Century Christian Fellowship" back in the early twentieth century, out of which was derived virtually all of the spiritual principles contained in the Twelve Steps. The cofounders and early members of *Alcoholics Anonymous* who came out of "the Oxfords" adhered to the movement's decidedly *religious* Christian teachings.

The reason that AA works is that it does not zero in on getting spiritual *first*, as churches tend to do—as the Oxfords did. Doing that is the ego trap perfected by the religions—religions that have failed most of us alkies so miserably in the past. The Twelve Steps work in getting us to God *first*. They go straight for the cause and not the effects. By zeroing in on our resentments the anger that each alcoholic spends a lifetime embracing points in the direction of the original scene of the crime causing every problem we have ever had in our lives. We go nowhere spiritually until resentments are handled.

Here is why: To think that "I am resenting, so therefore I must be spiritually sick" is backward—it should be, "I resent first, *then* I become spiritually sick secondly." We become sick *because* we resent—not resent because *we are sick*.

We can waste a whole lifetime trying to get spiritually well so that we won't suffer gagging on our own vitriolic backwash, but we will never succeed at it unless we understand this chronology and resist the idea that we need to be well *first*. We need to get the sequence out of reverse order, otherwise no growth is ever possible—just an ongoing continued search for spiritual wellness that never comes. This is why folks (sponsees *and* sponsors) can't stay in *Step Eleven* practice—in pure form—very well without adding to it (polluting it) to keep it "interesting."

Traditional religious teachings and New Age fads lure us into pursuing ego appealing, pink-elephant solutions promising complicated, highfalutin, perhaps somewhat spiritually robust philosophies. In these instances whims amount to rote indulgences in du jour spirituality.

Seeing the resentment *first* is the key to ever getting better and getting to the point from which spiritual growth becomes possible—otherwise only spiritual deterioration is possible—which is where most of us exist. (Even if we don't like to think so—even if we *think* we "practice these principles in *all* our affairs." It doesn't do us any good in the long term, because even though we are on "the path," we become increasingly less able to remain on it.)

In the Bill Wilson article from the January 1958 issue of *AA Grapevine,* mentioned in Chapter 2, Bill wrote in "The Next Frontier: Emotional Sobriety," a revealing self assessment of his spiritual progress. It was a major FAIL. Despite his wholehearted practicing of visualization techniques and contemplative prayers, devices he at one time believed to be "meditation", Wilson was as miserable as he was when he still drank, overwrought with debilitating depression. Many "sober" alcoholics find themselves in this predicament.

To the extent that Bill was able to lose his people dependency (which we know from human experience, occurs only as the result of his resenting and judging others with secret God-play in his own private head-kingdom), he was able to become free from the pain and despair that always follows God-separation.

Bill's "quiet place in bright sunshine" allowed him to break the binds of "people" (resenting and judging them) that tied him to despair. That is what also happens to us if we follow Bill Wilson's example; by giving up ambitious prayer and replacing it with the Wilsonesque paradigm comprised of *altruistic realization*. Then our prayer might have value.

Here is this basic universally spiritual order which is presented in "Alcoholics Anonymous".

"Resentment is the 'number one' offender. It destroys more alcoholics than anything else. From it (*'resentment'*) stem all forms of spiritual disease".[30] Resentment originates every kind of spiritual disease there is—not *some* spiritual disease, but *all* forms of it.

Yes the co-authors were aware of this spiritual chronology. Resentment first, *then* comes spiritual disease *second*. It is never in the reverse order.

Failing to understand this sequencing of spiritual disease kills more alcoholics than even alcohol does—so not drinking but not getting this can be deadly. This is why meditation is so vital—not doing it sends us on wild spiritual goose chases as we try to *get* spiritual and to *be* spiritual, *read* spiritual, talk spiritual, "sharing" spiritual even writing spiritual, and generally becoming feel-good devotees and agents for gurus and their philosophies while not first being well ourselves.

Alcoholics can go to one, two, or three meetings a week and to church on Sundays or Saturdays, serve soup at the Salvation Army,

---

[30]"Alcoholics Anonymous", 4th edition, Alcoholics Anonymous World Services, 64:3

and attend every Fellowship service gathering there is in a district, and what we *think* is spiritually fueled peace and serenity may serve well for a while—but eventually, at some point, it will prove itself to be just a show of a well-disguised spiritual *veneer* of goodness.

Unless we deal first with resentments past and present—and have in place the spiritual tools for dealing with new ones as they come along—we are screwed.

We speak of spiritual malady and spiritual sickness, and we can describe what it feels like when we've got it. But just exactly what is it? It is separation from God. This is something that those who consider themselves to be spiritual and who make intellectual affinity for a Creator a thoughtful priority, often cannot bear to admit. Realize your own agnosticism. Realize that every second, every moment that you are not in the *now* moment—every moment you are lost in your thoughts that you are not in the Sunlight of the Spirit and are disconnected consciously—you are in that moment, in fact, *agnostic*. As you go forward in life, those agnostic moments are to become less and less. The meditation exercise on my website will bring you to that experience.

"Resentment kills a fool, and envy slays the simple." - *Job*

8 OH THE PAIN!

The Benefits of a Guilty Conscience

If you are old enough, then perhaps you will recall the science fiction TV series from the 60s, *Lost in Space*. It was a campy serial show set aboard the Jupiter 2, an ill-fated American spacecraft that loses its way attempting to traverse the galaxy. The series featured a cast of interestingly developed characters, one being the always whining, not–so-likeable Dr. Zachary Smith, played by Jonathan Harris (Bronx boy, probably the best actor in the show).

Smith, a Soviet spy bent on sabotaging the ships launch is trapped aboard just as the crew – the lovably wholesome Robinson family, (Yes just like the "Swiss Family") blasts off for Alpha Centuri. He ends up an unwitting stowaway. Unfortunately, Smith's extra weight throws the crafts guidance system off and Smith, the family crew and one smarmy robot, end up stranded in space with not enough fuel to reach their original destination or return to Earth. They must wander the Milky Way conducting geologic studies in the search for enough fuel to get them back on a course. They are *Lost in Space*. It is Zachary Smiths fault; and he knows it.

Smith becomes the Jupiter 2's resident villain. Guilty as sin, he commits all of his energies toward chasing his own happiness and he does not hesitate to lie, cheat or steal, even at the expense of the safety and wellbeing of the rest of the Jupiter 2 crewmembers. Nothing stands in the way of his self-centered pursuits.

Smith is classic. If he were not *lost in space*, surely he would have been an alcoholic or a drug addict, forever slinking around in shadows, secretly planning, plotting and scheming—operating under the radar, out of view of wakeful eyes. He openly bitches like a little girl about everything, while quietly oozing guilt out of every pore.

One of Smith's most memorable, reoccurring lines was "Oh the pain," a catchphrase he wails whenever anything is not going his way, which was just about every episode. *Lost in Space* was highly popular and "Oh, the pain" became something of a meme in its day, a tag capturing Harris's portrayal of the self-serving, narcissistic Smith personality so well.

Harris's brilliant acting illustrates a despicable piece in the puzzle of human nature, easy to associate with the guilty alcoholic who does exactly the same thing. We spend a lifetime trying to rid ourselves of guilt by compensating with joys, pleasures and pursuits of happiness beyond what is practical or what we deserve. That is because it is always easier to consider effects rather than looking at causes.

This is why "Guilt Management," therapies like anger management, always fail, while permitting more and more underlying damage to go unchecked.

Truths, of anything, are quite a bit harder to accept than popular belief. Yet it happens all the time, especially when looking for a favorable outcome. This is especially common in medicine as well as in spiritual matters, anywhere that humans are trying to get well. It also happens while facing the truth of guilt.

Immediately prior to guilt is judgment (God-play). That is where you have been blocked off—and not by guilt. By the time guilt is felt, you have already been God-separated.

It is the effect of judgment and what you feel for having judged (played God), and from where comes *all* unexplained restless irritability, discontent, anxiety, depression, and so on. This happens at levels of which you are not always conscious. Guilt is the pain of that separation. It is God's call to unblock what is already blocked. The block is caused by resentment—not guilt.

Immediately before judgment (God-play) is resentment, the negative emotion that kicks off a sequence of spiraling descent that always ends up in obsession and unhappiness.

Here's the order: First, resentment, then judgment, then guilt. Finally, seeking solutions for the pain of the guilt comes in. Those solutions will provide anesthetic, pleasurable, white noise to drown out and hide the pain. Food and sex are the primary devices. But these attempts to squelch the pain do not stop it at its source. We develop more and more need to compensate as the pressures mount—we get worse.

Convinced that guilt is a cause of difficulties, you will always first try to get rid of guilt without getting down to what went before to cause it in the first place. When life begins to fall apart for having indulged instead of getting down to the cause, you will resort to treating the symptoms, and this path is a very dangerous and sly misdirection by a nefarious, mischievous ego.

Ego loves to believe it can manage things, ridding itself of guilt and character flaws and even praying for their removal so it can take credit for the diagnosis, for having identified them and asking God to assist in the cure. "I did all the work, God, all the self-analysis and inventories—now you go ahead and remove it!" as if He were the garbage collector. "There, there, that's a good little God" (*pat, pat, pat).

It is imperative to get to *causes* and not seek to correct effects—which are merely bedeviling symptoms of what is really wrong.

The coauthors of the *Big Book*, "Alcoholics Anonymous", were aware of the spiritual principles regulating the sequence of man's spiritual failure when they said, "From it (resentment) stem all forms of spiritual disease" (64:3).

These spiritually awakened and inspired ex–problem drinkers weren't kidding!

As it turns out, what is really wrong is that we resent at all. All bitterness, anger, frustration, and even petty annoyances initiate all spiritual dysfunction, and all misery, unhappiness, discomfort, and disorder that follows are just effects. A pained conscience is the evidence that we have turned our backs on God.

Just as the pain of placing a hand on a hot stove saves the cook from burning to death, guilt painfully calls us back to God and saves us from spiritual death. It tells us that we have stepped out of the God-guided Sunlight of the Spirit, that we have veered off the road of happy destiny into the shadowy, unpaved bramble where life is no longer a guided journey, where it is turned into directionless misadventure governed by unmanageability, chance, and random fate.

Guilt does not need to be fixed. It needs to be *felt* in order that we may get pushed back to reconnect with a loving God who summons us through it. The idea that guilt is some useless emotion or psychic boogieman is false. As long as you believe that, you will never be able to get beyond effects to guilt's causes.

Guilt is a lifesaver, not the life-destroyer that ego wants us to believe it is.

A guilty conscience is the single most powerful evidence humankind has that God exists, and it is an important way for us "kids" to experience His fatherly, corrective love. Resenting guilt is resenting God.

It is the dark nature in us that loves anger and loves to hate. It relishes languishing in bitter vitriol and self-importance—both forces from which we all need to be saved. That liberation is not anything we can do for ourselves. God's judgment, as it turns out, is actually God's love, something to be embraced and not resented or rejected.

Pain is produced by our own guilt. Most readers will already be familiar with the idea that there can only be one God. Acting as if we are God too, flies hard in the face of that idea. Ultimately it produces a conflict that hurts like hell. We are *not* God—we are merely *His*.

When we judge, we play God. We are like actors presumptuously wresting a role, which does not even exist, in a play, written and directed by a supreme playwright, God Himself. Arrogance tears us away from our true natural state of being as God's children and creates a painful experience for us. It is where the flesh of our soul tears and fills with our own life-blood. We bleed. We agonize, because what could have once been an ordered, manageable life—for ourselves and for those around us—begins to get messy and ugly. There are clinics dedicated to physical pain, but there is no such thing as a pain clinic for spiritual pain.

Conscience is the alcoholic's savior, not his enemy.

We are always touched by cruelty and injustice placed upon us by people, places, and things. What differentiates a spiritually awakened person from a spiritually sick one is how we respond to those who torment us. If we respond with patience, we grow—if we respond with anger, we die. Someone who believes they experience zero effect has already responded with anger and learned to go numb and unable to see the anger has likely suppressed it. That is how we became alkies!

Eliminate the effect of anger, and all our problems drop away. The *Big Book* coauthors demonstrated their understanding of this spiritual principle when they said, "If we were to live, we had to be free of anger".[31] We may infer from this that unless we are liberated from anger, we will die.

Being free from anger is not the same as *getting* free from it—and therein lies the trap into which so many of us fall. *Getting free* implies effort, and that effort invokes self-will. *Being free* implies that freedom *comes* to us *as* we become liberated—without effort and without the use of our own will.

Anger, or suppressed negative emotions, or hatred—call it anything you wish—feeds the ego-self, contaminating the spirit, the mind, and eventually the body to the point of mental insanity, physical sickness, and finally death. And all the way down we slide, living through bedeviling misfortune that we are sure we do not deserve, wondering, "*Why*, God?"

God does not cut us off —we sever spiritual flow ourselves by playing Him, and we do that each and every time we improperly meet a situation with resentment. Being resentful leaves us rudderless, frightened, and desperate for answers.

From the annoying mosquito in the room to the deadly car bomb exploding in the busy square, when we respond with anger, annoyance, or frustration, that is judging and playing God, which sets us apart from Him. That is where all pain and suffering comes from. That's why we drank. That's why we engage in any sensual distraction.

"The grouch and the brainstorm were not for us. They may be the dubious luxury of normal men, but for alcoholics these things are poison".[32]

As we suffer anger's unpleasing effects—anxiety, depression, and physical ailments related to the abusive use of food and sex—we might search for solutions in hope of restoring health and appearances. Armed with the discovery that stress is what is killing us, we feel enlightened and seek to rearrange or manage the stresses that are

---

[31]"Alcoholics Anonymous", 4th edition, Alcoholics Anonymous World Services, 66:2

[32]"Alcoholics Anonymous", 4th edition, Alcoholics Anonymous World Services, 66:2

around us. The idea that we might somehow manage anger becomes an appealing idea. Don't waste your time.

Clinical means for controlling emotions, such as anger management, are a deceptive lie to which many of those still suffering from spiritual illness fall prey.

Just look at today's cable TV programming and superficial, self-help infomercials, and you will see "experts" attempt to address the subject. They do not tell us how to become resilient to stress. They don't know how. They can only treat effects, not causes. Instead, they propose that the negative effects of stress ought to be *reduced* through diet, exercise, behavioral modification, self-hypnosis (sometimes disguised as spiritual meditations) are suggested to channel negative emotions out of us without ever getting to a real answer to our problems.

Drugs such as antidepressants and hormonal therapies are available to those already physically incapacitated by the debilitating effects of out-of-control emotions. Human-aid "treatments" are all temporary solutions to a permanent reality.

Stress, appearing as resentment, anger, and bitterness, isn't going to go away. Not in this lifetime, it isn't. It will always be waiting on the doorstep, poised and ready to crop up inside.

Stressful events will change as surely as the seasons will, but they will always be replaced by new events with new stresses—just like new seasons continue to stream on in the passage of time. As Gilda Radner's Roseanna Rosannadana would say on *Saturday Night Live*, "Well, Jane, it just goes to show you, it's always something. If it isn't one thing, it's another."

We are never without the heat of a summer or the cold of a winter.

In this world of feel-good pseudo-spirituality and clichés to the contrary, it can be a shock to realize that the cruel reality of life in this world is that, *even this shall never pass.* The best for which we can ever hope is that we learn a style of living that makes us resilient to resentment's inevitable force upon us.

That resiliency can be discovered in *Step Eleven* of the Twelve-Step program, which suggests a solution that is much simpler than any of the human aids provided by the psyche mechanics who may hold impressive degrees and paper pedigrees but who are meddling in matters they are ill equipped to understand or control. Their own intellects and ambitions form barriers to real helpfulness.

There is not so much psychology to the solution. There is no magic mantra or relaxation discipline. There is no uber enlightened recovery group, sponsor, pill, or knowledge. There is simply letting go of resentment and anger. Stop fighting anyone and everything. Give up anger. That's all there is to it. Simple. It is not easy—but it is vital. If you will try the meditation exercise that I propose in this book, you will see just how simple it is.

The spiritual pain of conscience will save the soul in the same way that the physical pain of body will save it from injury. It is the very same protection mechanism, expressed from different human realms.

One key characteristic of the guilty conscience is its relentlessness. It never stops pursing us. When we think of a guilty conscience, we immediately think of the things we did and now regret. Events of the past for which we hold remorse and perhaps require amends (or, at the very least, an apology) come to mind. Our conscience bothers us, or hurts us, for our misdeeds, and it is easy to see how drinking to forget may help alleviate that pain.

A woman who has a guilty conscience concerning promiscuity in her early years, a man who stole money from his mother's purse to go to the movies with his teenage friends; these are simple examples of common aberrant behaviors that can produce guilt which later require relief. We can bring these behaviors to the conscious memory with relative ease and deal with them, say, through counseling or some form of soul-searching (as is done in a fourth-step inventory built into the Twelve-Step process). A thorough rooting out of some events deeply lodged into the recesses of the subconscious will do wonders for relieving obsessive behaviors.

But what about the subconscious mind? Are there events lodged deep into those recessed corners of the mind which even the best and most thorough analysis cannot reach? Yes, there are. There is a plane of conscience that exists on a spiritual level that no secular practitioner can ever reach. That is the conscious and subconscious interaction with God. *Conscious contact* with God is the one and only stated purpose of prayer and meditation in the Twelve-Step process.

Just to be clear, I am talking about guilty *conscience* buried in the *subconscious*, and the distinction between these two forms is crucial. While we often speak of the pain of guilty conscience and how obvious pain throbs like an infected wound inside the conscious mind, we also need to include suffering that we are *not* able to bring to conscious thought and yet are somehow manifest negatively in our thoughts, behaviors, and treatments of others.

Oddly, you may think this must be a large task to inventory. I mean, how can we account for things in our craw that we cannot even bring to mind? It would require an exceptionally talented psychoanalyst under exhaustively long sessions to root *that* deep into the mind, no?

No.

It is simpler than even the most highly trained and skilled brain mechanic could ever imagine or would care to admit; so simple it is beyond their intellectual reach. It is beyond any human being except that each individual, each of us, reaches within ourselves as we relate to our Creator, one-on-one. I do it with alcoholics all the time.

You can review your entire life, look at every single grudge and regret through analysis and painstaking accounting, and yes, the result can be well worth the effort, offering a degree of relief from pain— enough to allow a pulling back from the obsession to drink. But there is something that cannot be reached through these human means. That something has to do with the relationship you have with your Creator and not with any clinician, counselor, or *any* human being.

That something, the commonality, is a pain that goes beyond our miscreant behaviors, errant actions and relations with people, places, and things. It has to do with our relationship with God and the internal turmoil we experience for having played God though our own judgment. That's right—that judgment, that God-playing, all stem from resentments mentioned in the previous chapters.

There is no doctor, counselor, sponsor, book, or guru who can bring you to the precipice of consciousness you need to reach in order to realize this. There is no spiritual advisor who can make it happen for you, except that you go through the light of truth, and it is only through meditation, the gift given to us all specifically for this very purpose, that that kind of "divine counseling" can be accessed. I am attempting to point you in that direction. I am not the way, but I am *a way to the way* for you. I have already discovered *the way* and live by it.

If you bought this book thinking it would provide you with the answer, you were wrong. Perhaps you ought to ask for your money back. As a way to the way, all I can do is point you to where the answer lies. If I had the answer to give you, if I had the magic and the ability to remove all of your problems, I wouldn't. Anything, any person or process that hands you the answer, becomes your God—you might as well go to Him first. At least, then God will be *your* God.

What was your mistake, way back when? You incorrectly thought that the pain of conscience that *could* have saved you was your enemy. It was not the enemy. Your conscience is the light of reality chasing you down to correct you and return you to alignment with God's will. You can only recognize this once you have had a spiritual awakening and have recovered from alcoholism.

Conscience saves people—not everyone who takes on the life of alcoholic abuse crosses the fine physical line into true alcoholism. Some people heed that gentle prodding and are able to break free from the continuous cycle of mental and physical torment. Conscious awareness provides a divine discipline that keeps most people from falling off the track of life. But the alcoholic rejects all such discipline from within and avoids the guiding principle we had stifled and all but silenced through abusing alcohol. Had we allowed truth to catch up with us, that discipline would have prevented us from falling off the track of life's purpose, and we never would have gotten so ill.

The alcoholic rejects the discipline of an earthly father just as completely as that of the heavenly One. Those of us who have been denied the *earthly* version have never learned much discipline at all. Alcoholics are nothing more than rebellious teenagers before their Father—regardless of how old they are, they adopt a lifestyle that cultivates and thrives in rebellious disorder. A rebel is a rebel internally—even without any obvious external cause. It is not always plain to see the cause, but it is there.

There is human consciousness and subconsciousness—most of us are already familiar with this idea and have practical, positive experiences with it. For example, many Twelve-Step practitioners who go through the rigors of a thorough inventory of past grudges, fears, and harms done to others see that they have played a selfishly inspired role to create their own problems. They see that they have put themselves before God and their fellows. This is a highly spiritual truth about their humanity. It requires a conscious spirituality.

Here secular specialists dare not tread. They aren't equipped. They haven't the authority. While guided inventories, psychoanalysis, and talking cures do help us at the human-animal level and to some degree also can and often do allow for spiritual awakening, meditation takes us deeper into our human-spiritual subconscious.

This brings us to a realm that can be frightening, and many of us will never wish to delve that deeply into our souls.

When alcoholics have a spiritual awaking as the result of the Twelve Steps, they awaken to the truth of what they have allowed to happen to themselves. If you have had a spiritual awakening as the result of these Steps, that that is exactly what has happened to you. That awakening broke the need to revisit alcohol over and over and over (obsession).

It does not matter anymore that your body had been damaged (except that you must be vigilant about your sensitivity to alcohol—just like someone with an allergy to hevea must be vigilant against exposure to products produced from that plant; that is, latex). Your conscience was restored to the forefront of your psyche. It reclaimed the seat of authority it had originally occupied before you squashed it in order to shut it up. *Now* you can listen. Now you welcome God's discipline. It is a miracle. But it won't last without your continued participation. That participation is made possible through meditation.

"Knowing your own darkness is the best method for dealing with the darknesses of other people." - *Carl Gustav Jung*

9 LEAKY TRASH BAGS

It's Dirty Hard Work—Playing God

*G*ary felt small and sore. *"Why would she say that?" he thought.*
"It's only two egg creams!" Betty said.
"Bitch."

The bell at the top of the door rang. Mrs. VeVerka came in for a New York Post. "Hot enough for ya?" Willie shouted backwards behind him and smacked the heel of his palm hard onto the pump button. WHUP OOMPH! WHUP OOMPH! WHUP OOMPH! Three long shots of brown chocolate syrup exploded into the bottom of the glass.

"Oh it's gonna be a warm one today," she shouted. "I swore I heard locusts this morning and it's still only June," Of course, they weren't really locusts. They were Cicadae, but hardly anyone in the Bronx knew the difference.

"You sure are lucky to have air-conditioning, Willie," she said. This was the first summer that Willie's candy store would have it. Most merchants in the neighborhood had been air-conditioned for at least the last couple of years. Willie was a holdout.

"I'm putting down ten cents for a Post," she yelled. "Looks like I'm taking your last one," she added. "And ya owe me two cents."

"All right Helen," Willie shouted back "We'll give you a discount tomorrow to make it up. Hey, tell Richard I was asking about him, will ya?"

"I sure will. Stay cool Willie!" Jingle Jingle. A blast of warm, Bronx new-summer air streamed in for a second, enough to flutter the top page of the Daily News on the stand just inside the door. Under a red brick that Willie used to keep the pages from flipping the big headline read,

Actress Shoots Andy Warhol
Cries 'He Controlled My Life'

Tomorrow in the same spot, on the same stand under the same brick there would be a new headline.

Kennedy Shot, Bullet In Brain, *it would read.*

"I will stay cool. See ya tomorrow." He got busy again.

WHUP OOMPH! WHUP OOMPH! WHUP OOMPH! The second glass was shot with chocolate.

Small talk did not distract Willie much. After all, he was a pro. He could make change, build two egg creams, a lime Rickey and a Cherry Coke Wingding while singing "God Bless America" and hoping on one foot, if he had to.

With one swipe of the leg, his foot slammed shut what sounded like a refrigerator door. Now in his hand he held something red, white and rectangular.

"These are three pumpers!" Betty said. "Good!"

"What do you mean?" Gary had no idea what a three pumper was.

"Now watch! He's gonna pour two glubs into each one. No more. No less."

With a squeeze and a flip of the forearm Willie pinched open the cardboard spout on the Dairylea milk container and splashed exactly twice into each glass. Just as Betty had predicted. The milk floated on top of the chocolate in a bubbly layer of cold moo juice.

"Now he's going to stir them, right?" Gary was wrong.

"No! He can't. It's too soon," Betty said. "Look at that chocolate and milk . . . . it's Ying and Yang."

Usually no one has to smell the breath of the alcoholic to conclude that he may be having a problem with the stuff. The scent of self-centered sick sprayed all around him is quite enough to make the determination. His lifestyle distresses his family, relationships and career. His whole world stinks...on ice.

Once an ego establishes itself as the source of direction in the life of an alcoholic, it continues to evolve an emboldened, egocentric existence in the role of "god"—judging people and conditions it sees in the world. Maintaining this *godly* stature is a lot of work for the unwitting human "host". The stress of it wears him down and the toll on those around him can be devastating.

So why doesn't he just slow it down? Doesn't he see the harms he brings upon himself, his loved ones, his own children? Yes, he does see it. Nevertheless, he is under a spell and cannot stop.

Circumstances around the alcoholic—as evidenced by people's reactions to his increasingly miscreant behaviors—constantly remind him of his true, diminutive place in the world. He must stay ahead of the game in order to forget. He has to reorder himself constantly—adjusting his thinking and his environment, to reset the stage for each new show. Each *Act* requires the performance of his life.

It is a restless existence as the alcoholic struggles, jumping through hoops, expending his energies trying to manufacture his own "self"-esteem—an imagined picture of himself he holds in his fantasies. As a slave to his prideful, false self; acting without awareness or regard for others—he wonders why he cannot ever seem to acquire and hold onto the white picket fence he ambitiously envisions. Failing to acquire all the creature comforts to which he feels he is entitled, he becomes haunted by a vague sense of dissatisfaction with life.

The first reaction many alcoholics have when the subject of their drinking comes up is *"Leave me alone."* An alcoholic can easily justify this kind of thinking. Never mind the havoc wreaked upon his own life and the ills he causes others. The constant acquisition of new self-esteem reinforces the effect, pressing him to act even more unconsciously selfish. Although it is clearly self-serving to say, *"I am not hurting anyone but myself,"* he never sees the folly of such a position.

The narcissistic *symptoms* of God-separation and guilty conscience that plague the alcoholic have become so widespread in our society that professionals have tagged them. Psychologists identify this condition as being a very real and destructive personality disorder. *Not all narcissists are alcoholic—but all alcoholics are narcissists.*

It is for good reason that others often charge alcoholics with being very negative people. Even an outwardly happy drunk, lost in his own thoughts, finds internal morass and despair at every turn. *Stinking thinking* is a popular AA term used to describe his demeanor.

Chapter 2 has already shown how the negative charge of resentment has invaded the psyche of the alcoholic. Once this violation has taken place, a repetitious cycle sets in and the mounting negativity can hardly be contained. Like a leaky trash bag, no matter how neatly and tight we tie the top, the bottom still drips, contaminating the environment with our seeping garbage. An unrecovered alcoholic *leaks disorder into the world around him.* It can get messy. We alcoholics in recovery know this uncontrollable condition as *unmanageability.*

Lack of discipline gets so bad we are unable to *self-contain* the problems it causes. As we unwittingly disassociate from our original state of *being,* we lose our birthright source of guidance and clarity. We begin to relate differently to the world around us through guilt-blurred vision, upsetting everyone around us. We harbor an unsacrificing attitude that is intolerant, impatient and…well, just plain ugly. The lack of perception is like wearing horse blinders and we go through life without much regard for the comfort of others.

A self-seeking alcoholic will always serve the pursuits of his personal advantage over the wellbeing of his fellows. Being selfish, his lost awareness places him into a self-absorbed, trancelike state where actions intending to serve his own interests carry more weight than the normal human desire for natural happiness.

Stepping on the toes of just about anyone touching his life—family, friends and loved ones, he cultivates an unearned, undeserved self-image. It is a reflection that will eventually turn most drunks into antisocial geeks as friends and loved ones, for their own sakes, pull away. Even when he is not *under the influence*, perhaps sober for many years, the unrecovered, un-awakened alcoholic still acts without regard to the rights or comfort of the people around him.

This is where the phrase "It's all about me" originates—in the behaviors and vainglorious attitude of narcissistic personalities. There are many ways to tick people off. Alcoholics seem to develop a knack for using their own inflated sense of self-worth to accomplish the task. They do it in spades. Even so-called *functioning* alcoholics, able to earn a decent living, eventually discover that their career is negatively affected. Ripping through the business and workaday world with all the aplomb and grace of a wounded bull in a china shop, certain reputations develop.

In 1939, at the time of the publication of the *Big Book*, "self-esteem," was not some coveted psychosomatic honor as it is today. Back then, it's definition leaned more toward the pejorative, meaning *a high mental valuation placed upon self, by self*—hardly an asset.

Most of us have an admirable capacity for honesty and have made positive contributions to the world around us; and there is nothing wrong with being "esteemed" or highly valued by others for good works done. A dispassionate awareness of our own assets and personal accomplishments is healthy, when such recognition is duly deserved. However, undue esteem which is installed by *self* is a lie—a delusion, calculated to compensate for the pain of a guilty, God-separated conscience.

There is something wrong with the spiritually sick human being that *needs* to feel right; hence it will seek any trick it can to "feel good" about It's *self*. If not through the abuse of substances, then by exploiting knowledge, approval, money, sex, food and even charity. An alcoholic seeking to self-heighten his "esteem" is in extreme danger.

Right before Bill Wilsons decent into the dark, sinister world of chronic alcoholism, he had become as addicted to his own overinflated view of his stature in the world as he would later be to the liquid solution to his problems. Self-important and overblown with a high opinion of himself, Bill later reconsidered, saying, "I, who had thought so well of myself and my abilities, of my capacity to surmount obstacles, was cornered at last."[33]

Recognizing that pride does indeed go before the destruction of man, it seems that Bill was becoming aware that it is not *too low* self-esteem that fells the alcoholic. It is *too high* self-esteem—the exact opposite of what most of us are lead to suppose.

---

[33]"Alcoholics Anonymous", 4th edition, Alcoholics Anonymous World Services, 8:0

Many of us believe the "self-esteem" fallacy because it is what psychologists and their intellectual minions have been taught and what they in turn teach us. Really, shouldn't this be expected of them? After all, self-esteem *boosters* are all that they have to sell; secular salve to smooth over the symptoms of spiritual disease without ever arriving at a remedy for what causes it: *Resentment.*

Those with self-esteem to sell have revised the original meaning of the term, placing a new rendition of understanding into the parlance of popular psychobabble. The psychological, clinical approach to all mental disorder, including alcoholic obsession, can be summed up in four words, "Self-esteem for Sale". This de facto motto is a motivation behind the PR groundwork in the furtherance of this concept. It helps define and develop a market while influencing public opinion, nurturing the idea that self-esteem is something we need more of; and if an alcoholic's deficiency can be restored, he can get well. It is quite a racket.

From 1995 to 2005, Americans have doubled their usage of prescription antidepressant medications.[34] Twenty percent of American adults are now prescribed at least one psychotropic medication, shelling out at least $11 billion a year on antidepressants alone.[35]

Medical solutions to spiritual problems do not work, and yet to an alcoholic faced with the choice between facing God or fixing things himself through a prescription medication…well, seriously, which do you think the down and dejected, self-pitying alcoholic would gravitate toward? Alcoholics are drawn to self-esteem vendors like counselors, self-help gurus offering weak, middle-of-the-road solutions not requiring too much change of heart, attitude or lifestyle. This is why treatment facilities are always full and must maintain waiting lists of sufferers who hope that their "talking cure" services will be key toward wellness. They will do anything to feel better about themselves, even if it takes pharmaceutical means.

I can best give an idea of what my pre-recovery choice would be by acquainting you with a man named Barry Gross. Here was a swaggering, gentle giant of a man—a quintessential New Yorker whose

---

[34]General Psychiatry, August, 2009, http://www.ncbi.nlm.nih.gov/pubmed/19652124

[35]American Psychiatric Association, June 2012, Vol 43, No. 6, http://www.apa.org/monitor/2012/06/prescribing.aspx

Jewish heritage and upbringing had been completely obscured by a Vietnam era Special Forces "inventory" acquired thirty years ago. He was the guy who first handed me the Twelve Steps and told me, "Here, this will save your life if you do what is in it."

I asked him, "Have you done it?"

He said, "I am making a beginning."

Barry had nearly five years of continuous sobriety under his belt. I thought this was amazing, considering he hadn't drawn a sober breath for the preceding twenty years. Still there were signs that his psychic innards were hurting badly from injuries received years ago. There were wounds inflicted in Vietnam, failed relationships, an estranged daughter and a childhood that was infected with the disease of a bullying, alcoholic father. These had piled onto him. Barry was well onto the spiritual road to full recovery, but he still ailed. Later on, conversations with him would reveal deep-rooted anger from the past – bitter emotions that tortured him every day, turning Barry into that which he had hated the most: his father.

There is a wordless identification that resonates between two guilty consciences; a certain empathic energy not unlike a magnetic force. It draws them toward each other. I shared this kind of understanding with Barry. I could feel his pain and clearly identify with the angry energy lurking inside him. Somewhere under a hulking body, controlled by an embittered brain was the real Barry—a loving, caring human spirit, trapped inside. Yes, that I could see.

What I could *not* see was the future and that this affable-angry new friend was only days away from a sudden, massive coronary that would end his life and that I was to cry and cry. Before then I would learn something important from Barry. As with many important lessons learned in life this one came unpredictably, while in the throes of struggle with the insane desire to drink.

Fresh into a three week spree of abstinence, mental obsession loomed. Most days were just like this one, in the fall of 1997, as I whiled away the time white knuckling both sobriety and living. This afternoon was especially difficult as all I could do was ponder the miserable past, fight images of a worse future and fear the inevitable arrival of the next insane idea; that a drink, just one, might take the edge off just long enough to give me a breather from the inner pain every alcoholic knows too well.

Any unrecovered alcoholic who has managed to stave off the desire a few times will tell you, *not drinking* most definitely is a contest. The knowledge borne out of bitter experience that eventually you *will* lose a round; that you *will drink,* no matter what, really sucks. It is one of the most depressing ideas that an arrogant human can ever face; the realization that *they have no control.*

While recuperating from drinking I was no longer able to maintain my Wall Street lifestyle. Counting down hours until the next AA meeting, I looked forward to a temporary feeling of relative safety there. Until then, a half empty box of Entenmanns Chocolate Donuts, a pot of coffee and the New York Post would help stem the stream of fear running through my head. Even better, there was my son.

After he was born, I was a house-dad. Nancy was a retail department store manager and was able to get right back to work. She commuted daily into midtown Manhattan bringing home a meager salary while I developed skills that in a million years I would never have dreamed I would.

The responsibility that comes with being a full-time father was having an effect. Yes, caring for another human being, someone who depends upon you for his life indeed does change a person. It changes them into a parent. Hairline cracks were beginning to shatter the selfish shell calcifying around my psyche.

But something also happens when a fresh *Huggie-load* of baby poop suddenly becomes the most urgent matter in your life; and nothing else counts but to get rid of it. This may or may not be a spiritual event but whatever it is, it does have a way of taking your mind off your *real* problems, if only for a few minutes.

There is also nothing quite like the fleeting moments of delicious freedom that come in the middle of the afternoon with the realization that the baby has fallen asleep. Fixing a sandwich, stealing a fast shower, peaceably thumbing through a newspaper from page one to the last page, without interruption, feels like bliss.

I strapped Danny into his bouncy chair, (Whoever invented bouncy infant chairs needs to receive a Nobel prize) wedged a binky nipple into his mouth and rocked him until his eyes rolled back into his head and there was that slight pause in his sucking, the one where the suck circuits switch over from waking suck into involuntary suck-mode. It meant he was out like a light. In twelve minutes I was showered and toweled. In eighteen, a tall turkey and Muenster on rye, stood high on a plate, waiting to be devoured. A little drippy, me still with water, the sandwich from copious Hellmann's Mayonnaise, I plopped onto the living room couch. With The New York Post splayed across the coffee table I thought, *"I wonder what the poor people are doing?"*

Then I saw it. A small display ad in the back section next to the TV listings.

Are you unhappy? Do you tire easily? Are you having trouble sleeping? Are you having digestive problems? Are you restless? Are you irritable? Do you feel fatigued?

"Yes! Yes! Yes!"

If you answered "Yes" to at least four of these six questions, then you may be eligible to receive free treatment with a new antidepressant medication. Come be a part of our new drug testing trials. Must be 18 or older.

"Anti-depressant medication!" I was already in the habit of taking four aspirins every morning, *just in case,* so I was certainly not averse to solutions in a pill.

"Oh, my God. Alcohol may not be my problem after all. I might just be depressed." I lunged for the telephone like a starving Florida alligator at a Yorkshire terrier.

It took six seconds to punch up Barry's phone number. Four rings...fourteen seconds later... he answered. Those twenty seconds was all the time it took to write a script for the next whole year. I would enroll in the pharmaceutical clinical trial and life would soon be better.

Doctors flanked by hot, brainiac blonde assistants in white lab coats with horn-rimmed glasses, cradling clipboards, would hook me up to electronic devices, take fluid samples, and mutter and nod among themselves. Needles and dials on sophisticated instrument panels would measure the progress in my brain, as they would marvel at how well I was doing. Yes, new self-assuredness and confidence might restore me once again to splendor; the kind only similarly endowed He-men of the Universe can ever know.

With new and improved thinking I would triumphantly return to Wall Street to take care of much unfinished business. All it would take is the miracle of modern chemistry to correct some slight chemical imbalance in my brain; an anomaly that existed through no fault of my own.

Yes, this was an answer. Soon the limos and the Cohiba cigars would be back. A table next to Rush Limbaugh at the 21 Club, porterhouse steak lunches at Peter Lugers, and a parade of entrepreneurs kissing my butt for money to invest in their enterprises—back in the saddle. Nancy would not be upset with me anymore, even if I came home late. It would be just like it was before. This was hope. These thoughts held more optimism than I had experienced in quite a while. I was sticking to it.

"Listen Barry ... I had an idea."

"Uh-oh." He said. Barry had made it clear to me in the past that he respected my intellect, but when a newly sober alcoholic opens a conversation with, "I had an idea," more often than not, you will need to brace for impact. It's for your own protection.

"I know this going to sound a little strange to you ... and I know you may not like what I am about to say..."

"Uh-oh."

"Barry, just hear me out, okay?"

"Uh-oh."

"What!" He was beginning to piss me off. *Royally*, as only a Royal can be so pissed.

"Go ahead...tell me." This was smarm I did not appreciate. I ignored it.

"You know how hard this not drinking stuff is for me. I mean not just how crummy I feel and all ... but just now Barry ... I am starting to see that this is not new. I have felt miserable a very long time."

"Uh-oh."

"Please hear me out." I waited. *He's still listening. Good.*

"Barry, I swear to God, I have been feeling like shit since I was a kid." Memories of odd restlessness and discomfort and feeling uneasy about so many things, so many situations with so many people edged into my head and I pushed these thoughts out of my mind, stuffing the reminiscence back and down, deep into my solar plexus. Tears rolled down my face.

"I don't think I have ever felt quite right." *I listened. Still no "Uh Oh".*

"Barry, I think I may have depression."

"No shit!"

"No, really. I came across this ad in the *Post*, and it listed almost every symptom that I have. I think I am a candidate for an antidepressant medication. For free!"

I could see Barry's face through the phone receiver. His cheeks contracted, and his eyebrows stiffened. His trimmed mustache curled at the ends like fiddlehead greens.

"*This* is your big discovery?"

"Yea. I mean I think so. I mean…what else could it be?

"We're *all* depressed, Schmuck!" he said. "Why don't we see how long this lasts without the booze first, before we go running to the pharmaceutical solutions?"

It seemed to me that sobriety should not have to be such a miserable state of mind. "Barry I don't know what to do. I don't think I can make it. I feel like such a shit!"

"You're supposed to feel like shit. You're an alcoholic and you don't have any. Alcoholics with no booze feel like shit," Barry was serious and he wasn't going for my wonderful discovery. Still I persisted, "Man, if only I could get my self-esteem back," I said. "I could glide through this not-drinking thing like nothin' if my self-esteem weren't so damned low."

"*Low* self-esteem? Danny, we haven't been trying to *build* your self-esteem. We have been looking to *knock you down* a few notches."

Knock me down? This was stunning.

"Why?" I couldn't wrap my head around that idea all. My new career as a clinical drug trial guinea pig *(Medically supervised, mind you—very legit)* had just ended before it got started.

"Look, the reason you feel so lousy isn't because you have *low* self-esteem. It's your *high* self-esteem fuckin' you up. *Danny* has an unrealistic opinion of *Danny*."

This seemed impossible. It was counterintuitive. Yet later it would prove to be true. *If you are an alcoholic and come away from this book with this single idea, you will have come a very long way toward solving all of your problems.*

"Tell you what…let's keep the spiritual solution going, then if in six months from now you still feel this way, *then* we'll talk about getting you some meds. Okay?" he said.

Barry's strategy was sound. As he got better, as he went through the Twelve Steps, he would take me along with him. His intentions were good. After all, he had gotten me through Steps 1 and Step 2 without a snag. Ultimately, he could not take me through the complete spiritual awakening course because like me, Barry had not yet gotten on the path. He could not give away what he did not already posses. All he could do was give me a book and a start. Yet for the first time in his adult life, Barry was sober and he was taking action that was moving him toward God. He knew about alcoholism in a way that I had never before heard, the way it was for me; and so he had my attention.

I agreed to hang around. Barry was further along the spiritual road than I was and so I listened, because although he had not yet fully recovered from his spiritual malady, Barry's obsession to drink had been removed. It seemed to be a miracle. He had made a decision to turn life and will over to God; a compelling resolution that had empowered him enough to point others in the direction he too was going. He could *at least* do that much.

The depth and weight of Barry's talking carried authority. It flowed with power he would not live long enough to recognize; but the lesson he conveyed would change how I viewed alcoholism, the human condition and myself forever.

How could I have mistaken *high* self-esteem for *low*? *All* alcoholics do. We go about our lives donning boorish, thick, self-absorbed mannerisms—rooting self-centered and selfish taint into the matrix of our environment. In our own eyes, we might be leader of the pack when really we are just another small, angry set of snarling teeth scrounging for treats in a much larger, unfair, dog-eat-dog world.

The alcoholic, plagued by his own negativity, never seems to establish vitally important resentment-free relationships with other people. He always seems to find himself in situations where either he is overwhelmed with love for someone or harboring anger for another; as he alternately places some people and situations on pedestals or resorts to derisive, resentment-laden temperament directed at others. (This attitude is the crux of gossip, slander even racism.)

It is impossible to maintain anything like healthy associations with other people under such extremes: first loving and hating; then hating and loving. Ultimately, hate wins out, and those he *thought* he had admired and appreciated now become objects of bitterness. Their very presence or the thought of interacting with them brings discomfort. This is very often the principle behind the idea that someone "makes my skin crawl."

This kind of disturbing, reactionary behavior makes it very difficult to make a living or to experience the advances in social or career networks that the alcoholic sees others enjoy—at least not to the level he feels is due him. Now, handicapped by his own inability to work and play well with others, the alcoholic's restricted social position gives him cause for even more resentment and anger.

After a while, he begins to feel that the world owes him a living and does not appreciate him. With the mounting pressure of a suppressed and repressed emotional state bearing down on him, the alcoholic's discomfort becomes so objectionable that a fear of people, places, and situations develops.

Situations that may further provoke his soreness are avoided, and he may tend toward reclusiveness, dodging social situations. Unless he can overcome the fear of his own resentment, social phobias can develop. It is not the fear of people that is really the problem. It is fear of his own hostile *reactions* to others that leads the alcoholic to seek isolation, avoiding confrontation and the secret irritation that conviviality brings.

He is not merely a victim of circumstances. The alcoholic himself has set in motion a series of unfortunate consequences he is sure he doesn't deserve. He has done this through his own fears—his own resentment and worry about events that have not even occurred yet. Troubles gnawing away in his imagination are set-ups for disappointment, as each new failure becomes just one more symptom in a growing roster of bedevilments signaling lost faith and continued placement of reliance upon himself before God. It is doubt manifested in his life.

In chains of events such as these, there are always originating causes and a finalizing effect. Nothing ever happens without consequences. We can either like them or not. Accept them or object to them—either way, chains of causes and effects, each dependent upon the other to sustain the sequence of conditions, lead up to delivery of the final event. These conditions are easily identified as "symptoms" of each other; especially when they are dependent upon a preceding causal link in the chain.

One link is an effect, caused by the link preceding it, which is the effect of a causal link preceding that one, and so on, each causal link becoming the effect of the link immediately preceding in the sequence. All links are both effectual and causal, with the exception of the first and last links. One man's ceiling can be another man's floor, just as one causal condition can be the effect of another equally dichotomous cause. Identifying a "root cause" of a problem doesn't necessarily mean we have identified the originating source of the trouble. Getting to a root cause of any situation is usually merely identifying one of several effects in the sequence of causes and effects. Getting to root causes can be exhilarating, but the question always remains, "What caused the root?"

The root cause of any situation is also only one of many effects, the difference being that it is the effect which anchors the sequence firmly into place, making it difficult to solve. One effect is usually the cause of another effect. Only when we get to the germinating cause that sets a sequence of cause and effect in motion, can we see how a problem may be solved, or even whether or not it *can* be solved.

Herein lies a problem when trying to solve our troubles. Mistaking effects for causes, we may conclude that since one cause has been responsible for one effect, then we will have solved our problem if only we resolve that cause. This is not so. It fails to go far enough, far back enough to the originating cause of the problem to which there is no cause itself. Get to *that* original cause, and we can see the truth about troublesome effects.

Getting to a root cause can be moving in the right direction, as long as we don't fool ourselves into thinking our troubles are over once we discover them. We must really get to *origins*. Even roots have a cause of their own. Observing the symptomatic conditions—the detrimental, painful effects along the way—as signposts is extremely helpful, as they are clues pointing us toward the first cause. The first cause is always resentment, which comes in many flavors.

From resentment comes all of our problems and other causes and effects. It is the original cause we must not shrink from discovering. (The original "sin," if you will.) Selfishness and self-centeredness is a root in that it anchors our egos in the world and holds us as slave of our worldly selves. Once that bondage is broken, we are free from ourselves, our roots become uprooted, available to be planted into new soil.

Until then, we anchor our ever-inflating ego-self into terra firma; the matrix of worldly affairs, stepping on the toes of our fellows as we go along; spawning the very same type of confusion that first caused our own downfall.

In his 1889 essay "The Decay of Lying," playwright and aesthete Oscar Wilde held that "Life imitates art, more than art imitates life." Wilde was not complaining. He approved of the phenomenon. And why not? He was, after all, himself an artist.

There are modern-day examples all around us. Every time we compare our lives to those in a TV show; or copy a fashion trend, aren't we imitating art? This is not limited to the decorative or visual arts. Performing artists are also known to affect society with prophetic projections, especially in writing, music and film. There are many examples where such artists seem to have a prophetic knack for presenting us with hauntingly realistic perspectives of truth, sometimes masquerading as fiction. The line between what is real life and what is creative work or art can blur where it is difficult to tell which mimics which.

Take for example science fiction film directors and screenwriters Andy and Lana Wachowski. In *The Matrix* these two depict our human existence with horrifying accuracy, under the guise of sci-fi movie making. The Wachowskis introduce us to the Blue Pill-Red Pill idea. It is an ancient concept but very effective in this futuristic presentation.

In *The Matrix*, the world's human population has been conquered by evil machines. Every human being on earth has, from birth, been reduced to living a pod-like existence—each of their bodies plugged in to a "matrix" life-support system. With their brains interfaced with a highly advanced virtual reality computer nicknamed *the Matrix*, they are injected with an alien-programmed presentation of virtual human life that is indistinguishable from anything they know or can recall.

The aliens, who have constructed the system, have just about annihilated the earth as humans have known it, reducing it to cinders and smoldering rubble. Those who have survived blissfully sleep, plugged into the matrix programming that is supplying them with a stream of thought and presenting a virtual reality that appears to be the world as they have always experienced it. They see cities and homes and other people just as they have always appeared, giving the illusion that all is well, when in reality not only is all *not* well, but also, it could not possibly be any worse.

In essence, they are all asleep, dreaming that they are awake—all accomplished through a canned, computer-generated reality that the evil aliens pump into their brains. Save for a very few, the world population does not even realize that they are being duped, that they cannot tell truth from falsehood. To them, their homogenized, preprogrammed life seems the only normal one. Upon closer examination, we begin to see that nothing—not their interpersonal relationships, careers, or even their meals, with the flavor of the food they *think* they are eating—is actually happening except that the matrix provides a false reality of its occurrence to their brains. And so the world goes on, running like a bad movie—just one big algorhythmic loop of a projection, inside that false reality where every inhabitant exists only to serve the alien machines keeping them alive.

(By the way, the collective neuro-electric life-force of humanity is being tapped and stored as a power source for the machines to run on. The human "pods" are being used as a giant battery of power cells for the alien machines.)

There is an underground force of people who have somehow managed to wake up and unhook themselves from The Matrix and who see the new world for what it has become. Horrified by what their once beautiful world has become, they chose to live in reality, holding onto the hope of overcoming the evil force enslaving their fellow humans. The decision to live in the real world or in the Matrix is symbolized by the taking of a pill. A person is awakened, and given a choice—to go back to their dreamscape existence oblivious to their own enslavement and false existence or to remain awake, fighting for freedom, even if that means living in a horrible world—its original beauty obliterated by the ugliness of the Matrix.

All right, so you are probably wondering, "Why has he just spent two pages playing Roger Ebert?" (Ebert, by the way, is an alcoholic who admits never having recovered from alcoholism and did not care for *The Matrix*. He thought the story was "kind of disappointing.") I am making an important allegorical point. Take the red pill and wake up to the tragic, horrible truth about your existence and the world in which you live, or take the blue pill and return to "sleep" in a false reality that seems much more comfortable.

While you still have a choice, you make the wrong decision, and with that, you instantly lose your freedom to choose further. This is why, under some circumstances, the alcoholic really *does* have choice over whether he drinks or not, or when he will drink or not drink.[36] It

---

[36]Very rare, but it does happen where the obsession can be temporality staved.

is in those situations that he does not have a choice, that kicks him off. Then, to make matters worse, once he drinks obsessively in this manner, he immediately loses the power to choose whether or not he will stop or when. How screwed up is that?

It is very likely you have heard the expression *crossing the line*. This is a term sometimes used by recovering and recovered alcoholics. Typically they are referring to that physical "point of no return" where the potential alcoholic, who is been repeatedly abusing alcohol, now begins a new irreversible era in his alcohol-abusing days.

Drinking and drinking for years, the alkie finally *breaks* his body and loses the ability to metabolize alcohol. One day he can drink with impunity—the next he cannot without experiencing the abnormal phenomenon of craving. This is a condition where the body's ability to metabolize alcohol has been so severely compromised that the harm done cannot be undone. (Save for hiring a surgeon to perform an organ transplant.) His injurious abuse of the food *alcohol* has reduced his physiology to a certain level of harm, so that any amount of alcohol whatsoever entering his system will kick off a craving.

No matter how hard he tries or how high his hopes of ever normally drinking alcohol again, the real alcoholic will not process it with the same ease he used to—not like anyone with a fully functioning body. His body is not working fully anymore. He is physically broken.

It doesn't matter how the alcohol enters the body, either. It might be through chugging a glass of straight vodka, or it might simply enter the bloodstream through traces of unevaporated rice wine the Chinese chef used preparing a take-out container of moo-shu pork. It could be shot up with an enema hose or delivered in a single drop of vanilla extract placed under an eyelid; whichever way the alcohol enters is unimportant. What is important is recognizing that as the alcohol is absorbed into the system, it will need to be properly metabolized through his liver, pancreas, and brain—and it will not be.

Once this line is crossed, the abnormal reaction of craving will be triggered each time alcohol enters the body, whether wittingly or unwittingly. (For me, the craving would trigger in about twenty minutes after the first exposure.)

But it is not only this physical defect that is the problem. Remember, alcoholism has that one-two punch—mental *plus* physical. Not only are alcoholics physically screwed, but they are mentally deranged too.

I mean to say that there is another line to cross on the road to chronic alcoholism. Long before the physical line just described is so much as approached, the heavy-drinking potential alcoholic will have to cross a mental threshold. This barrier in the brain, once traversed, guarantees the commencement of alcoholic obsession. From that moment on, the alcoholic no longer draws a sane breath, for he has abdicated all power of choice over whether he will abuse alcohol or leave it alone.

Unlike the physical line, this mental line *can* be reversed through a spiritual awakening, and sanity can be maintained as long as the alcoholic remains awakened. This is exactly the kind of maintenance you will have access to when you meditate properly using the technique I will demonstrate.

It will help you stay awake. Any alcoholic who is handling resentments in the manner that will be revealed through meditation will have a diminishing source of pain instead of an increasing one, probably for the first time in his or her life since childhood.

The breakthrough pain threshold crossed through overreacting to daily stress will be lowered, requiring less anesthetic such as alcohol, less numbing, and less obsessive behavior in order to live. (Many people do not realize that alcoholics, prior to recovery, need alcohol in order to continue living.) You will not have immunity from alcohol, but you will definitely receive immunity from drinking. This is the reprieve written about by the co-authors of the *Big Book*, "Alcoholics Anonymous".

Along with your alcoholic obsession diminishing—and then disappearing—you will also soon discover that you are incompatible with, and finally immune from, many other mental obsessions with which you have been plagued; vile behaviors negatively affecting health and well-being, slowly destroying the quality of life and your relationships. Unnatural obsessions with food and normal sex through abusing sexuality, sugar, masturbation, the use of porn and so on, will subside and fall away. If you are getting the impression that this is not just for alcoholics, you are quite correct.

But, after all, has alcohol *really* been your problem? Or has it been a *symptom* of an underlying spiritual disease?

One of the great hoaxes in recovery circles is that once alcohol has been removed and the alcoholic has recovered—adopting spiritual principles, replete with spiritual-sounding phrases, philosophies, and displays—that he automatically attains some sort of spiritual maturity, and sophistication has been reached. He will attempt to prove it to his fellows through accumulating spiritual platitudes and studying theoretic pseudo-spiritualism, many times unrelated to the principles which first brought him his initial chance at peace.

The truth is that even though he may be abstinent and has had a very real spiritual experience, unless the alcoholic develops a way of life that allows him to be free from anger, he will never properly detach from the self-centeredness that continues to kill him. He will remain a spiritual derelict, and it won't matter *how* well he "knows" his *Big Book* text, how many meetings he goes to or doesn't go to, how many protégés or "sponsees" he has, or how many graduate degrees in spirituality he thinks he has earned through books he has read outside of *Alcoholics Anonymous*. Ignoring anger is fatal. You hold in your hands a way out of such spiritual recklessness.

Once that reckless road has been taken, the alcoholic has entered the new mode of existence when it becomes impossible for him to distinguish the true from the false.

Seeing the choice between the two possible existences is important. Even more important is the realization that someone has done this to you. It isn't by accident. A force wants you to remain sleeping, because that is how it is able to suck the life out of you for its own existence. On its own, it has no lifeblood—only yours.

Yes, the Matrix's red pill-blue pill is used as a metaphor. It is a cinematic device written into a movie treatment by screenwriters. But do not take this obvious allegory too lightly. The meditation I am going to show you is *The Matrix* metaphor come to life. It is an astoundingly accurate parable that will make even more sense to you in a short while, if you follow the meditation direction on my website.

Not only has the human race been put to sleep, but they are not even the original victims. They are offspring, progeny of generations who have never *tasted* freedom or the real world—who have *always* been under the sleeping spell of the illusion. They have inherited, so to speak, their own bondage, and their eyes have never seen the real world. The light burns. Just like in the movie, there is some difficulty and great pain in waking up. "Why do my eyes hurt?" Neo asks Morpheus. "You've never used them," Morpheus replies.

So it is when we meditate. There can be some difficulty adjusting in the beginning, until we get used to seeing the world, how it really is and just where we fit in. Sometimes there is difficulty and some pain, and it can be quite shocking. Having been misled and tricked into an altered state of consciousness, we quickly begin to discover that life is not as we had supposed. Now we are becoming more and more aware as our original state of consciousness is being restored and we are perceiving truth. We may want to run from it.

Like the whole human race in *The Matrix*, we have been duped, suckered, tricked, and placed into a deep trance state. Alcoholics are not suffering from trite psychological aberrations that respond to slogans, mantras, and affirmations. If that were so, then the hospitals and sanitariums and rehab centers would be turning out well folks instead of benzodiazepine- and antidepressant-addicted zombies. The problem has been worse than supposed, more sinister and having much *deeper* connotations that go beyond mere mechanical dysfunction of our brain machinery or emotional disorder. Real recovery is not within the scope and ability of clinicians and secular theorists.

It turns out that the spiritual awakening and subsequent removal of the desire to drink has only been a tiny reprieve and a solution to one very small aspect of a much larger problem. We are in a full-blown psychotic state—a somnambulant, mesmerized condition. Instead of being fully conscious beings traversing a path illuminated by divine sunlight, we have walked the earth as dull, self-absorbed creatures in a world that we had not realized has become a living hell. If only it would remain a private hell; but it is not, as we spread the infection, doing unto others as has been done onto us.

Fooled by the humanoid image of ourselves in the mirror, our insides bore closer resemblance to the flesh-eating zombielike creatures of science fiction stories. All unrecovered alcoholics are psychotic with respect to their lives—not just to their involvement with alcohol. There is no such thing as an alcoholic who escapes this horrifying description.

"You have enemies? Good. That means you've stood up for something, sometime in your life." – *Winston Churchill*

10 HEDGES AND WEDGES

Devices To Save Ourselves From Obsessions

Trauma and everyday stresses in the Stream of Life are good for us humans if these are properly met. If not, then they will invariably be a source of upsetting pressures, causing all misery imaginable. Animals live solely on instinct. Their existences are void of inspiration or spiritually actualized intuition. This is a natural state for the critters. It is quite another thing, however, when humans, being born of spirit, attempt to live through the cunning of their own sensuality. The discomfort brought on by playing God (through judging) excites the need for a solution to the painful friction it draws.

The judgmental human who is in conflict with God in this manner must find relief, and he must do it within his lifetime or else die in order to attain it. That is because the unflinching love of God's correction bears down on every alcoholic who judges—in order to force a reunion with his Creator. It is a *heavenly* stress, the kind that spawns ever-evolving human virtue.

First having made the wrong choice—that is, choosing human "will" and vision over His will and vision—we will soon become subject to the pain delivered through this wrong choice. Once painted into a corner, we might face the horrible prospect of a *final* solution. When we can no longer play God, we can only return to His care or else make the supreme sacrifice. Suicide is a spiritual solution to this spiritual problem—the *final* solution to the conflict. *This is why those who postpone proper choice, taking antidepressant medications, eventually discover that the drugs no longer work and begin to think about taking their own lives. Ideation is not a side effect of such medications; it is the predictable conclusion.* Either God becomes the answer with which to side, or not. Either way, a solution *will* be found.

So we search for answers to gain access to one side or the other of the spiritual realm.

Alcohol is not the only solution that the delusional alcoholic might find while trying to maintain order and a sense of manageability over his life. He can access other devices as well. If you are alcoholic, then you will undoubtedly already be quite familiar with many of these. Hedges and wedges, I call them.

Before looking at some specific examples, let us first see what I mean by these terms.

*A **hedge*** is a row of bushes or trees planted together in close formation to construct boundaries. *A **wedge*** is different. It is something more solid than a hedge. It is a more forceful separator that splits apart and divides objects or ideas. Typically, it is hammered or driven in between things to solidly sever them.

These simple terms help characterize some of the methods by which the alcoholic is *typically* able to separate and isolate himself from antisocial behaviors (that would otherwise make life more difficult) and to maintain a personal sense of sanity. It helps him feel some relief from his internalized pain while still remaining on the socially acceptable side of the communities in which he lives and works. At least until he discovers the *atypical*, more enduring solution. You can make *that* discovery right now, should you choose to live in an aware and awake state. The way to *that* choice lies in the meditation technique now proposed through this book and found on my website.[37]

If you are a *real* alcoholic who is *really* serious about recovering from spiritual illness, then whether your last drink was a minute ago or two decades ago, you are definitely going to have to reorder your perception of what recovery is and what healing and wellness is all about. You are going to have to get honest and look at the truth about some of the methods you have used in the past in hopes of permanently solving your alcohol problem and *all* your problems. They have not worked. Admit it. Although you may not have had a drink in years,

---

[37]Please visit the "How To Get There," page in the back of this book for fast access to the meditation exercise. It is available for streaming or download. It is free and always will be.

perfect ease and peace of mind has still eluded you. Something has risen up inside you and lied to you, telling you it was impossible to attain the highly cherished serenity and joy that comes from liberation from the deadly burden of supplying life to your lower nature. Be assured that you can attain that serenity and joy. All you have to do is recognize the horrible truth about the way you have lived your life up until now.

Naturally, you would want to know just how you have become subject to this *thing*-identity living within. First you would need to see that this identity wants more than anything else to be God, and has placed its nature inside you, so possessing your thoughts and actions that while It thinks and acts through you, all you can do is believe that It *is* you doing the thinking and acting. Its energy is derived out of the electric-like universal forces that manifest through anger, bitterness, and all forms of resentment. As it feeds and grows, it casts judgment upon others as only a God could. It is playing God.

Meanwhile, the real God stands ready to save you from this possession. He has set up this seemingly bizarre existence so that rescue from it is possible. He has allowed an entire universe to spin into existence, solely in order to house the process. For it to work in your, *and in His,* favor, you must move toward Him. That much, He has left in *your* hands. He'll meet you halfway, but you have to make the first move. Although He could cancel this course of human development in one fell swoop, He doesn't. Rather, He allows for the formation of a host of spiritual legionaries. As willing humans, we are in the final test and can opt to be of His mind and spirit or else not. It is our choice.

Each life is a single chip in the whole purification process—impurities being burned out of precious universal product. This identity within intelligently seeks to exploit our vulnerabilities during this process. It gains life for itself through our weakness, feeding and nourishing its envy and hatred for God in order to overthrow Him and sit in His place. This thing doesn't care if you consciously select It over Him. It knows the very idea would be so abhorrent to you that you would not. Therefore, anything that can shed doubt on Its existence, preserve Its stealth, or distract you from present awareness will suffice, as long as in the end, you reject God.

With no life of Its own, It knows that Its only hope for survival is to take up residence inside you, hooking up to your need for sensual fulfillment, so you might select your own gratification over God. Creating a need to seek pleasure through abounding injustices and cruelties in the world, It masquerades *as* you, and as you believe that you are selecting your *self* and your need for relief from your discomforts—over God, really, you are choosing It.

Your anger is not really your own. It is *Its* anger. Your hate is really Its hate. Your judgment of others is really It playing God—and so God forgives you for making this classic error, and He calls you back to Him. You experience His loving judgment as something we call *guilt*. It feels like pain, in your fallen state. It is not your pain. The *It* inside you writhes in agony under the lash of God's judgment. As long as you are attached to It, you believe *Its* pain is *your* pain, and so you clamor for the things that offer relief. Although there is easy access to food, sex, and drugs, these can become unwieldy. When abused, they become vices. There are alternative "saviors" that will save you from your misery at least as well as these. They will serve to assist in running from God—hiding in order to avoid facing Him.

In the preceding chapters, you have already been reminded that God isn't going anywhere. He never gives up on you. You have seen that His pursuit of us is unremitting, and so, since God cannot be eliminated, you can do the next best thing. You can take the same route that Adam and Eve took in the Garden of Eden. You can hide from God. You can pursue activities to help override your pained conscience with happy endeavors—you can engage in socially acceptable, pleasurable activities—behaviors that will not gain condemnation and disapproval of your fellows, perhaps activities that they themselves similarly enjoy in order to accomplish the same thing you seek to achieve: bliss in the face of pain and feeling comfortable in your own dissipated skin.

You can build socially manageable hedges, and you can drive socially acceptable wedges between you, God, and the observable activities that can be embarrassing threats to your public image. Usually these are behaviors that we feel comfortable letting others see us engage in, things that folks might quite naturally do anyway, without abusing the habits or themselves. I have often said that an alcoholic could abuse a ham sandwich if he had a need. Not only does this principle extend to the eating of an innocuous, normally wholesome ham sandwich, it is also a fair classification accommodating a host of human activities. These are the things that fill the dark void created through separating from God—a hole that should instead be wholesomely filled by *conscious contact* with Him.

We revert to what is thought to be moral conduct, readily convertible into socially acceptable substances of abuse; stand-ins for alcohol, which substitutes for God. Our attitude is, "I don't want to face God. I also do not want to drink, overeat, or appear promiscuous, but I still need relief. So I will obtain it through <*fill in your favorite hedge/wedge.*>

To make it a little easier to see what this means (and at the risk of having this sound a bit like a textbook), I have loosely categorized examples of these devices into distinct areas: institutional, practical, and social. Each of these categories of devices serves one purpose: to keep us distracted so we can never stay on the path leading to the discovery of God.

Like alcohol, these devices are highly addictive and so commonly abused, just as any substance—pharmaceutical, gastronomical, or otherwise—would be. Without attempting to establish any sort of nomenclature, let's look briefly at a few examples. Some of these items even overlap. The perverse inventiveness of the spiritually corrupted human being is practically boundless, and so this is not a comprehensive list or analysis. But these should give you some rough ideas.

Institutional devices can be either secular or spiritual. Spiritual hedges and wedges, like churches, cults, religions, and mystical-spiritual movements that follow gurus and personalities are in many ways incomparable, but in one respect they are identical. They all serve to allow the God-separated alcoholic to feel as though he is being saved—while, more often than not, serving as mere distractions to dull awareness of the ever-pursuing pain of his guilty conscience.

For instance, if I could convince you through some absurd doctrine or manipulation of scripture, that all the world is an illusion—that everything you have ever seen and experienced in your lifetime is nothing more than a fantasy, with no true or false, only what you create in your mind—the very concept would shock you. The absurd suggestion that there is no right or wrong would so traumatize your sensibilities, it would disrupt your inherent faith—placing me in a very unique position. I could step in as a new authority and pretend to have a solution to your conflict.

You become desperate for a new "truth" to replace the discredited one, and I come to your rescue, becoming your savior. At this point, it is possible to have you believe almost anything I want you to accept. Your indoctrination would be so cunningly subtle, you would not even know you were being seduced. The purpose behind this sowing of doubt is to exploit your already weak faith by cultivating and taking advantage of the fear it raises.

By cajoling you into distrusting what your heart already knows to be true, I could gain access to your mind and control your behavior by replacing your *lost* will with a *newfound* will of my own. By taking your old, objectionable thoughts that have caused you so much trouble and replacing them with new thoughts—*mine*—I employ classic hypnotism. This kind of mind-screwing occurs every day. It is an effective method used by mind-control specialists in the military, police departments, sales organizations, and the education system. Religions, cults, and charismatic leaders also have learned to manipulate inductees and the "faithful" using such powerfully simple brainwashing techniques.

The meditation technique being proposed in this book and detailed on my website,[38] unlike most any other you will encounter anywhere, represents the complete opposite of this unwholesome phenomenon and is an effective preventative against it. Instead of catering to your weaknesses in order to direct your thinking, encoding your mind through confusion, this exercise frees the spirit from the lower self, restoring your access to original intuition. That intuition should be the guiding force for your thoughts, not doctrines, concepts, or philosophies, especially not those implanted through religions,

---

[38]Please visit the "How To Get There," page in the back of this book for fast access to the meditation exercise. It is available for streaming or download. It is free and always will be.

movements, organizations, and institutions that seek to own your mind.

The truth is that there is *both* true and false in the world; and there is no absence of right and wrong. Light and dark, good and evil, Heaven and Hell really exist, just as your heart has told you all your life, and you *can* live for what is right without judging and playing God, simply by letting go of the lying self—the ego identity that tells you otherwise.

Perish the thought that anyone should ever detach you from your God-given birthright of discernment—that they should become your source of knowing right from wrong. That you have not been able to know the difference up until now is symptomatic of having been linked with the lower side of you, the side that loves lies. It has blocked your own ability to discern. This meditation exercise will break you free from this psychic slavery.

Although there is much chimera in the world, being awake and aware reveals that all is *not* an illusion; that there is truth and reality in God's world. Yearning for what is real about God's universe can move you to cry out to Him—to become a living, conscious component of His creation. As an aware human being, you can finally grow in faith, no longer relying upon human aid or men to tell you what truth is. Instead, you can allow intuitive inspiration and understanding to guide you away from what is false and toward what is true. This liberation comes only through conscious contact with God. It awakens the uncommon sense, enabling a capacity for distinguishing the true from the false. While this is God's gift to the awakened, the absence of this ability to discern is a curse upon the spiritually asleep, causing the spiritually hardened to deny reality, believing none exists. To be stuck living such a skeptical existence is no way to be useful.

Sometimes we seek spiritual bypaths that seem shortcuts to solutions. Failing to find freedom from the *bondage of self* through childish pursuits, pain returns more intensely than before. Along come the rescuing arms of worldly saviors like counseling, therapy, fellowship, and support groups. Some folks use the *Alcoholics Anonymous* style of social fellowship as an emotional dumping-ground for the disposal of their cares and worries; their meetings serving the spiritually ailing as a place to share and vent frustration, fear, and anxiety—all problems created because other secular and spiritual pursuits have proven to be futile. Venting in these places is valued as an inexpensive form of self-therapy, where the fellowship meeting becomes an ersatz dollar-an-hour self-help support group. For them, the fellowship becomes a hedge. That is only one side of the fellowship extreme.

At the other end of the spectrum are those who use Twelve-Step fellowship gatherings as a ritualistic, almost OCD indulgence. For them the fellowship becomes an entire life, converting written spiritual principles into doctrine—transforming what was once a spiritual place into a "not drinking today" clubhouse of caffeine- and people-addicted chain-smokers. No longer is it a place where unrecovered, still sick and suffering alkies can meet up with recovered, healed, and whole alkies. Instead we see how the recovery fellowship experience is a sharp wedge. These tend to be the unrecovered (still-recovering) alcoholics; the most self-centered, self-absorbed, narcissistic people on the face of the earth, although they don't think so. Perched in church basements and eager to dispense advice, these folks want to help you remain as unrecovered as they are and will even show you how to brag about it as they do.

There are plenty who fall in between. They stay sober but *not* enslaved to the Fellowship at all. They remain useful, recovered, participating members, availing themselves of the fellowship as it was originally intended. *Recovered* alcoholics such as these are some of the most patient, tolerant, kind, and loving people on the face of the earth—and as few as they may be, they are aware of this change in their thinking, and they too are sitting in church basements, but instead of proffering advice to the forlorn, these folks are more eager to help you learn *how* they found peace and ease in life. These former drunken boors will put their life on hold in order to show you what they did to recover from alcoholism. They bring to the table a life badly lived, that had been rooted in narcissistic, self-absorbed attitudes and tell of how that nightmarish past has been transformed into productive living, full of helpfulness and love.

When it comes to telling others what to do, these folks will be a little more gun-shy than their *still-recovering* brethren. They lean more toward conveying what it is that *they did,* making no bones that if their actions can be emulated, it is a safe bet that you will get what they got: *a spiritual awakening*—a new relationship with God and a bunch of components for a lifestyle that will answer not only the problem with alcohol but *all* of your problems.

For them, AA-style fellowship and it's Twelve-Step program are not about to be abused. It becomes neither a wedge nor a hedge. It remains a spiritual entity; its spiritual principles come to life; a gathering place for sufferers to meet others for whom problems, alcoholic and otherwise, have already been solved. They insist on placing reliance upon God, realizing that the only thing within their power to save themselves—is nothing. But that once the leap of faith is taken, they have become amazingly active and useful, without trying.

Then there are secular institutions: rehabs and treatment facilities that take a more clinical, formal approach to recovery. These are mostly the *for-profit* and the *not-for-profit* organizations and institutions that employ the purported salaried "pros" of alcoholism treatment—classically trained administrators bearing an array of clinical tricks, tools, and philosophies of varying complexity. These make use of the recovery models, programs, and even pharmaceutical applications prescribed by doctors, counselors, and trained and untrained facilitators—all hired to man the offices and halls of substance-abuse treatment centers.

Any treatment that either ignores or distracts from this simple truth, that spiritual problems demand spiritual solutions, falls flat. It is an egregious affront that fails to address this single cause and is *exactly* why real alcoholics continue to suffer from their affliction, even after admitting they have a problem and sought help.

While under the care of financially focused rehab administrators, miseducated addictions counselors and improperly accredited clinicians, the real disease, spiritual disconnect from God, continues to ravish these unfortunates as they get worse, not better. Even AA folks, promulgating similar secular solutions under the guise of "meeting makers make it," are equally culpable—perhaps even more so.

The only permanent solution to alcoholism is spiritual awakening and sustained *conscious contact* with God—a solution for which doctors and professionals are untrained and ill-equipped to deliver.

This assertion is apt to stir some disagreement among some readers and reviewers alike. This will be especially true among those for whom the ideas and experiences presented in this book represent a direct financial threat.

Social solutions gleaned out of relationships are an excellent source of comfort for the discomforted. When Bill Wilson, first cofounder of *Alcoholics Anonymous*, found himself dejected, standing at the bad end of a failed business trip, he was abstinent but broke and discontent. His first call for relief did not go out to booze. It was for romance. This is an area where all men fail. Many will betray family, country and God for the sake of personal lasciviousness.

Before the thought of breaking his sobriety even entered his head, Bill's emotionally charged, still-obsessive nature aimed him toward sex. There, in the musty lobby of the Mayflower Hotel, he estimated that a weekend holed up in his hotel room with an Akron babe, would be a suitable solution to his distress—a substitute for his former master, King Alcohol. (The actual term he writes was "companionship and release." If you have even been out of town on business and stayed at a socially active hotel adjoined with busy bars and restaurants, then you may well recognize this *call of the wild* and understand what "companionship and release" means within Bill's context.)

It was only *after* he had fantasized and made the decision to indulge, to cheat on his wife, did his thoughts *then* turn to alcohol.

That is because when it comes to hiding from God, sexual relationships answer an obsession even more base than alcohol-food. Fortunately for Bill, his sensual obsessions—to find pleasure through alcohol-food and sex—were spontaneously removed in that moment; he thanked God for his restored clarity and *then* moved forward into a series of activities leading to steadily maintaining his God consciousness.

This *awakening* event, on the ground-floor lobby of a busy urban hotel, was the founding dawn of the granddaddy of all Twelve Step Fellowships, *Alcoholics Anonymous*, a worldwide spiritual fellowship that flowered out of a single spore of conscious awareness in the mind of one man, in one moment of one day in 1934.

Here we are nearly a century later and literally, nothing has changed about human nature. Behaviorally, quite a bit more has changed. We seem to have gotten worse. Society has deteriorated to a place where in many circles, the social lines that have normally separated relationships into categories like friendship, romance, and sex have been blurred.

Much later in his spiritual development, Bill would discover the horror of depending upon people, his pains so great it would nearly destroy him. He would discover that his reliance upon people and circumstances to supply esteem and security, even though he was sober, was a fatal flaw in his makeup.

Do you remember the song from the old Broadway musical *Funny Girl* sung by Barbara Streisand, "People Who Need People"? According to the song's lyrics, these needy folks are "the luckiest people in the world." Oh boy, did the songwriter get that one wrong. As it turns out, dependency upon others for any emotional fulfillment is not all it has been cracked up to be. Relying solely upon social stimulants like relationships places us in a position where we will honor other men before we honor God.

Even the most innocuous relationships can be cultivated for this purpose. There is nothing wrong with encouraging the company of others for the enjoyment this brings, graciously accepting their companionship. But when we suck on the life-force of people, being paid with a sense of well-being, we abuse the reward mechanisms in the brain. Like horror-film vampires, moving from victim to victim, we join a vast matrix of life-suckers who roam the earth, believing themselves to be human.

Having no real life of our own, we become parasitic and dependent upon each other, sucking a sick emotional substance out of the psyches of others. Sure, relationship building and social activities can *feel* like a solution. From the simple pat on the back, good word of approval, to the wildest sexual fantasy fulfilled—and every alluring, pleasure-producing activity in between, delivers relief. At what price? We pay with our humanity.

Heaping heavy, not to mention addictive, doses of praise and verbal support to artificially inflate self-esteem, these types of social endeavors feed and inflate the hungry ego through nurturing whatever willpower already exists. The addictive quality of these compels the abuser to seek opportunities to people please and to serve others—oftentimes selfishly. The alcoholic doesn't see it as selfish. He believes he is being of altruistic service to others, but since the comfort of living in his own skin now hinges upon such service, is he not really cultivating more people dependency than ever? Engagements like these are especially attractive, since they are so available and produce an immediate dopaminergic response[39] which supplies the anesthetic value that numbs the pain of the conflicted conscience.

Can you clearly see that such human barriers cannot be maintained indefinitely? If you have been meditating as I show you on the website and have been reading along with this book, or if you have ever experienced the anguish of repetitive relapse or known the frustration and emotional torment from hitting a spiritual brick wall in sobriety, then something should be becoming clear to you. It should be plain enough to see that although the initial effects of the typical *fixes* for alcoholism might be highly desirable, their precarious natures prove dangerous and oftentimes deadly when relied upon for too long.

There are many *practical* ways to wrest pleasure out of the world too—ways that seem to be quite compatible with cultivating a normal social existence among our fellows. Most people would concede that money and power are sexy. What they mean to say is that these are as exciting as sex. But like sex, money and power can be taken beyond their intended purposes and become misused—for the same corruptive reason. The pursuit of money and power is an astonishingly powerful anesthetic.

Men caught up with an unhealthy quest for power and money will also be oversexed, their need for some form of guilt-compensating pain therapy being the common element. These men are not so much driven to success as they are running away from their inescapable

---

[39]This refers to pleasure center, neurotransmitter activity in the human brain and is addressed in the next chapter.

truth. Infidelity, sex-for-hire, and pornography fixations are very common themes among the powerful and fabulously wealthy. Not *because* they are powerful or wealthy, but because of the kind of people they have become while improperly chasing the creature comforts power and wealth provide.

Money is a practical necessity. Typically, there is some degree of command and power necessary to amass and manage it well. However, even the very thought of wealth will help conjure up a powerful brain-salad of pleasure-producing fantasies that can so enthrall the pained person, becoming obsession onto itself.

But it does not necessarily take a truckload of dough to feel good. In the Velvet Underground song "Waiting for the Man," Lou Reed wrote that with just twenty-six dollars in his hand, "waiting for my man," even before copping the package of heroin from the drug-dealer "man," Lou says, "I'm feeling good. I'm feeling oh so fine."

Lou knows. All junkies know. There is a euphoric effect in waiting to get high. It is not so much an *ecstasy* as it is a *relief* borne out of an absence of pain through self-induced expectation. Anticipation can feel like getting well. It is a drug, and it is addictive.

A person can become so seduced by the ambitious prospect of wealth, fame, and recognition that the potential of accessing an endless supply of distractions can set the person into a state of mesmerized living.

Hyper-focusing on career or the excessive preoccupation with "the climb" to the top has claimed many victims. There is nothing wrong with being powerful or being rich, if these have been acquired by *non-obsessive* means. Just as there is nothing wrong with food or sex, as long as they have not been used as a means to placate the guilty conscience for a life improperly lived through anger and judgment.

If you will recall, it was mentioned earlier that a guilt-plagued alcoholic could even manage to abuse a ham sandwich. The converse is also true. The very same sandwich could just as easily provide nourishment and sustenance to the person who would *not* abuse it. Sex used for procreation instead of purely for the exchange of gratification is a healthy component of human life.

Likewise, preoccupation with self-enrichment through education, academics, and study is another common utensil allowing for the cultivation of the alien identity within. It could be in business, spirituality, theology—it really doesn't matter, any course of study can do the trick. Not only are certifications, grades, and being impressed with one's own knowledge a powerful stimulant, but also the job of earning them can be so all-consuming that abject unconsciousness can be sustained for years as a student dives headlong into the conscience numbing, self-absorbed role of being a perpetual, professional pupil. Learning for learning's sake provides a very special kind of glory, one that can be displayed as well as reserved as a private stock of *self*-esteem.

Generic altruism, the kind not performed under the auspices of organizations or institutions, can also be an effective appliance to help manage the growing load of guilt and pain. Even sober, an alcoholic can override feelings of inferiority and guilt by congesting his life with overly philanthropic activities, helping others through volunteerism and acting out the role of sober goody-two-shoes. Everyone knows someone who seems to *get off* on being the servile "nice guy," who bows and scrapes before everyone, making them comfortable and happy, forever opening doors, pulling out chairs, pouring drinks, and falling over backward to make sure everyone is pleased.

Pastimes, like avocations and hobbies, can also be abused, providing ways to decrease a person's awareness of unresolved anger, only staving off inevitable bedevilments. What is normally a harmless diversion can become an obsessive alternative to more-obviously seductive behaviors. Music, video games, and spectator sports are particularly prone. Many incredibly talented musicians, athletes and artists have become worshiped progenies not solely out of pursuit of their artistic or athletic passions but from obsessively over-practicing their skills. They have overindulged in their own crafts.

Addictions are rampant in the arts for this reason. If you peek into the early backgrounds of many of the rock stars plagued by alcohol and drug problems, particularly those who self-destructed through alcohol and drug abuse, you invariably discover histories of dysfunctional parenting and patterns of escape, plunging these individuals deep into their passions in compensation.

It is possible to become so focused on one thing that one hones a degree of proficiency that could not normally be developed under better circumstance. Skills can be developed out of obsessive flight from God. Overdeveloped talents and skills are often celebrated as genius, but sometimes they are symptoms of neurosis.

Obsessed, all-encompassing involvement with anything, similar to the way an attention-deficit-disorder sufferer hyper-focuses upon tasks, is antisocial, neurotic behavior. It is the result of a spiritual rebellion that leads to becoming outrageously good at the performance of their obsessive indulgence. One of the most influential musicians ever, Jimi Hendrix, spent a mere three years in the public eye and yet became the greatest electric guitarist in history. Yet no one should become as good a guitar player as Jimi Hendrix became.

If it were not for the need to survive the terror of his home life, if not for having been raised in poverty by abusive, alcoholic parents and sexually molested as a child, little Jimmy Hendrix would have grown up to be just another excellent guitar player.

I assure you that Jimi Hendrix rarely ever really played his guitar as much as his guitar played him. Sports, music, the arts, and many other fields are replete with examples just like this. Those so entrenched into the performing arts rarely ever climb out of the obsessive pit of the mind.

Sometimes a hedge or wedge can be very ***personal*** and hidden: closely held, sometimes done in secret solitude, and not requiring any social interaction at all. They can be done in isolation. Such is the case with our own intellect. Thoughts, yes—streams of imagery found embedded in words, pictures, and sounds inside your own head can be very spellbinding.

This area surely could support an entire book on its own. But you can abuse the power of your own brain. From there emerges fear, projection, and irritants—seemingly out of nowhere. Some become so deeply rapt by the stream of thought, they cannot muster the presence of mind to pause for much-needed emotional rest.

Whatever the category, the anesthetic value of all these human-aid solutions are undeniable and highly overrated. Although these devices certainly have their place, they are most often overused and misused. This happens more often than not as the pain of God-separation continues to mount in the typically unrecovered alcoholic.

The pain eventually catches up and overwhelms, neutralizing whatever positive effect the effort at first seems to provide. Typically, an alcoholic trying to solve his drinking problem will resort to this nonalcoholic buffet, borrowing from some or all categories of these varying devices. Oftentimes their conflicting natures adding to a deadly confusion that guarantees relapse and failure.

The question remains: aside from the continuation of the species, just what is it about a human being that causes him to engage in such activities? These distractions are all devices we will use to manage the load of increasing guilt and pain. They can work for only so long, perhaps many years, until finally we reach a breaking point and attain a level of anesthetic numbness where our self-hypnotic indulgences are no longer able to keep up. Life turns that exact moment from being manageable into unmanageable.

"The light of the body is the eye: if therefore thine eye be single, thy whole body shall be full of light. But if thine eye be evil, thy whole body shall be full of darkness. If therefore the light that is in thee be darkness, how great is that darkness."
- *Matthew 6:22, 23*

11 PLEASURE CENTERS

Just This Side Of Suicide

"*N**o! He can't stir it. Not yet,*" *Betty said. "Look at that chocolate and milk . . . . it's Ying and Yang."*

Gary wanted Willie to stir it immediately, to mix it together, now. The layers of brown and white reminded him of the sand terrarium he made in Sister James's art class a few weeks ago. Instead of layering sands the color of a rainbow, Gary had poured two layers— the bottom black, the top white. Sister James didn't like it much.

"It's a zebra design," he told her.

"Well, zebras have many stripes Mr. Greengrass, but you have only used two." She held the glass up to the light and peered over the rim of her glasses.

"This looks like you put a penguin in a blender," she said.

Willie brought the glass over to the chrome plated seltzer spurting spigot and put it down directly under one large black nozzle. Attached to the top, just above the nozzle was a handle. It stood straight up.

Gary had a non-stop mind this morning. His thoughts careened through him like a runaway subway train barreling through a tunnel; one car after the other passing each station, going faster and faster.

"What's a tree humper?"

"A three pumper!"

Betty's voice seemed far away; from another place or time. It was off somewhere in the distance, like when he and Buddy Bloss made telephones out of paper cups and string.

It seemed to him that she was coming from a dream. A dream inside a cup. It didn't even sound like Betty talking, yet it was her. Most definitely it was.

"What's a three pumper? Why didn't I order a coke? Why won't she answer me? What is a Ying-Yang, anyway?"he thought.

Willie tilted the glass to a precise thirty-seven and a half degree angle and smacked the spigot handle backward. He held it for one and a quarter seconds as a flush of seltzer fizzed in—not directly into the glass. Instead, the bubbling soda hit off the inside wall, rapidly pooling into a sparkling mixture.

Through the side of the glass, Gary could see the ingredients sitting on top of each other like geologic layers of earth; dark, viscous chocolate stuck defiantly to the glass bottom; whole, white milk over it—a tempest of clear seltzer clouding white with milk on top.

"I'd like to put her in a blender...," he thought.

"...and Mr. Greengrass, black and white are not colors. You must not forget your primary colors."

"...and then hold the button down on 'puree' or 'liquefy'."

"Mr. Greengrass, here...look." She stretched one arm toward the window sill. Folds of cloth in the black sleeve of her habit fluttered; rosary beads depended from her side, at the end of them a tiny Jesus rode across her skirts, like he were swinging helplessly from a Six Flags ride gone wild. Out of a colorful row of glasses filled with sand and gravel she grabbed one.

"Here, look at Anthony's terrarium." She held up a striking parfait of rainbow colors in a stemmed glass that was truly beautiful.

"Did a girl make that?" Gary asked.

"No, Anthony Damiano made it. He has exhibited quite a bit more imagination then you have... wouldn't you say Mr. Greengrass?

"Yes sister".

"But you will have a chance to be more creative next time." The nuns voice trailed off in an echo down a hallway inside Gary's head.

Willie drew the lever toward him and instantly clear bubbling seltzer cascaded hard into the glass. He abruptly and purposefully slapped the lever back with a thud! The flow stopped. Then he pulled out a long chrome spoon with a rifled stem and dropped it into the glass. It rang off the side like a bell clapper.

With one hand on the lever and the other holding the spoon, Willie drew the seltzer spigot lever forward for the final rush. Seltzer bounced, first off the spoon, then splashed into the liquid below.

Somewhere half way between three quarters and all-full, Willie slapped the lever back up again.

Gary's eyes widened as Willie's hand began a rapid flourish of spoon that was neither stirring nor was it whipping. It was somewhere in between.

This is a spiritual book, not a scientific one. Nevertheless, we need to talk about the brain a little bit because it is the place where spirit and physiology finally meet—where the human mind and the soul co-mingle currents and essence, constructing what we know to be our total *humanness*.

In the past, alcoholism has been thought to be a weakness of character and immoral behavior. In recent decades, research has increasingly found that obsessive maladies like drug addiction and alcoholism (and other food disorders) are scientific matters of brain chemistry. That may be true to *some* extent and so there is every reason to trust their analyses—but if it is merely a matter of faulty brain chemistry, then what has caused the problem? Why is brain chemistry malfunctioning? *That* they cannot answer because the answer lies beyond scientific scope. Brain imbalances and almost all physical dysfunction is caused by spiritual imbalance. Period.

You are not going to come away from this chapter with a full understanding of brain neurochemistry. Even some extraordinarily smart and educated folks with advanced degrees, who study the human

> **Dopamine Does Not Function Alone.**
>
> *Dopamine is only one of the catecholamines, a particular class of substances produced by your brain and adrenal glands. The best-known catecholamine is epinephrine (What used to be called adrenaline.) Other catecholamines include norepinephrine, metanephrine and normetanephrine. All of these organic compounds work together to direct blood pressure and glucose levels, cardiac function and neurological responses to stress, including fight-or-flight responses. How you respond to all events in your life is directly related to the levels of each of these compounds.*

brain professionally cannot seem to get that properly together. We can at least have a base understanding that will help make some sense out of why we do the things we do; especially the things we do when we don't want to do them. This should be of utmost interest to the alcoholic since it characterizes such a large part of his life.

Our spiritual connectivity is designed to take dominion over the sensual, thinking side of our humanness. Our human design dictates that we should be guided and disciplined through a God-vision, which flows through the conscious individual. It does that *only* when we are free from the "bondage of self." Then we become channels of heaven on earth as it flows through us and onto others.

But s*elf* is a bully. It constantly works to extort and maintain control, rivaling spirit for authority over our actions and behavior. *Self* is a lower nature residing inside, with the intent of interrupting the flow of Gods vision and Spirit into and through us – to thwart heavens coming to earth. In contrast, when are free from the bondage of self, life becomes ordered and we are at peace and ease. Heavenly.

This is a freedom we definitely cannot do without if we are to live a full, useful life doing God's will instead of the will of *Self.*

While attached to *self*, we cannot help but permit Its control over our conduct and intellectual reasoning. We get caught up in the workings of our mind and our thoughts prevail over intuition. Under this intellectual regime, our spirit is squelched and we are left swinging in the wind, subjected to fate, chance and the cruel stresses flowing in the Stream of Life. The whims of those "people, places and things," eat us alive and begin to control us. We become mesmerized by life and our problems seem astonishingly complex and difficult to solve.

Your brain is a physical co-conspirator in this diabolical scheme that along with the traitorous ego, infects us with spiritual disease. Generating thoughts to snare you out of awareness, it places you into a bedeviled, spellbound existence. You become a prisoner of your own brain. That is because all thoughts and all behavior are controlled through the neurological processes of the brain.

The brain is a massive clump of tissue inside your skull that is made of a large group of cells called neurons. Those neurons are all interconnected in a network, comprising the brains portion of the human nervous system. Not only are biological processes controlled here, but so is all conscious and subconscious thought affecting emotions and feelings like love, anger and guilt as well as pain and pleasure.

Please recall from the Chapter on guilt, that guilt-pain is relentless. Naturally, the alcoholic seeks relief. His relief-seeking must be at least as unrelenting, at least as potent as the pain pursuing him lest he experience the deficit. The more pain there is the greater the need for pleasure. It does not remove the pain. During these abusive pursuits, the feeling of pleasure masks the pain.

In sound masking, undesirable noise can be neutralized by transmitting "opposite" sounds where frequencies cover-up but do not eliminate an objectionable sound. Likewise, pain stemming from God-separation can be ignored through the issue of pain's masking counterpart: *Pleasure.* The concealing of pain by issuing the "white noise" of pleasure, generated through neurotransmitter brain processes, most notably dopamine, seems to be the antidote. As in this *sound* example, pain being the undesirable condition, is merely overridden. Pain and its source remain unaffected and as vital as ever while we receive emotional gratification for an unseen, subconscious purpose—to anesthetize the conscience of painful guilt.

The anesthesia is always available. The alcoholic, or anyone suffering from the guilt of playing God, finds relief through his own private apothecary, located inside the brain – specifically, a wonderful little place called the Nucleus Accumbens, which houses the human apparatus we call the Pleasure Center. Like CVS, it is always open with a pharmacist on duty, 24/7.

Here are the reward pathways. It is a neuro-circuit board to which the alcoholic learns he has easy access. The potential for abuse is enormous as this takes the pleasure neurotransmitter chemicals beyond their naturally intended purpose: *Human survival and the continuation of the species.*

Dopaminergic substances, activities and experiences fall into two categories both necessary for human life – food and sex. God wants us to reproduce and he wants us to have the fuel to do it. We can't spend all our days having sex and eating food. (Although some of us have managed to establish lifestyles that seem to contain more and more of each.) If we did, our lives would become too unsightly; too unmanageable. In time, we would be obese sex fiends unable to do much more than stuff our gross bodies with satisfying sugars and carbohydrates, *sexing* until we drop.

Transmitter dopamine is a key element that provides the reward "pleasure." The more dopamine, the greater the pleasure. The reward we get through this circuitry of axons and neuro-wiring is the sensation of pleasure—given in exchange for helping God expand His creation, for without sex and the energy to do it, the human race would not continue beyond our immediate lifetimes.

Just what causes us to pursue this most natural behavior? Chemistry! The brain's pharmacist on duty stands ready to dispense the most sought after drug in the store: Dopamine.

This Nucleus Accumbens is very closely associated with another area of the brain called the ventral tagmental area (VTA). It is here that dopamine is synthesized and then sent to the Nucleus Accumbens. Connecting these two areas of the brain is a network of *wires*—a bundle of axons serving as the pathway for the neurotransmitters. Eight such pathways comprise the complete reward circuitry needed to transmit euphoric sensations, even a general sense of wellbeing. In the case of alcohol, this sensational conveyance is done through two chief neurotransmitters, dopamine and GABBA. *I say chief transmitters because there are many others too.*

Simply defining these euphoria-producing neurotransmitters does not really do the two substances much justice. There is a lot more to know, but for our purposes, this is enough.

With each neuron connecting with all of the other neurons at tiny connection points or junctions called *synapses,* a circuitry forms. The synapse represents a break in the circuitry; that break is called a synaptic canal. In order for the signal to jump the canal, the connection needs to be made across and that is done through the neurotransmitter completing the circuit so that the communication between neurons occurs.

Dopamine is stored in the nerve terminals, inside fatty bubbles called vesicles. These tiny bubbles wait until a nerve impulse of electricity comes shooting down the pre-synaptic neuron, sending the vesicle to the inside-edge of the cell wall where it releases its dopamine into the canal. Once released, dopamine crosses the synaptic canal, fastens onto a postsynaptic neuron receptor at the other side, causing it to fire. Bam! You feel good. It becomes a primary neurotransmitter that also activates other neurons. In binding to the other neuron receptor, its presence (or absence) either completes or severs the connection.

When dopamine neurotransmitters are doing the job they have been sent to do, inciting your pleasurable feelings, they cling to a receptor for a few microseconds. Then they are released and picked up by neat little mechanisms called reuptake pumps that pull the little buggers out of the canal, shipping them back to where they came from. There they wait to be reused. It's the ultimate recycling plant. It is all quite an amazing and complex process that we are only just beginning to understand.

Another name scientists have for this nervy little network is "Reward Bundle." Why *reward*? Well, a reward is a "prize" you receive in exchange for some performance. This ties into motivating you into performing some action. You carry out an action

> ## What Every Coke Fiend Loves
>
> *When you take cocaine, it isn't the "blow" that makes you feel euphoric. The only effect the drug really has is to block the functioning of neurotransmitter reuptake pumps by sitting on them. That is when dopamine that has been released into the synaptic canal accumulates. When these are not pulled out of the synapse for recycling, they pool, causing the cell to fire and fire and fire—for way longer duration than they are supposed to. Cocaine will sit there for an hour or two causing a big accumulation of dopamine, extending its effect on the body functions, the first being feeling of pleasure and wellbeing. That is what every coke fiend loves – pleasure, and the elusive sensation that all is well and life is good. That is why so many alcoholics also become users of chemical stimulants like cocaine.*

with the hope of receiving the prize. (If there were no prize, your self-centeredness might prevent you from even doing it.)

That's roughly how the pleasure center works. At least so far that's how we *think* it works. The study and the understanding of the

176

subject is still in its infancy. By the time you read this there undoubtedly will be even more information available, but considering how limited our brains are in comparison with God's creation, this fair approximation will do for now.

The central idea to remember is that *dopamine-generated pleasure sensations become elevated, creating the obsession to perform actions that are normally reserved for simple survival; sex and food are the main ones.*

This understanding begs a couple of questions. First, what is it that creates the need to seek pleasure? But also, why do some people obsessively seek to access the reward circuits of their brains while others seem to get by well enough with much lower levels of pleasure stimulation? The answers to these lie in spirituality – not in physiology.

The lower we go on the scale of human spirituality, the more dopaminergic activities we will tend to weave into our personal lifestyles. Some of these may not be attractive. To avoid embarrassment we keep some of these activities in secret or at least limit them to avoid personal, negative "publicity". Most people do not have too much difficulty maintaining access to chemicals like nicotine, caffeine and in some social circles, cocaine or other recreations drugs—all of which are shortcuts to the pleasure center, bypassing the need for awkward anti-social activities. They help to short-circuit all of the complications that go along with excessive, overindulging in the food and sex categories.

There is always some base level of dopamine being produced in our bodies, no matter how minimal, just to feel normal. The ideal level renders us feeling neutral about any given situation.

There is currently no way to reliably measure the levels of dopamine since these neurotransmitters are constantly changing from second to second in response to encounters in the Stream of Life.

But there have been studies performed on our fine furry friends, lab rats. Scientists have also established what they believe to be normal dopaminergic values, sampling the amount of the substance that can be measured in urine over a 24-hour period. With 65 - 400 micrograms (mcg)/24 hours being within normal parameters, it is thought that the base level for the average human being to feel normal is about 300 units. (For the purposes of discussion in this book, a "unit" equals 1 microgram as measured through a urine test) Anything over 400 units is attributed to overstimulation and much under 100 would be considered dangerously low.[40]

According to the boys with the clipboards and the white coats, (and the rat cages) alcohol causes a 1-200 unit (mcg/24 hours) release of dopamine—pretty much the same as nicotine. If you need a bigger rush than that, then cocaine will do the trick, kicking it up to a 350-unit dose. Methamphetamine will get users an incredible 1250 unit shot of dopamine. We are talking about some *serious* pain squelching here. Morphine is 200 units, about the same as an orgasm. These represent unit doses above preexisting, normal levels necessary for ordinary human living.

> **Work hard – Play hard.**
>
> *When I worked on Wall Street, many brokers and traders drank, did drugs and frequented strip clubs – often with the attitude that they had earned the privilege. We really thought we needed these pleasures as a justifiable counterbalance to the stress we endured during the day in the high-pressured securities business. This may seem a reasonable assumption, but what about those who do not work so hard and yet still have the same need for prurient recreation. Where does that need come from? It comes from somewhere, and it does not always come from the stresses of a high-pressured business lifestyle.*

When we mess with the base dopamine levels—or when we allow others, such as doctors, to pharmaceutically tinker with our equilibrium level of dopamine in order to control feelings and behaviors, then we are tampering with things not fully understood.

Some limited physiologic understanding exists; but clinicians and other secular professionals do not appreciate the spiritual ramifications. Artificial manipulation represents damaging interference with ancient, spiritual corollary that will be difficult if not impossible to later correct.

Pleasurable neurotransmission within the food and sex reward pathways are necessary for the continuation of the species and are

---

[40]According to laboratory standards published by MedlinePlus. http://www.nlm.nih.gov/medlineplus/ency/article/003561.htm

most often the first and most abused. Eating is usually more accessible than sex and therefore eating is the first activity to be misused. The foods most often abused are sugar and alcohol. Both are very effective dopamine boosters. *(In addition to their drinking problems, most alcoholics also suffer from grave eating disorders.)*

You might think that you love Hagen Das Chocolate ice cream. You might think that you enjoy sex. You may even believe that a good deep-tissue back massage or that moving Sunday church sermons are soothing events for the soul, but it is not true. None of these activities actually make you feel good. When you associate good feelings with activities and behaviors, it appears as though you become fixated to that activity for the sake of its continuance. But what is *really* floating your boat is the biochemical activity just described; the biochemistry occurring in your brain as the *result* of engagement. It isn't the activity itself.

Each indulgence does essentially the same thing inside your brain by writing a little prescription for that dopamine. You might think you like a wild orgasm and a gulp of gin but it is the dopaminergic reaction inside, to which you have learned to associate with those activities that you *really* find so delectable and pleasing.

It does not take that much to get a little dosing either. A pleasant memory, say a vision of little lambs and green pastures to a sublimely blissful orgasm and everything in-between, all have corresponding dopaminergic values.

A kiss, a pat on the back, a compliment; a dose of Beethoven, Metallica, a moving piece of poetry or viewing a magnificent oil painting can all help produce dopamine, the true *drug of choice*. We want it because it is dopamine that delivers the therapeutic feeling we want, *pleasure* that mimics the absence of pain by drowning it out (never eliminating it). Multiply and eat! Eat so you can multiply. Then multiply so your species never dies out—and feel wonderful doing it.

Scientists believe that the reason dopaminergic substances, events and behaviors are "addictive" is that ... *uhmm, they don't know.* They can tell you the obvious, that you *want* to keep doing it, but they cannot tell you *why* you want to keep doing it.

They will use words like "satiety," "expectation," "conditioning" and "reinforcement," and conduct studies addressing these topics, accumulating data, pronouncing unsupported corollaries and arriving at some reasonable conclusions. But this reasoning still falls short and despite much studying, scientists still cannot arrive at the "Why?" this happens. This only raises more questions they cannot answer. Why do you expect pleasure? Why are you conditioned? Why can you not be satiated? Why do you keep repeating the dopaminergic behaviors?

Is it only because it *feels* good? Yes, but why do you keep seeking to feel good? Why are some people able to have a glass of wine once or twice a week over a fine meal and never become alcoholics? Why is someone who has been prescribed opiates to help manage surgical pain, or someone who got high on grass a few times in college not destroyed by alcoholism or drug addiction? For that matter, why can some folks indulge in a giant hot fudge Sundae once in a blue moon and not become addicted, food obsessed gourmands.

Something must be must be going on for some people, that is not going on for others; something outside of the realm of physiology; something mystical—spiritual. When you meditate properly, as I will show you, you will begin to see just what this is. You will discover why, despite all effort, you have never been able to solve your own problems. This will be revealed to you without me or any human being spoiling the power of discovery by forcing you to learn what it is.[41]

The study of the brain, the neurology and biochemistry involved, is enormous. The most authoritative, scientific minds can hardly be blamed for knowing so little. They can barely keep up with each other as new discoveries constantly dispel assumptions derived out of past findings. It is incredibly complex.

Doctors are always presenting varying theories about physiological causes of alcoholism, drug abuse and vulnerability as they try to construct a full dimensional picture of just what alcoholism

---

[41] Please visit the "How To Get There," page in the back of this book for fast access to the meditation exercise. It is available for streaming or download. It is free and always will be.

and addiction is—or to explain how it progresses. They are wasting their time. They are wasting everyone's time.

It is a field where yesterdays understanding is continually being challenged by new discoveries. Trying to wrap ones head around the contradictory and oftentimes convoluted data science generates out of their study of the human brain is an exercise in never-ending futility. So it is not difficult to see why even your doctor's training barely provides him with enough understanding or information to generate much more than talking points.

Their efforts might do well if substance abuse were solely a physiological problem. The problems of addiction to any substance-- any behavior, begins with spiritual disease. Alcoholism and addiction are merely *symptoms* of spiritual disease—not a disease itself.

The closer a scientist gets to the truth, the closer his investigation brings him to finding God – a discovery that every died in the wool intellectual must avoid, or else admit, deep within his humanity, that it isn't him.

And so everything we find when looking up the physiology of the brain is laced with noncommittal phrases like, "suggest that" or "finding indicate" – even "we don't know for sure, but . . ." You would think that adjuncts such as these would be far too ambiguous for the scientific mind; but even the scientist has a personal spirituality with which he was born. Covered in layers of intellectuality, self-importance and rote knowledge, he finds it difficult to reconcile God with *self* because it means the deflation of ego.

Albert Einstein rode the wave of his discoveries toward the heavens in a way resulting in his standing humbly in wonderment of a Creator – while Steven Hawkins, discontent with the very same discovery that he is not God, ambitiously sets out to uncover evidence that he is. Can you now see why some scientists become more God conscious while others, cherishing their own intellects more than God Himself, only become increasingly resentful of their own ignorance?

Have you ever heard the expression, "Heart over mind"? Spiritual intuition arcs into the physically neurological side found in 'thinking', but it can't happen unless we sit still long enough to let it catch up. Devotionals don't do that. Affirmations don't do it. Mantras don't do it. These mental devices hinder intuition because, as with the over-studious, overly intellectual scientist, they help him erect walls of thought that only block the Sunlight of the Spirit – God's vision – grace, term it however you like.

Only sitting still, allowing conscience, God's loving judgment to catch up will do it. The very special meditation exercise to which I am introducing you through this book allows a psychic arc over from the outer spiritual realm, some call heaven, into the inner spiritual psyche where God can govern life and will. This is the meditative experience and the only purpose meditation serves.

No matter how beautiful or seemingly profound, whenever we latch onto the thoughts in our head, it is for the purpose of hiding from the pain of the truth that we have played God. Attachments to thought hinders the wordless, thought-free, God-vision that manifests as intuition—never as thought. It is the interminable force of guilt, that pain of conscience, which compels the alcoholic out of his natural conscious and aware state and into his brain-hell where he becomes trapped.

The crack addict who is "stuck" sitting on the floor of a crack house for days at a time, while his family frantically searches for him, until his bank account has been depleted, his jewelry and car gone, parallels what goes on inside the mind of the alcoholic. Once locked into the prison of obsessive thinking, this behavior must continue, no matter what the personal or social consequences, until conscience ceases its pursuit. It does not. This is why human behavior under siege of full-blown alcoholism is so baffling.

If left to their own devices *all* alcoholics will eventually find some way to escape guilty conscience from catching up with them – yes, even to the point of killing themselves. Death by alcohol is not usually intentional, but it is frequent enough to call it a common side effect of alcoholism. That is not to say that premeditation is at all uncommon. Many alcoholics end up in such states of pain that their only release from such torturous bind is had through suicide. Suicide, the deliberate and final relief, is a solution that works. Dead men do not drink. They also do not think. There is no longer a need for them to do either once the dark side wins.

Still, just *short* of suicide, there are *substitute* solutions, which the alcoholic has not yet exhausted. The next chapter explores the mechanics of how he manages to access some of these and not kill himself—buying some time—at least for a while. If you haven't already guessed, we are getting around to talking about *obsession*.

There is *what* happens. There is *how* it happens. There is also *why* it happens. *What* and *How* things happen have only limited values and while these can be studied, analyzed and argued—reasoning still does not change anything. It is only through understanding *why*, that we see the root of a problem and can move toward a solution instead of speculation and theorizing. You see, the cause of alcoholism is spiritual in nature, and by learning *why*, we get to appreciate the course of the spiritual answer.

There is a lot to know on this subject and we have only peeked at as much as we need to see right now for the purposes of understanding the need for meditation. Trying to wrap ones head around the contradictory and often confusing scientific data regarding the brain and the effect alcohol has is very difficult. One day I will write a more exhaustive study but right now, I am happy to stick with scientific descriptions using a layman's narrative to allude to some highly scientific stuff, lest my own brain sizzle and fry into a disintegrating puff of smoke as I write.

"I don't do drugs. I am drugs." – *Salvador Dali*

12 ALCOHOLIC OBSESSION

The Pursuit Of Equilibrium

If you will recall, it was mentioned in the previous chapter that guilt is an inexorable, unrelenting force. It is as universal a force as is gravity, light, love or hate. The truth about what resentment is should also be becoming clear to you. As it turns out, resentment is not what you may have supposed it is. It is not merely some natural, human feeling generated from within. It is a universal, cosmic force which gets inside, invading the psyche, every time you unwittingly allow Self to feed upon it.

Whereas resentment is a cosmic force for evil, guilt is a lifesaving force for good. As the result of playing God, vis-à-vis resentment-fueled judgment, we sense the pursuing pain of guilt through our conscience. This unshakably ferocious "hound of heaven"[42] is always nipping at our heels, compelling us to find solutions through the pleasure center's reward circuitry buried deep in our skulls. When we apply alcohol, it invokes the neurotransmitter anesthetics of the brain to override feelings of guilt. It does not eliminate guilt or the source of it, but it squelches the consciousness of its pain.

We experience relief when we drink. Through the numbing characteristic of alcohol, an effect most men and women chase even when it is not attained through alcohol, we become ignorant of the hound chasing us, believing the pursuit has been called off. It is no wonder that people from all walks—alcoholic, non-alcoholic, or potential alcoholic—like to drink.

---

[42]The "Hound of Heaven" is a 182-line poem written by English poet Francis Thompson (1859-1907) depicting an ancient spiritual and psychological metaphor representing God's hunt for the souls of men hiding from truth.

The discomfort of guilty conscience does not cause itself—it is an effect. Whenever we drink, eat, study, work or even pray to arrest pain, we only forestall the inevitable.

Once you have been violated with resentment, its negative emotional energy becomes something we call judgment. Now being the *judge*, you are playing God. Since there is only one God (and it isn't you), you have separated your being from the one true God in order to play the role yourself. Presently you feel guilt—the pain that automatically comes out of being a fake God. You subconsciously see the guilt as the problem needing to be fixed. To find relief, you need to access the pleasure mechanism of your brain. There are many ways to do this, but food and sex pretty much head up the two categories.

If you decide, for example, to use sugar, it will produce the necessary biochemical brain stimuli to anesthetize the subconscious pain of guilt. *Krispy Kreme, baby! Here we come!* With your donuts come obscene carbohydrates, and that means plenty of rewarding dopamine—your *real* "drug of choice." Now you find you are also unconsciously moved toward consuming more and more bread, pasta, and other sweets, packing on more and more weight. Every dose of sugar does indeed solve your pain problem, but since the guilt is relentless, you must refresh the dosage over and over again—hence the repetitiveness that we can observe as *addiction*.

If you knew the true nature of resentment, and if you knew what your ego really was, you would realize that doctors, addictions counselors, psychologists and the like cannot help you. Even ministers, theologians, mystics, fellowships and spiritual movements will fall short. Many of these can only teach you new ways to suppress your anger. If they really wanted you to be free of anger, they would lead you to God. Then you would be free of them, too.

You now obsess over sweets and foods, because failure to eat sugar means experiencing pain—the conflict created by your original resentment setting the whole hellish train in motion.

Alcoholism is not the cause of the alcoholic's troubles; it is an effect—just one possible syndrome of symptoms that indicates "spiritual disease." Attempts to treat effects rather than looking at their causes never fails to allow matters to worsen. This is why classifying alcoholism as a disease is so dangerous.

Such attempts result in little more than brief solutions, for they will fail to nip the problem at its beginning. And so we develop a daily grind—wrought, from beginning to end, with pain-relieving activities, all carefully orchestrated to ensure that the Royal Majesty, us, is not inconvenienced.

Soon our only measure for a good day is by how free from personal nuisance and displeasure we feel or how well others have served us, whether or not they have avoided our disdain by not interfering with our plans.

We will praise God for such days, and bemoan when we feel He has slacked in His Godly duty to supply us with happiness, serenity, or whatever other sensations we feel we deserve.

If an alcoholic could reserve major drunken episodes and the negative consequences of a spree solely for major traumas like divorce, job losses, and other big disappointments, then life would be manageable. Of course, for the alcoholic that would also mean managing alcohol consumption—something every real alcoholic must come to see he cannot do. Sprees would be a breeze. Counterbalancing pain with pleasure is the prime object of an alcoholic's life, and under such conditions, he would be able to do it.

The problem for the real alcoholic is that new pains only mount on top of the old, even after applying alcohol. Each new drunken episode solves nothing. New problems continue to build upon the ever-increasing load; the sum of an ever-growing negative inventory of resentments, fears and harms.

Any means to abate discomfort never amounts to more than a temporary cover-up. The moment we let up on the booze-switch (stop drinking), the tenacity of God's pursuing love is revealed and it's very special agony resumes. It is only through continual refreshment of gratifications, like drinking again, that the alcoholic finds relief from the constant reminder of his inner conflict.

Please do not think for a second that this degradation of humanness need be a long, complicated process. It is not. It takes only a moment, but in that instant, hate has caused you to go from *fit* to *fatty* or *drinker to drunk*.

This is one reason why eating and sex disorders are more stubborn than alcohol or drug addictions. Unless you get to the original cause, which means dealing with your resentment problem, you will struggle for the rest of your life with food (or sex). You cannot abstain from eating and so dieting, willfully controlling intake, will only further exasperate the *battle of the bulge,* inducing still more resentment as you get fatter and fatter. If you have ever wondered why diets do not work very well, now you know.

This is what those who struggle their entire lives with a weight problem go through, often bringing on food-related illnesses like diabetes, cardiovascular diseases, and even certain cancers. Believing that their problem is food, they go through life struggling with dieting and a futile attempt to control appetite—lust for food, really. This doesn't work. What they really need to find is not freedom from food, but freedom from anger. Then all lust falls away, even the obsessive desire for eating. Anger creates abnormal desire, and there is no such thing as an obese person who is not full of anger.

This is also exactly what happens to the alcoholic. Instead of sugar and carbohydrates, he has discovered that alcohol, also a food, will serve the same purpose (without so quickly adding much weight). He will abuse it in order to deal with the pain of his judgment and will at some point irreversibly cross a *line* into chronic alcoholism, just the same as a sugar abuser can cross the line into type II diabetes. He has begun to treat his guilty conscience by blotting out the pain—accessing alcohol-food as one selection on the smorgasbord table of dopaminergic actions.

This is not a very healthy way of dealing with problems, is it?

The only hope to truly break free from this pain-pleasure cycle is to reduce the need for pleasure by being saved from pain. The only way to do that is to reestablish the lost bond with God. When we awaken, we do just that. To awaken you will need to practice being very still, very objective, and very observant of your own thoughts and temptation to hate or love and judge. There is only one way to do that. It is to meditate in a very special way.

Faced with the daunting task of setting aside his prejudice toward spirituality, the alcoholic will always face doubt. While a spiritual awakening is necessary for durable recovery, it is not uncommon for a person in early sobriety to ask, "Why should I go through it?" For him this seems to be such a tall order. It is. It's dammed tall.

Getting honest is the hardest thing a dishonest person will ever have to do, yet without it he will never know peace. Something inside quivers in fear at the prospect of facing itself, of losing It's stranglehold and power over the alcoholic's twisted thinking and immoral, antisocial behaviors. But as long as he remains attached to the sinister *Thing*, the alcoholic will still think it is him. It isn't him. Breaking the ties he has to the Self will expose him to the truth – knowing what he has become.

I am going to tell you something that I have told many people in helping them overcome their alcoholism.

I tell them of a man—a man who right now *is sitting in a bar. The bar is not closed, but it is only four in the afternoon, and so it is uncrowded. He sits alone. His head is down on the bar. He isn't passed out, just wiped out. He has been wearing the same clothes for couple of days now and smells a bit. His wife has no idea where he is. He has missed work. The last anyone has heard from him was when he left a message on his wife's voicemail telling her he was on his way home. That was Tuesday. Today is Thursday. Now his wife sits wondering where he is. She is sitting at the kitchen table, her eyes red and swollen from countless hours of crying. Is he dead or alive? Is he passed out in a downtown alleyway or lying in some urine stained subway stairwell, robbed, stabbed, and bleeding? Has he got into an accident? Should I call 911? Is he cheating on me? The couple's daughter, maybe six, seven, or ten years old, it doesn't matter, asks "Mommy, where's Daddy?"*

"I don't know, honey," she says.

"He's been gone for so long."

This little girl is beginning to hate her father. Her bitterness grows and before long it will ripen into anger toward Daddy. Hatred will become the food for a developing self-entity inside her. She will repress it for many years. The struggle will steal her consciousness, dragging her into her own head to wonder. Eventually this uncertainty will commandeer her thought-stream entirely, turning into daydreams and fantasies—an unrealistic dream world from which she will find it impossible to break free. Anxious, she will find it difficult to concentrate on her schoolwork and although once an honor roll A student, now she will barely find the patience to scrape through grade school. She will enter high school resenting even having to attend. As she matures into womanhood, she will project her acquired bitterness toward Daddy onto all men. It will affect every relationship she ever has. Her thirst for control will drive all decent men away from her, while drawing users to her like flies to honey.

Imprinted deep in her mind is the suppressed memory of how Daddy hurt Mommy, how he made her cry, how his behaviors—his lack of patient, manly love for his wife and family and the conditions created in the home—have sucked all the fun out of living, replacing what were once carefree child-years with into days filed with worry, fear, depression, and anxiety. By the time she is fifteen, she will have already found some solution to these stresses, some of her own "wedges and hedges." She will even seek to compensate through chemical and social solutions. By her sixteenth birthday she will have already smoked cigarettes and become a periodic cannabis smoker. She will have discovered how easy it is to override her naturally protective inhibitions and will have no problem with fellating boys on movie dates. In order to get their approval, she will regularly allow men to use her body for their own gratification. It will have become easy to mistake their need to overcome their own problems as love for her. By the time she is eighteen, she will move out of the house—pregnant and worn, and she will move in with her boyfriend, a twenty-year-old who is too self-absorbed to marry her, and for whom she already has repressed deep resentments. This father who has sired her baby makes enough money to valiantly or reluctantly pay for Pampers and baby formula. But within a year or two, he will move out and move on—to another, more "fun," understanding woman. And all of this will happen unless her daddy, that man who is slumped at the bar right now, with his head down, gets a tap on the shoulder, lifts his head, and sees you—a recovered alcoholic who holds an answer to all his problems. If not— then everything I just said happens. But if he does discover you, and if you can get his attention and present the answer you have found, then none of it happens.

189

That is what I tell him. And now I tell you this:

Right now, while you are reading this very page, someone is sitting at the edge of a bed tearfully looking up to the heavens and crying, "Oh God, why did he do it again?" For ages, wives, husbands, sons, and daughters of alcoholics whose lives are torn apart, their hearts broken and their own sanity in ruins, have asked this question. Precious few have been presented with the answer, and for those who have heard it, even fewer have embraced it. Alcoholics themselves have tossed their own clarity of thought and awareness aside to crawl into the abyss of their own minds, cowering in shame and horror. "Why ... oh, why ... oh, why?" wails through their heads. Even after seeking clinical help, following medically supervised detoxification—after all the alcohol has been drained out of his body with no chance of craving or need to mitigate the effects of withdrawal—despite all the misery and horror it brings upon him, why does the alcoholic still drink again? Emotionally rubbed raw from repeated episodes, loved ones finally ask, "What happened to the person I married—to the beautiful son or daughter we brought into the world and raised? Is it my fault? Doesn't he love me enough to stop?" Finally, one of the most humanly distressing cries, rises up: "God, are you punishing me?"

Standard recovery methods, even those espousing vestiges of spirituality in the mix, venture to provide some answers to questions like these. Some of their theories are accurate, to a degree—but they are not accurate enough. Often, the answer to the question, "Why doesn't he just stop?" recklessly blames something called *obsession*. I say "recklessly" not because it isn't true, but because of the cavalier usage of the word without much understanding as to the true nature and origin of human obsessions.

To the classically trained clinician, an *obsession* is a recurring, distressing idea, thought, or impulse that feels "foreign" or alien to the individual. According to the *Gales Encyclopedia of Medicine*, anxiety disorders and obsessive-compulsive disorders are all obsessions. These ideas sound about right, but they do not explain much.

It is true the alcoholic *is* obsessed. His drinking certainly *is* insane behavior. But what is *obsession* really? Just as experts do not know what *resentment* is—they also do not know *why* obsessive human behaviors develop. They only know that they do. That is why they cannot cure mental illnesses or help an alcoholic recover from alcoholism.

In 1956, the American Medical Association made its proclamation regarding alcoholism. They decided it was a disease, fitting five criteria: a pattern of symptoms, chronicity, progression, subject to relapse and treatability. What a brilliant move—sort of like a *National Hammer Association* declaring that all "screws" shall now be called "nails". Never mind that a screw will be ruined by a hammer when hit with one.

Doctors are skilled in establishing massive amounts of academic nomenclature, giving names to physiological bases for disease. But in the field of alcoholism, these professionals fail to construct a full dimensional picture of just what alcoholism and addiction is or how it progresses. In skirting the spiritual dimension, they do not even come close to discovering the real solution that works.

That is because alcoholism isn't a disease. It is a simple syndrome of symptoms that are the *effects* of a disease, a spiritual one, for which they have no solution. And it frustrates the hell out of them. They are so close, they can smell it.

Modern medicine has never once, in any case, ever cured one single person of alcoholism; nor has a clinical approach ever caused an alcoholic to recover. Yet how many alcoholics over the last several thousands of years of human existence have awakened spiritually and crawled out of their cups without the help of an addictions specialist, clinician, or psychologist? Millions. How haughty, then, it is to conclude that recovery from alcoholism is not possible.

When I was about ten years old, I developed a horrible red, itchy rash on one of my fingers. My entire ring finger was scaled and painfully irritated. My mother brought me to a doctor who gave me a prescription for a cortisone cream and told me I had *dermatitis*. "Oh ... dermatitis! What is it? What causes it?" It would be helpful to know, right? But there were no further explanations. The condition had been given a name and that would have to be good enough. And for then it was. I received my cream, applied it, and within a week or so, I was "cured." I relapsed many times over the next ten years, but at least I *did* have a name for the recurring condition. I also had a handy prescription for a skin cream to refill every once in a while.

A quizzical kid, I went to the local library, did some research and found out that *derma* means *skin* and *itus* just means inflamed. This was my first inkling as to just how smart doctors *really* are.

The doctor came to the brainy conclusion that this boy with a skin inflammation was suffering from a condition known as—get ready for it—"SKIN INFLAMMATION!" Brilliant! For this, you need a three-hundred-thousand-dollar student loan?

Years went by, and, growing into my teens, I developed what my mother diagnosed as a "nervous stomach." I would know hours and hours of painful, episodic diarrhea and public embarrassment. Finally, when I was seventeen someone would think to stick a periscope up my butt and see what the problem was. "By *Jove! He's got*"—are you ready?—"colitis." That's right: *colon inflammation.* What sleuthing! No shortage of intellectual brilliance here; and yet no one would ever come close to discovering a cause or to prescribe and effective remedy (other than a three-times-a-day cocktail of benzodiazepines and Metamucil). That is because despite having a name for it, they didn't really know what was wrong with me. What they *did* know was that by tapping a Latin dictionary they could bury their ignorance in etymology, presenting the appearance of knowledge and training. It's phony medicine, and it's still prevalent today among those in the "healing" professions. It cannot be helped, really. (The real cause of my colitis was left untreated and brought me to near-death years later.)

If someone came to you with, say, an eye that was red, bloodshot and oozing fluid, how smart would you sound if you said, "I know what it is!" making the pronouncement, *"Oculitus!"* Ooh!

(I am reminded of the Wizard of Oz speaking to Tin Man: "Back where I come from, there are men who do nothing all day but good deeds. They are called phil ... er ... er ... phil ... er, yes ... good-deed-doers." Ahh! Now we have an official title! How... official!)

Intellectuals have a nasty habit of appearing smart by merely identifying problems, giving effects names without much more to offer than that. Causes and solutions escape when they do this. This practice is a far cry from understanding *why* these problems occur. Without understanding, there will be little motivation to seek true answers, because only the hopelessness that comes from seeing how truly impossible our situation is can move a person toward accepting the drastic solution necessary. Alcoholics are helped little by knowing they have an obsession. They will be helped better when they know what is the cause of that obsession and how it might be removed. The problem is that not everyone *wants* to be sane. They just want to manipulate their obsessions, making them manageable.

Isn't this what you have been learning all along in this book: that unconsciousness is tantamount to insanity? No alcoholic draws a sane breath as long as he lives within the sometimes dark, frequently colorful recesses of his imagination—where thoughts keep him from ever seeing the truth about the present or the past.

It is good and necessary to identify and establish a name for a condition, such as "mental obsession." Labels are useful in organizing approaches to describing the conditions—but it is better to know *why*.

I have worked in several major rehabilitation and treatment facilities. Most of the clients whom I dealt with on a daily basis where not there for the first time. Very many had been through multiple facilities multiple times. "Retreads," they call themselves, and "frequent flyers." Whatever the term, alcoholics drink again despite being fully detoxed beyond the physical urge to drink. So why is it then that despite all the misery and pain, despite that every chemical reason to drink has been drained out of their bodies, do they do it again? This is because alcoholic recidivism is not only physical.

Crossing the line is a common term heard in recovery circles, and it refers to someone who has been repeatedly abusing alcohol but who has reached a physical point from where there is no return, where any amount of alcohol whatsoever will kick off a craving in the body. It is when the body's ability to metabolize alcohol has been so unusually compromised that the irreparable harm done cannot be reversed. From then on, he will crave alcohol every time it enters him. It doesn't matter if it is hidden in foods, diluted with water, injected, swallowed— on purpose or accidently. It does not matter if he can taste it or even if he can feel its effect. If it gets in him, he is going to crave more. It is as if his body screams for it.

There is another "line" the alcoholic crosses. It is not a physical line. It is a mental line. The line, once crossed, guarantees the commencement of obsession as he enters a certain mode of attitude guaranteeing unsound bondage to his lower self for as long as he remains subject to this insanity. He will be subjected to his obsessive need for relief before all else, even before God. This is not his body looking for more alcohol. It is his mind steering him toward quenching the pain in his soul.

The cofounders of *Alcoholics Anonymous* referred to the alcoholic's obsession as a "mental blank spot." What is a mental blank spot but unconsciousness? Consciousness means the elimination of mental blank spots. The "strange mental blank spot" cannot occur when a person is spiritually fit, awake, aware, and conscious. It just is not possible.

This repetitive mitigation of guilt keeps pain and pleasure balanced, so the alcoholic can live with a facsimile of sanity and maintain appearances. "I got my shit together," he thinks. This continuous cycle of action, beyond our conscious control, is what society terms *addiction*. It is the way *the guilty* can maintain balance.

Maintaining this equilibrium eventually becomes the main object of the alcoholic's life. Anything that becomes the main object of a life is an obsession. He seeks a very special kind of mindlessness, one that is in response to pain and is a method of escaping from the guilt brought on by playing God. The alcoholic who is dependent upon this in order to live with ease and comfort looses a piece of his mind as he forces counterfeit *peace of mind* he knows he does not deserve—and so he becomes a slave to whatever courses of action or substances he can incorporate into his life. It is a drinking lifestyle common to *all* alcoholics in *all* walks of life.

An alcoholic who has recovered from alcoholism, and who meditates properly, using the exercise I am presenting to you in this book, will not be able to abuse alcohol, ever again.

His obsession lifts. It will never return for as long as he maintains the God-conscious state, which this meditation helps him establish. It will not matter how many meetings, he goes to—how many sponsors he has, how much coffee he makes or how much service work he does for any organization. He will be useful, sober and awakened, independent of anyone's measure of how he is doing. Yes, he may show up in an AA meeting, and he may carry a spiritual message to others; he may show up praying in church or working at a soup kitchen, he may write checks to charities—but none of that is any of your or my business. That is an affair between him and his Creator. What he *will* be is a happily whole and useful human being who can raise a strong family, be an example to others, and hold a God-given power to help other alcoholics regardless of anyone's estimation of how he ought to go about it. He will be a conductor for God's will and vision on earth— as it is in Heaven.

So the answer to the question in the beginning of this chapter ("Why does he do it again?") is easily answered. Equilibrium must be maintained in order to feel right. That balance occurs in the place in the alcoholic's psyche, where pleasure rises at least to the point where it matches the pain. If accessing the pleasure centers in the reward circuitry of the brain is how to reach equilibrium, then obsessive behavior is the way to maintain that balance; where pleasure is accessed to continually mask unrelenting pain. When pursuing God-consciousness is no longer painful, this pain becomes a "good" guilt and we will have truly recovered from our spiritual malady—able to walk in the Sunlight of the Spirit of God.

". . . the multitude of persons who exhibit misbehavior conduct through faulty upbringing or complexes, who are oppressed by a sense of humiliation or inferiority because of unfriendly or disapproving associates or because of some physical defect, and find that a few drinks enable them to consider themselves the equals of any or even superior to all others, are not to be classed as chronic alcoholics merely because they indulge in alcohol regularly." - Dr. William G. Silkworth – "Alcoholism as a Manifestation of Allergy," Medical Record (March 17, 1937)

13 GOING FORWARD

Awake and Aware

Gary's eyes widened as Willie's spoon spun. Was it stirring? Was is whipping? It was too fast to be either. It was something else.

"Willie is no ordinary soda jerk," thought Gary. "Holy Moly . . . he's an artist."

Whirling the spoon with swordsman-like skill, Willie chopped and whipped; beating in and out, up and down, back and forth. His hand moved so fast it blurred, nearly undetectable to the human eye.

A fine white cloud of silky foam rose up out of the concoction and when it had reached barely above the rim, just about to run over and down the sides of the glass, it stopped – as if by magic.

Two paper napkins and two paper-sheathed straws appeared next to it and with the cold clunk of glass on stone, two egg creams had landed. Fed by the sweet creamy froth rising up from the fizzy chocolate liquid, their tops bulged out of the glasses with life of their own.

"In about two seconds, we are going have foamy mustaches," Betty muttered aloud.

"Not me. I'm using a straw," Gary corrected her.

"Drink it fast, before the foam melts."

Indeed the sweet suds on top of each glass were already shrinking. They would last only less than a minute and forever be gone.

Each time Betty Wilson spoke, the sound of her voice stirred up something from deep inside Gary. A voltage foamed up inside him and made him squirm. She was starting to annoy him. He thought, "Shut the fuck up, Betty," and smiled at her. It made him feel odd. He wished he could stop smiling—that this pulse inside him would go away.

It wasn't going to go away. Not in his lifetime, although Gary would soon discover some relief. There would be a remedy that would change his life forever.

Gary picked up the glass, put his lips to the rim, tilted and swallowed. He pulled the glass away and rolled his eyes upward under closed lids just as the bells on top of the door rang once more. He did not open his eyes to see who walked in; he didn't even noticed the bells. Under a thick foamy mustache, Gary's mouth widened.

"Ahhhh," he said.

Then Gary Greengrass grinned like an idiot.

The hope is that you have at least attempted to use the meditation technique[43] on a regular basis. Even better, perhaps you have incorporated the state of consciousness it brings into your daily routine. If you have, then you have already begun to experience amazing changes in your life. Things look a little different to you. You might feel a little detached—a little at odds with the world. That is because you are. You will become accustomed to it.

You are seeing that people and situations are not as they have long seemed to you. You are discovering your place in this world and your life is taking on a new meaning—a significance that you had not previously imagined. You are beginning to acquire a sense of just how significant your insignificance really is. You are seeing the real wisdom in the idea of living *in* this world while not being *of* this world—and you are seeing that there is no effort to gracious living; that your source of strength is always available, right here, right now, in this very moment. You are experiencing what it means to be free from the bondage of self, at first just in tiny slices; but then, that little bit goes a very long way.

Going forward now, if you decide to incorporate this new state of consciousness into your life, there are some questions that will soon come up. There is no possible way to answer all of them here but in anticipation, I can at least bring your attention to several, making a

---

[43]Please visit the "How To Get There," page in the back of this book for fast access to the meditation exercise. It is available for streaming or download. It is free and always will be.

few informed predictions and present some tips and reminders. All of these come from practical experience garnered over thirty years of practicing this way of life, in assisting my family with it and, over a decade of working with alcoholics.

There will likely come the question, "Am I doing it right?" or you may wonder if your efforts are good enough. Trying to make this determination, if done too willfully, can be counterproductive. It will help to know that when it comes to this exercise, keeping score of your progress is discouraged; and that *longer* is not necessarily better. Extended meditation sessions, going on for hours, are not only unnecessary, they are deleterious. Please don't do that.

Remember, this is a waking-up proposition; meditating deeply or for too long will have the effect of putting you to sleep instead of waking you up. It takes only a single moment to move from awareness to unconsciousness, and another moment to move back to awareness again. This is all you are doing when practicing meditation. It is after all, only an exercise.

A few minutes in the morning, a few minutes at night, and then any time you can during the day, even if it is while sitting at your desk at work, on a subway, or walking down the supermarket aisle while shopping. One of the most important times to meditate is before you go to sleep at night. This is an extremely important interlude that allows you to have some time, before falling asleep, where you are awake and disconnected from the thought stream. If you are to meet unfinished business in your dreams, then let it present itself to you, rather than you unwittingly dragging negative, emotional baggage into your subconscious mind.

After a while, you will find that you will be able to fall asleep effortlessly, while awake and aware. Your sleeping may become very light. If you have a bed partner, he or she may notice that your sleep-full breathing is becoming much lighter, more shallow, and shorter than usual. Many people find that they need less sleep than they did before. Do not be surprised to find yourself rising earlier in the morning than usual, feeling fully rested; this is quite common. If this does happen, and you can avoid going back to sleep, you will not suffer any. If you have sleep apnea, you may experience improvement or a complete resolution to problematic snoring.

As the weeks and months go by and you continue to practice the exercise, you will see that spiritual growth is more about living in the aware state, in *conscious contact* with God at all times, than it is about the mechanics of meditation[44] and making that contact merely once or twice a day. Meditation is only a device that helps us arrive at that spiritual state. It serves as a reminder of how it's done, so we *can*. Your most profound revelations, the so-called spiritual "aha" moments, will not occur during meditation sessions, but as you are *not* meditating, simply going though your day *meditatively*—awake and aware.

Admittedly, when you first begin to meditate, the exercise recording on the website is substantially longer than a few minutes. This is temporary, and allows slow and safe acclimation through the exercise without too much shock. I hope that by now you have listened to the pep-talk recording on the website and been alerted to the seriousness and immeasurable spiritual consequence of this meditation, and know that this exercise is no toy. Your psyche would not survive if you were suddenly infused with the spiritual energy you will be receiving as you increasingly become more aware. In time, as you become used to it, you will only need to meditate for a few minutes each morning and each evening. By doing this you will find an increasing strength to extend seconds and minutes of awareness all throughout the day, as increase consciousness becomes more natural to you. This strength is your "daily bread".

If meditating for too long is an issue, then so is meditating deeply. Notice I did not say "too" deeply; I mean to say, to meditate with any depth at all. Depth does not characterize the experience. If you are going deep into anything, it means you are losing awareness, not gaining it. Keep it light. Keep it subtle, and do not overshoot the runway with effort. Your awareness of your surroundings, noise, and distractions in the environment will increase, not decrease, as you awaken. If you are earnest about your *conscious contact*, the old tendency to nap or to go into a trance will diminish in just a few days

---

[44]Please visit the "How To Get There," page in the back of this book for fast access to the meditation exercise. It is available for streaming or download. It is free and always will be.

as your natural wakefulness escalates back to its original state, as when you were a child.

When sitting down to meditate, avoid pretension and ritualizing. Do not intentionally try to create what you feel are *meditative* environments. If you have ever meditated before and taken to suggestions like using sensory stimulants such as incense, music, sound effects, or other ceremonious affectations, you are now seeing the danger of such seductive practices and how these keep you comfortably attached to your physical world, edging out true spiritual connection. A simple, empty space with no one around is sufficient.

There could be a temptation to integrate old habits into this exercise. Techniques that focus on imagery, recitations, affirmations, visualization and especially those that use mantras, readings, breath control or techniques that induce feelings of elation, perhaps through hyperventilation and over-relaxation, can produce ill-fated results. These are narcotic in nature. We are looking for freedom, not only from substances, which seduce you into a false sense of safety and relief, but from thoughts as well.

Be on guard for practices that include the melding of physical exercise into this meditation, as it is an attempt to inexorably bind the human animal with spirit. Bringing physical exercise and spiritual exercise together will ultimately decrease your awareness, since muscle and spirit are to be separated in two—not homogenized as one. Anything which blurs the distinction between the physical and spiritual worlds is extremely dangerous. We are trying to practice *separating* human physique from spirit—not to fuse them into one. The avoidance of all physical activity and eschewing showy habits while meditating will be helpful. Such activities may seem to provide benefit, but they are mortally hypnotic and will cancel the spiritual benefits from this consciousness *wakening* exercise.

Voices inside the head are sometimes an issue. If you find yourself in a conversation with a voice, treat it as you would any other intrusion into your awareness. You have been learning that this is merely your lower Self moving in to distract you. You will find that by stepping back and observing voices just the same as you would any other distraction, that the voices will diminish and fall away. The more you practice this, the more you will be able to do it with ease, even during the day. Also, do not listen to the voice that tells you that any of these realizations is an objective.

Noticing these psychic intrusions is merely one step toward the truth. Awareness can be raised many ways. It can even happen accidentally in a yoga class, a movie theater, or while stirring a pot of spaghetti sauce. The world is full of awake and aware individuals who have never meditated in their lives. It is what happens *after* you wake up that makes the difference between living a God-directed life and rejecting Him.

Realize that every thought especially those which have "voice" inside your thinking is suspect. After a while you will be able to distinguish between thinking and knowing. Watch the voice that tells you to discontinue meditating, that compares, that judges me, others, or the spiritual progress you may or may not have made. In the meditative state of awareness, you will discover that you are able to observe without judging—so keep it up.

You will worry less about outcomes. You will become less goal-oriented and more inspired. You aren't losing aptitude, aspiration, or ability—you are losing self-centered ambition.

As you continue to notice the generic mind-chatter inside your head, remember that becoming aware of this mental noise is no great spiritual feat. Even the most puerile of mental training can accomplish that much. The "trick" continues to lie in resisting the inevitable urges to struggle with it, to silence it. Do not resent the mental noise. Do not try to make it go away. Simply notice it. As long as you do not struggle as if to silence, repress, or suppress your thoughts and instead simply notice them, you will be okay.

The chatter, the volume of thought and the barrage of resentment and irritation you encounter every day, will seem to get worse before it gets better. You may feel as though you are being bombarded with more distraction and thoughts than ever before. This is just a little illusion set up through your previous lack of awareness—as it becomes a little shocking to discover how distracted, bombarded, and unconscious you have been. Don't listen to the voice that tells you that you are different; that you are *worse* than everybody else; that the cannonade of irritation is a sign of failure. It isn't.

There may be a temptation to abuse this meditation by thinking it is a way to quiet the mind or to relax. As attractive as this idea may initially seem, once you have been using the exercise a short while you will come to see how extraordinarily dangerous this is. Just calmly notice such errant thought as you would any other. These thoughts are for the purpose of manipulating your newfound awareness and to bring you into a stressed relationship with your own thoughts. That struggle will remove awareness. Rather cunning, isn't it?

You have begun to take on a calm, natural posture of indifference to the cruelties and injustices that other people inflict on you, themselves, and each other. You will see that this resilience to evil is not callousness but a developing attitude that is free of anger, full of love, and a sure sign of true forgiveness. You are losing emotional entanglements, allowing you to exhibit love. You will see this trait as a central feature to maximize usefulness—an enhanced spiritual attribute that has evaded you all your life. Now not only are you able to forgive but also because you forgive, you are also *forgivable*. This has always been the case. Now you are for the first time seeing this great truth.

You'll also begin to notice little things about your behaviors, known only to you. You will be more thoughtful toward others than you have ever been before, more conscious of their presence and of their needs. Less and less will you be inadvertently stepping on the toes of your fellows, and you will not even notice as your narcissism falls away. You are developing humility now, so as you notice these changes, do not pat yourself on the back. Just observe. See how others need to experience your patience; and how the world benefits from your bringing tolerance and love forward; especially to little children, perhaps even your own. As sick, symbiotic relationships with others wither and drop off you will find that your newfound natural life means routinely packing into the Stream of Life instead of mindlessly drawing out of it.

Before long—*remain patient for this, now*—you will notice bad habits like smoking and overeating change. *All* of your obsessive vices will begin to make you very uncomfortable. Eventually they will fall away—if not immediately, then down the road. In either case, you will not enjoy them as you once did. Even your sexual attitude will begin to take on a new healthy meaning as you become less selfish in your pursuits in this area.

While meditating, you may notice your breathing begin to change. This is normal. It is also normal for your heart rate to adjust. Notice it happening. Nothing more. It is typical, and there is no need to analyze it, because your body is being altered at levels so deep we could never approach understanding the details of this alteration in this lifetime. (This is why doctors and psychiatrists become so baffled by miracle cures and sudden remissions of mental and physical diseases.)

You may also feel a heaviness, a pressure or an energy up through the torso, perhaps emanating out from the center of your chest. Some people also experience tenseness rising up out of the belly, through the throat, and into the face. This is a very common part of the awakening process that is unique to this particular meditation. Do not try to induce it. Do not inhibit it. Just notice it, and do not be frightened. You have already learned what causes this. You will be safe. You may have to suffer through it. There is more about this effect found on my website. Please feel free to assuage your fears and be confident that this may be unavoidable if you are to pursue a spiritual path.

You will see how the world is asleep and how most people are just like zombies, vampires, and werewolves, roaming the planet lost in an unconscious state, seducing and being seduced. You will be gaining an increasing ability to ignore their errors by watching your annoyance arise in response to their absentee lifestyles and their lack of awareness. Watch yourself *as* the irritation arises in you. You can do this just the same as you would *any* resentment. You will find yourself nonjudgmental of them, which is experiencing true love, knowing that "they know not what they do."

Don't beat yourself up each time you have lost awareness, not while meditating nor during the day. Although there will be a tendency to do that for a while, you can now be grateful for being shown your inevitable *slip*. I predict it.

There might be a temptation to become evangelistic over your new discoveries and the special adventures you are having through this meditation. When that happens, you will see what a bad idea it is to try teaching this technique to others right now. A whole chapter could be written on this subject, but rather, go with the hunch that cries, "Stop!" For now, anyway. If need be, feel free to direct others to the free download, but do not try to become an ersatz guru in the matter. This of course would be a distraction from your own "now." There will be plenty of opportunities in times to come, as you have more to offer, after *all* your problems have been answered. That will be once others have vetted your progress by the examples set through the fruits of your own life, much the same way I have done with you. This will happen soon enough. You'll intuitively know when. Perhaps one day you will write a book conveying this spirituality.

Occasionally, after you have been practicing this for a long time, you may find yourself trying too hard to meditate properly. What has happened then is that you are allowing willfulness to wrestle control over your own wakefulness. Take a breather. Recall the madness of injecting willfulness into anything, let alone meditation—and then you can leave effort behind. Relax. Just be aware without trying to create your own awareness, knowing that you cannot, anyway—that it a gift, for which you can be grateful to God.

Make the choice to be aware independent of thoughts, not in reaction to those thoughts. In time, you will see that simply *choosing* to be awake automatically results in doing the right thing, without responding to conditions. You are becoming proactive to life and less reactive. Put your awareness first, not any single issue at hand. Do not use your awareness as you would a sword, to cut down unwanted emotions, thoughts, or feelings. Consciousness is not a defensive weapon; it is a protective shield. To abuse it would mean becoming selfishly selective and tempted to bask in good feelings while repelling unpleasant ones. That would be playing God again. There will come a time when you will foolishly test your own faith and try to beat up your enemy with your armor. If you do, you will lose it. When this happens, simply stand back and start over again. You may have to endure this kind of pain for a while. These will be lessons well learned if you stick with it, calmly observing your doubts. You will be developing patience.

Memories from the past will come up. Some will develop out of familiar themes, while others will surface out of incidents that you have never remembered before, not even through fourth-step inventories, counseling, or psychoanalysis.

In time, you will learn to appreciate the pain these memories summon instead of letting them aggravate you. Then you will be able to sincerely concede your weaknesses, gaining the strength to suffer through them without regret. With repentance, yes—however, morose remorsefulness will no longer be part of your recall experience, because now you are able to see how progress and growth comes out of patiently enduring the daily stresses presented in each moment. Each potential conflict is an occasion to love—an opportunity to escape anger. Soon your life will be free from anger, and the people close to you will no longer be harmed by the vitriol emanating out of your negative reactions. You will no longer be reacting with bitterness.

You will begin to see that you exhibit patience and tolerance for others—not merely in appearance but through serenity within. You will not feel elated. You will just feel naturally present and comfortable in your own skin. *Confident* is a good word.

As that confidence builds, your thoughts will seemingly purify themselves, becoming congruent with God's vision, and you will see how foolish it is to measure your successes as you go along. More importantly, you will lose that perverse, faithless need to keep a scorecard on God, as if to evaluate His performance. God doesn't have to pass your "Good God" test.

And now, one last thing: Obviously, I cannot answer every single question in a single book. I can, however, tell you that you will make mistakes. If I could anticipate them all, there would not be enough paper, time, or cyberspace to address them. Most of the questions that come up derive out of uncertainty and a natural insecurity that new experiences entail. Most of these will be answered all by themselves. Just remain patient.

In addition, please feel free to come to my blog, where I answer questions regarding the experiences you are having. Many of these are addressed in articles, and it is a lively blog with frequent updates.

Although we may never meet in person, this will be a good way for there to be personal contact on some level, at least while you are still a beginner on this journey. As you proceed on the path, you will not need the benefit of any contact whatsoever. Your ongoing contact instead will be through your new consciousness with God and through helping others as you carry a message of love to your family, your friends, and especially to your children. May they also receive this message, and may they encounter my children along the way.

"The meeting of two personalities is like the contact of two chemical substances; if there is any reaction, both are transformed." – *Carl Gustav Jung*

ABOUT DANNY J. SCHWARZHOFF

Danny is a recovered alcoholic. He writes several popular and enduring blogs about alcoholism, meditation, recovery, and the spirituality-based solutions to life's problems. For eight years standing, both Google and Yahoo have ranked Danny as the number one, top rated "Recovered Alcoholic."

He calls himself a "Real Live Recovered Alcoholic"—an *ex*-problem drinker, no longer suffering from the syndrome called *chronic alcoholism.* Danny stopped drinking in 1997; after a relapse in 1999 he has been sober ever since. He has over thirty years experience with a special form of nonreligious, spiritual meditation, through which he uniquely integrates a classical style of carrying a standard message of recovery. He claims the technique is the *missing link* in Twelve-Step recovery and has devoted his life to delivering it to the world, beginning with the alcoholic.

Danny is a born and bred New Yorker (b. 1957) who grew up in "Da Bronx" and has lived most of his adult life in the borough of Queens. He now lives on Cape Cod in Massachusetts with his wife Nancy and their two children, Danny Jr. and Kristen. The Schwarzhoffs are a complete family unit, enjoying emotional, mental, and physical health and a harmonious lifestyle free from harmful stress. Both children are honor roll students in their schools and are socially active and well balanced in all areas of their lives. In July 2012 the Schwarzhoffs celebrated their thirty-third wedding anniversary.

Danny was first exposed to the meditation technique he prescribes in the winter of 1963 when he was about six years old. It happened following a traumatic experience with his mother's violent, alcoholic live-in boyfriend. In order to deal with the humiliation and resentment he experienced at the hands of this troubled man, Danny stumbled upon the technique of bringing light from inside his head to the inner surface of his eyelids—an activity which produced a sense of detachment. He later recognized this to be the state of *meditation*—a state of consciousness that shielded him from emotional harm caused by that painful traumatic experience. Miraculously, when the experience was over, he realized that he no longer hated the man for beating him, his mother, and his sisters. Armed with his secret '"gimmick," life could never be quite the same.

Later, in his teen years, he discontinued the mystic "dislocation" practice and descended into the perverse world of active alcoholism, suffering mental and physical dysfunction for nearly two decades. In 1999, during a "white light" spiritual experience, everything changed and he was able once again to truly meditate. He has never needed to look back. He continues to apply this method in all areas of life and has continued to enjoy mental, emotional, and physical well-being as well as spiritual healthfulness. All physical, mental, and emotional disorders have fallen away as continued spiritual wellness has been restored.

Now he teaches the technique to others, frequently through intensive work with alcoholics who are attempting to go through the Twelve-Step recovery process.

Not only has Danny fully recovered from alcoholism and substance abuse, but through this technique, integrated into the Twelve-Step process, he has also been able to overcome major depression, anxiety, smoking, onset type II diabetes, obesity, high cholesterol, sugar addiction, colitis, hemorrhoids, and other dysfunctions. His doctors have stopped prescriptions for virtually all of the medications he has been given in the past decade including Lipitor, TriCore, and ADD medications like Adderall, as well as the antidepressant drugs Effexor, Welbutrin, and Lexapro.

He first began writing in the mid '70s, landing a job as publicist and advertising director for a Bronx produce company. He wrote advertising copy and press releases for the company and directed all of their marketing and promotion until 1982, when he left to start a weekly tabloid newspaper where he was editor-in chief, writing most of the tabloid's feature stories and much of the news copy. Danny has published articles in *Grapevine*, AA's magazine for alcoholics, and also in the *Barnstable Patriot* on Cape Cod.

The late '80s and '90s brought Danny to Wall Street in New York City when he became a stockbroker and an Investment Banker. One of the firms he worked for became the subject of the movie *Boiler Room*—a factoid that fuels some of his storytelling on the subject of alcoholism, spiritual dysfunction, and substance abuse in the workplace. In the late '90s he moved to Cape Cod, where he began writing, working with alcoholics, and breeding thoroughbred racing pigeons. He also began working for several rehab centers, aiding addiction counselors with rehabilitating alcoholics and drug addicts.

Today, Danny gives regular public talks on alcoholism, recovery, and spirituality. He has conducted Twelve-Step workshops at recovery conferences in Boston, New York and in Denmark as well as at Dartmouth College (UMass).

Although frequently consulted by treatment facility administrators and those in the recovery business, Danny does not affiliate with any treatment center or rehab. He hasn't got any recovery models to sell. He gives his meditation exercise away *for free* on his website and writes of his experience on the subject with only one goal in mind: he wants to persuade others to try the meditation technique detailed on his website and to experience an entire change of being and lifestyle through it. He is not a member of any organized religion or cult and has no axe to grind. He does, however, express his experience and observations as a spiritually awakened and recovered alcoholic. He does *not* write as a form of "Twelve Step" work for *Alcoholics Anonymous* or as a form of therapy.

Biographic disclaimer: Sometimes the question of anonymity arises—along with the issue of whether or not Danny is a member of Alcoholics Anonymous (AA). If Danny were a member of AA, he would violate AA's traditions by saying so publicly. He would also be lying if he were a member and denied it. So in order to respect the traditions of that organization, he does not answer that question publicly. However, Danny does want his readers to know that the spiritual Fellowship of AA has earned his respect, and he approves of AAs Twelve-Step program. He also does not think that AA has a monopoly on recovery from alcoholism, spiritual recovery or that AA is for everyone. He has attended AA meetings and has done extensive research into its history and Twelve-Step program, and is an ardent practitioner of the spiritual principles contained within the Twelve Step proposals. He typically writes about some of these observations regarding AA's program, fellowship, and history in his blog articles, pamphlets and in this book.

"HOW TO GET THERE"

Free download, streaming audio

1. Pep Talk
Not a "Pep Talk" in the traditional, emotionally arousing sense, but a brief introduction to some of the ideas behind this meditation and suggestions on how to approach the exercise. It is suggested that you listen to this first, before trying the sample and then decide if you would like to continue. Many find this audio preface helpful, especially those not yet familiar with my writing on the subject of meditation. www.bit.ly/samplepeptalk

2. Sample Meditation
Just a small introduction, a "taste" of what the full meditation is. This is a "mini" version which, over the past decade, I have distributed to alcoholics seeking conscious contact with God, all over the world. Even this tiny chip has been enough to transform lives. www.bit.ly/realmedsample

3. Pre-Meditation Talk
Another *"Pep Talk"* but a little more informative than the first one. It is suggested to listen to this prior to using the full 30 minute version because it provides some valuable "tips" and some very important caveats for the inexperienced but especially for those who feel they already are experienced with some variety of meditation. *www.bit.ly/rmedpep*

4. "Real Meditation for Real Alcoholics"
This is the full 30 minute exercise that will allow you to get free from anger, separate you from your thoughts so that you can get connected to God immediately. This is the non-religious, non-commercial, pure exercise that will open your mind, heart and eyes and break you free from the bondage of self. *www.bit.ly/realdaily*

Sites To Visit

5. *Frunobulax57*, (aka "Danny S, Recovered Alcoholic")
A popular and enduring blog about alcoholism, The Twelve Steps, recovery and the spirituality-based solution to life's problems. Contains over a thousand articles on issues of interest to those involved in Twelve Step recovery. This site is Google and Yahoo ranked as the #1 "Recovered Alcoholic," site on the Web. *www.bit.ly/Frunobulax57*

6. *Meditation for Alcoholics*
In addition to article about meditation, alcoholism and excerpts from this book, this site also contains handy links to the free exercise. It is my *blog*, a place to communicate, connect and ask questions; or just read about the journey through recovery and the path that leads to the discovery of God. Yes, I do answer comments when I am able. You will not be bombarded with "offers" here. I do not *sell* any events and seminars. There will be no meditation retreat weekends or *courses* in spirituality. At most, I will have links to my Amazon bookstore. (I am a writer you know). But that's it. This is non-commercial and the Meditation for Alcoholics experience is free to use and distribute by anyone – and it *always will be. www.bit.ly/MeditationBlog*

Special Download

7. My Medical File
This download contains my full, unadulterated medical file. In it are copies of the actual pages of my files obtained through my personal physician. Yes, this is very personal information to open up for public scrutiny but it lends authority to the claims I make about the meditation experience proposed through this book. It is a chronicle of my mental and physical condition spanning almost the entire last decade. You are free to examine every physical exam, blood test, x-ray, ailment and prescription –every pound I've lost or gained, every ache and pain for nearly ten years – with accompanying physician's notes. In summary, you will see how I

have recovered not only from alcoholism but also major depression, anxiety, smoking, onset type II diabetes, obesity, high cholesterol, sugar addiction, colitis, diverticulitis, hemorrhoids, and even erectile dysfunction. Doctors have un-prescribed virtually all of the medications I have ever been given in the past decade including Lipitor, TriCore, and ADD medications like Adderall as well as the antidepressant drugs Effexor, Welbutrin and Lexapro. *www.bit.ly/Dannysmedicals*

Please consider these records as my evidence-based, *curriculum vitae* and authority to pass on what I have truly experienced myself, not what I have been taught, or picked up in reading.

I believe that real life experience and the "fruits" of one's labors are the best accreditation one can earn and carry far more depth and weight than any institutionally issued degree. I propose that it is possible for almost anyone to recover from such illnesses. *Oh yeah... and alcoholism too.* In the absence of getting to know me personally or to meet my wife and my kids, the facts in this file are some of the best "written" proof I am able to offer. If credentials are important to you, then here they are.

~ danny j schwarzhoff

TO THE PROFESSIONAL

Anything that helps a mental health counselor assist clients who are in recovery to better cope with their feelings can also help transform the negative patterns in their minds into more constructive thinking. Clear thinking helps them approach optimal functioning as human beings. Today it is not at all unusual for psychotherapists to incorporate yoga and meditation techniques into contemporary professional counseling.

Although the approach presented in this book is chiefly spiritual, it has strong and direct physiological connections with mental, emotional, and physical functioning. It would serve no useful purpose to impugn the millions of men and women who work in the treatment industry and who dedicate their lives to helping others through the countless numbers of recovery and addiction models. I recognize that there are many devoted, informed and dedicated people in the field.

When *some* clinical approaches are integrated into spiritual solutions, amazing progress is possible. It must be recognized that the cause of alcoholism is spiritual disease, that the solution is spiritual in nature, not medical or psychological. As Clint Eastwood's Inspector (Dirty) Harry Callahan says in *Magnum Force*, "A man's got to know his limitations". There are certain things a clinician *can* do but also many things they cannot and often *should* not do.

Accordingly, it is not the aim of this book to demean the efforts of rehabs and treatment facilities, nor is it to completely disparage all psychological solutions. I have experience in the clinical field of treatment for alcoholism and drug addiction.[45] I also am experienced approaching problems from an exclusively spiritual perspective. There is no doubt that under the right conditions, some of the typical ad hoc barriers to destructive drinking—the kind applied through the work of a properly trained clinician, can be useful.

---

[45]Danny has worked *with* and *for* several rehab centers and treatment facilities specializing in rehabilitating alcoholics and drug addicts.

If the body and spirit can unite to form a whole human being, then surely the healing forces of both physical and spiritual realms can be combined in treatment when there is a malfunction.

If you are flexible enough to include spirituality with clinical conventions, then the meditation exercise proposed through this book can be of enormous value to you in your practice.

We know that ongoing, continuing education is crucial to learning about new and developing areas in the field of mental health. If broadening the knowledge base of psychological theory and a rigorous clinical training in counseling techniques are useful in maintaining professional competence, then why not also expanding that base to include an ancient, time-tested technique designed to do nothing more than raise awareness?

If you would recommend yoga, transcendental meditation, New Age training or even the AA fellowship—each of these having strong spiritual, even pseudo-religious implications—then surely you could recommend to a client a technique not containing any religious doctrine at all.

After all, addressing issues that lead to the repression and suppression of emotions, while encouraging clients to develop non-judgmental self-awareness, can only add value to the practice of a mental health professional.

Your experience will abundantly confirm that issues concerning anger, stress, and strained relationships can all be addressed when *self* is appropriately put in its place. That being the case, I propose to you a form of meditation, different from anything you have ever considered before, which develops immunity to anger and promotes an awareness of the truth about *self* in the first place, so that there is no judgment in the second place. Well, that is the meditation technique proposed in this book, which is free for all, and can be accessed by anyone.

If you have clients who have difficult to break associations, who would benefit from the liberation of unhealthy dependencies, to not only substances, but also their own morbid thinking, then please feel free to make use of the meditation proposed in this book. Instead of linking behavioral responses to external cues, this exercise will allow them to break free. It is non-religious. It will not offend a client's Judeo

216

Christian proclivities and is a perfectly reconcilable practice with most approaches, Twelve Step or otherwise.

You will find your patients much more open and honest to speak with—their recollections and willingness to look at themselves will quickly reach levels you prefer to deal with. You will also find that personality barriers break down quicker and more completely, making your professional work much more effective.

With the many recovered or recovering alcoholics and addicts in the treatment industry, who have moved from being student to teacher—from patient to clinician—this exercise can be as much a boon to your personal peace and happiness as it will be to those you treat. Try it yourself. It is my sincerest belief that you, your client and your professional relationships will only benefit.

ABOUT THE TITLE

The term "Real Alcoholic" used in the title can sometimes seem a dog's bone of contention. There is no need. This book probably could have been titled without the *Real* thrown in. "Meditation for Alcoholics" still would have made a good title, but I decided to include the term *Real Alcoholics* – and for good reason.

I did not choose it because it sounds cute. I also did not invent the term. I have simply borrowed the expression, and the supporting concept of the malady behind it, from some people who were very knowledgeable on the subject of recovery and alcoholism: The co-authors of "Alcoholics Anonymous" a magnificent volume that delineates the complete, simple Twelve Step process in 164 pages.

Aside from their particular description of the illness and the specific solution they propose, there are many other explanations proliferating in the world of recovery and alcoholism too. Rather than sort through them or to invent a brand new "description of the alcoholic" I mean to remain congruent with the *"actual"* and the *"true"* alcoholic description as depicted by those one hundred men and women who recovered from alcoholism and wrote a book to tell the world about how it happened.[46]

I have done this for several important reasons.

First, writers such as myself hate when people don't *get* what they mean or when some slight ambiguity betrays what is on their minds. To avoid confusion communicating with readers, some standard has to be set. Since this a book dedicated to alcoholics, my readers and me must be on the same page in as far the description of alcoholism.

There are two conditions to real alcoholism according the "Alcoholics Anonymous" description. One is *mental*, the other, *physical*. Having either one alones is no picnic, but both have to be present to fit the book's description of alcoholism.

---

[46]"actual", "true", and "real" alcoholic are each coined in "Alcoholics Anonymous", 4th edition, Alcoholics Anonymous World Services, pp. 21,22,23,30,31,34,35,39,44, 92,149

One condition, the physical side, is the sheer inability to stop drinking once an alcoholic starts drinking. This is called "craving." It is an abnormal physical response to alcohol since only a small portion of the total population experiences it. Hence, some have come to see it as an allergy by this definition - *an exaggerated or pathological immunological reaction to substances, situations or physical states that are without comparable effect on the average individual.*[47] The phenomenon is activated by the introduction of alcohol into the alcoholic's digestive system.

Real alcoholics do not crave alcohol until they first take it into their bodies – most often by intentionally drinking it, but eating or accidental ingestion too. Alcohol contaminated Tiramisu, Moo-Shoo Pork cooked in rice wine or a New York cheesecake baked with 80 proof vanilla extract will do the trick. People who are affected this way can pretty much solve this problem in the same way *anyone* with *any* food sensitivity can: *"Just don't drink the alcohol."*

Someone sensitive to tree nuts or shellfish would naturally recoil from those. *My wife is allergic to gluten. It causes all kinds of digestive and nutritional harms when she eats it. This isn't a great obstacle. She just doesn't eat food products containing the stuff. Problem solved.*

The other condition is an obsession; a mental phenomenon where the alcoholic is *compelled* to drink alcohol. He does it regardless of his own will against the idea, in order to overcome the pain caused by some internal, psychic disruption. Alcohol does *not* have to be physically introduced into the body first in order for this obsession to kick in. It is a *mental* component that causes the sufferer to drink even though his history shows that he will experience the aforementioned physical reaction and not be able to stop once he starts. *By the way, my wife has never, at least to my knowledge, snuck into our basement to access a secret stash of semolina pasta; and she has never suffered the humiliation caused by a Kaiser roll or garlic bagel rolling out from under the car seat at a sudden stoplight. She isn't nuts. She's just allergic.*

---

[47] Merriam-Webster.com. http://www.merriam-webster.com/dictionary/allergy (8 May 2011)

A person can have just one of these conditions present, resulting in alcoholic styled behavior that is quite distressing, yet still their problems can be solved through human aid – such as rehabs, support groups and counseling. However, if one cannot stop once they start—*and* they are unable to *not start—then* they fit the "Our description of the alcoholic" offered by *Alcoholics Anonymous* and depicted in their book; and no amount of human will be effective. They are a candidate for the drastic spiritual solution proposed by that Fellowship through their book.

This doesn't mean that other people who have problems with alcohol ought not to be free to refer to themselves as "real alcoholics" or to imply that experiences other than the *Alcoholics Anonymous* explanation to drinking problems might not also be "real," "actual" or "true". It is just the description chosen here. The meditation talked about here can be used by anyone; even if they do not fit the description or even they are not if full disagreement with it.

Secondly, the "Alcoholics Anonymous" description is the one I happen to fit. All discussion of my experience as an alcoholic depends upon it. Therefore, anytime the word "alcoholic" appears in this book, it is referring to the "real," "actual," "true," alcoholic, as represented in the first forty-three pages of the book "Alcoholics Anonymous."

What about the term *Real Meditation*. Here the term *real* applies to the results, not to the technique. The meditation method spoken of in this book induces effective experience that frees the practitioner from the bondage of self and maintains unadulterated *conscious contact* with God. I know of no meditation that does this and so therefore, I can see that it is 'real'. It really works.

In order to see how this may be so, you will just have to try the meditation—since words cannot possibly do it proper justice. The overhauling of attitude that you will begin to experience—towards life, towards God, spirituality and sobriety as the result of this practice, speaks volumes of praise that I have only barely begun to convey in this book.

I could have called the book *Special Meditation for a Particular Kind of Alcoholic – And their Families,* but it didn't have the right *ring* to it—not to mention that graphically it would have looked terrible on the front cover.

The subtitle, "and those who love them" was added at the last minute for a two reasons. I want to extend the reach of my writing to as many people as possible (writing is after all my livelihood) but also in honor of my wife Nancy and my two kids, Danny and Kristen.

We are each united and completely in touch with this style of meditation, living each moment of each day as a family, walking increasingly in the Sunlight of The Spirit as the result.

Is there guidance from Dad? Of course! Fathers are naturally preordained to guide their families – but we are supposed to guide them toward God and be the conduit for His will. Whenever a father instills certain spiritual principles in his family—demonstrating how to have God consciousness, that guidance becomes operative and the family progresses as a spiritual entity.

It is that way in our family. It can be in yours too. Pointing you toward the Source of this kind of contentment is the simple, main purpose of this book.

I assure you that my teenage son could write his own book, containing the very same principles as those presented here, without any help from me. My wife and daughter can converse on the spiritual aspects and understanding imparted them as feely as talking about the weather or buying a new sweater at Hollister.

While some of the ideas written about in this book may at first blush seem deep and profound—really, they are not. If *profound* then they are *profoundly* simple. Once you have practiced the meditation exercise for a short while, nothing here will seem as foreign or deep as they may first appear upon an initial read.

So when I added "and those who love them" I had those who love *me* in mind when I wrote it, but it was also added knowing that *anyone* who has an alcoholic in their life, will benefit from the exercise and the spiritual Principles revealed to them through it. It will not matter whether the alcoholic in their life is recovered, still recovering, dry drunk or actively engaged in the life. I have taught many non-alcoholics this technique whose lives have experienced instantaneous reversals of harms.

In our family there is no posturing of personalities from atop spiritual mountains; nor is there any spiritual rocket science to complicate simple living. There has been no study, instruction and there are no rigid commandments to follow. We exist sans any self-proclaimed religious piety. There is only understanding, acquired through a non-religious, but spiritually *conscious contact* with God. It is an unspoken guidance system, to gently lead us through the treacherous streams and keeps us safe, healthy and useful.

APPENDIX I

What follows is the original transcript of an email sent to an alcoholic I was helping to recover from alcoholism back in 2004. He was a Marine Corp. Chaplain and. (His copy of the meditation CD was the first one I even recorded). I forget when the text from this email was originally composed, but I recall cutting and pasting it out of a previous writing I had posted on an Internet message board. I have reprinted this and distributed it many time to many people all over the world, who have found it useful. I hope you do too. (With the exception of the Chaplain's email address, this text has been left intact and is exactly as sent.)

-----Original Message-----
From: Trudger57@aol.com [mailto:Trudger57@aol.com]
Sent: Tuesday, September 07, 2004 8:00 AM
To: XXXX@XXX.com
Subject: (no subject)

This may be helpful to anyone following along who is just starting out on this path. I keep a printed sheet of my night morning prayers on my nightstand next to my bed so I don't' forget any of the prayers which my Big Book tells me are part of this Program.

Maybe its it's just me, but I WILL get lazy and complacent over time and probably cut short these procedures unless I keep some prescription in this manner. The following is exactly what I do each night and morning in keeping up a healthy meditation and prayer life.

I believe this is how my Big Book tells me I should do this, but I do not represent AA as a whole. These actions and prayers are not any official part of this study, they are my own only, as I have extrapolated from out Big Book, Alcoholics Anonymous.

If I have left anything out, or if there is anything in this which does not adhere precisely to the prayer portions of our Program of recovery as outlined in the Big Book, then please ignore it. And please correct me.

(But it is as exacting as I could get it)

EACH EVENING
I start with the 12 evening questions from P. 86 I try to be constructive as much as possible. I try to look at the good I have done during the day so I am not zeroing in on my objectionable traits only. After all, God has made some changes in me.
1. Where was I resentful?
2. Where was I selfish?
3. Where was I dishonest?
4. Where was I afraid?
5. Do I owe an apology?
6. Have I kept something to myself, which should be discussed with another person at once?
7. Where was I kind toward all?
8. Where was I Loving toward all?
9. What could I have done better?
10. Where was I thinking of myself most of the time?
11. Where was I thinking of what I could do for others?
12. Where was I thinking of what I could pack into the stream of life?

"Forgive me God for each of these areas where I have failed you and fallen short of being able to be as effective as I could have been for you. Forgive me and help me live Thy will better tomorrow by showing me how to correct these errors. Guide me and direct me to do better tomorrow. Remove my arrogance and my fear. Show me how to make my relationships with my others right. Grant me the humility and strength to do Thy will. Amen"

If I was resentful, dishonest, selfish, unkind, unloving, if I owe an apology or if I have kept things to myself, I remember these for my morning prayers so I can include these specifically and ask God for help and improvement in these areas. If an answer comes to me, try to remember it. (Some people do this as a written exercise, I personally do not) When I say my morning prayers, I ask God for help in those areas, if it is His will.
Now I spend 10-15 minute in meditation.

EACH MORNING
Upon awakening, prior to even rising out from bed, I take care of these areas:

1) I think about the 24 hours ahead: I contemplate what I would like to be and what God might want me to be.

2) I consider my plans for the day: I think about what God wants me to do and how I am to live His will. I determine what my vision for what God's will is for me today. I already am remembering the amends I've discovered from last night's 10th step. I start out my day with the making of these amends in my plan and I ask myself what else would God want me to do today?

Now, I usually need to use the bathroom. I do so.

Upon returning I start these Big Book prayers. These are in addition to my meditation, (Which many confuse with reading anything called "Meditation" and contemplative prayers) I keep my prayers & meditation as two very distinct activities.

"God I am yours to build with me and to do with me as Thou wilt. Release me at long last God from the bondage of self, that I may better do Thy will.
Take away my difficulties, especially the trouble I am having with
_____ that YOUR victory these may bear witness to those I would help of Love, Thy Power and Thy Way of life. May I do Thy will always! Remove my fears and direct my attention toward what you would have me be, not what I would have me be. Instead God give me whatever intuitive thought, and inspirations you require for me to have in order that I may know your will and receive the power you give to carry that out. Help me to have an intuitive thought or a decision with regard to _____ which I face today. Father, help me to not struggle with this. Help me to relax and take it easy instead. Help me know what I should do, keeping me mindful that You are running the show.

Direct my thinking today God, and keep it divorced from self-pity, dishonesty and self-seeking motives. Help me employ my mental faculties, that my thought-life may be placed on the higher plane of inspiration and help me to pay attention throughout the day to this vital sixth sense."

"My Creator, I am now willing that you should have all of me, both good and bad. I ask that you now remove from me every single defect of character, which stands in the way of my usefulness to you and my fellows. Grant me strength, God as I go out from here to do Thy bidding. Show me today how to find Patience, Tolerance, Kindness and Love in my heart, my mind and my soul and help me demonstrate these to my family and to those about me.

Remove from me my selfishness, all dishonesty, resentment and fear. Whichever of these crop up today God, help me to immediately share these feelings with others and guide me toward making immediate amends if need be, that I might live serenely with the people about me.

Lord, help me to not think of myself, instead, help me think of others and help me be loving and tolerant toward them. Father, keep me spiritually fit today, by helping me to not fight with anything or anyone -- even alcohol. Show me what I can do today for the man who is still sick."

"My Father, help me live the twelve steps of my recovery life, the twelve traditions of my Group and my family life and all the principles of AA in my entire life. Remove from me my character defects, specifically profanity, dishonesty, arrogance, false pride, sarcasm, judgment of others and fear, especially God the fear of what others think of and about me.

Watch over me, protect me and care for me. Give me the strength, courage and faith I need to do Thy bidding. Keep me mindful of Thy presence Lord and help me know you better and help keep my house in order.

"God, should I find myself agitated, doubtful or indecisive today, give me inspiration. Show me all through this day, what my next step is to be. Give me the strength, faith and courage I need to take care of the problems in my life today. I ask especially Lord, that you free me from self-will and fear. Amen"

Then I spend 10-15 minute in meditation. I use a simple non-religious non "Eastern" method, which I find non-hypnotic, and extremely effective.

In Service with Love,
Danny S
508-315-9878
http://recoveredalcoholic.blogspot.com

APPENDIX II

***This is what my current daily morning "routine" sounds and looks
like today:***[48]

The prayers emailed to the Marine Chaplain in Appendix I came
from an early 2000's message board post I had shared with others.
Subsequently it has been shared and used by protégés all over the
world. I have been giving that old sheet to those who have needed it as
a matter of course for years. It is also what I have personally followed.
However, over time this is no longer the case.

While I still believe it to be worthwhile, these days my personal
morning prayer and meditation has trimmed down quite a bit, omitting
much of the self-centered stuff contained in the original version.

Several years ago I came across the old email prayer and noticed
that it is quite differently from how I pray anymore (even though
textually printed in this book) Part of the old version has melted away
quietly. Not consciously, just practically, over the years. Directions
have been separated from predictions and what to do in conjunction
with the actual prayers. It is stuff riding alongside the prayer but not
actually the prayers.

I consider the later evolution to be more genuine and much
better reconciled with the *Big Book* prayers than the previous ever
was, as virtually all of the "self" centered wording, the stuff I must
have subconsciously inserted into the prayers years ago is now filtered
out.

(*While kneeling upright with no physical support other than a
small pillow placed on the floor under the knees, fingertips lightly
touching.*)

Prayer: "God, I am yours to build with and to do with as Thou
wilt. Release me from the bondage of self, so I may better do Thy will.

---

[48]This prayer, in it's entirely, is most often done together with the entire family at the
start the day.

231

Take away my difficulties God, so that your victory over them may bear witness to those I would help of Thy love, Thy power, and Thy way of life. May I do Thy will always.

Remove my fears today God, and direct my attentions toward what you would have me be, not what I would have me be, keeping my thought processes divorced from self-pity, dishonesty and self-seeking motives. Instead, God give me whatever intuitive thoughts and inspiration I need in order to know what *Your* will is for me; and give me the power to carry it out.

Show me where I can be helpful to others today God, (especially alcoholics) and show me how to show patience, kindliness, tolerance and love toward everyone I meet, especially my family members. My Creator, I am now ready that you should have all of me both good and bad. I asked that you now release from me every single defect of character which stands in the way of my usefulness to you and my fellows. Grant me strength God as I go out from here to do your bidding"

In meditation: *(Begin the meditation "exercise" along with this idea.)* Our Father in heaven, hallowed be thy name. Thy kingdom come. Thy will be done on earth as it is in heaven. Give us this day our daily bread. Forgive us our trespasses *as* we forgive those who trespass against *us*. Lead us away from temptation and deliver us from the Evil One. For *thine* is the kingdom and the power and the glory forever. Amen

The Lord's Prayer is not in the Big Book. However, "If not members of religious bodies, we sometimes select and memorize a few set prayers which emphasize the principles we have been discussing."[49] It seems a good idea to me and has been foundational in daily living.

---

[49]"Alcoholics Anonymous", 4th edition, Alcoholics Anonymous World Services, 87:2

232